BLACK MAN IN THE NETHERLANDS

BLACK MAN

IN THE
NETHERLANDS

AN AFRO-ANTILLEAN
ANTHROPOLOGY

FRANCIO
GUADELOUPE

UNIVERSITY PRESS OF MISSISSIPPI / JACKSON

The University Press of Mississippi is the scholarly publishing agency of the Mississippi Institutions of Higher Learning: Alcorn State University, Delta State University, Jackson State University, Mississippi State University, Mississippi University for Women, Mississippi Valley State University, University of Mississippi, and University of Southern Mississippi.

www.upress.state.ms.us

The University Press of Mississippi is a member of the Association of University Presses.

First printing 2022
∞

Library of Congress Cataloging-in-Publication Data

Names: Guadeloupe, Francio, 1971– author.
Title: Black man in the Netherlands: an Afro-Antillean anthropology / Francio Guadeloupe.
Description: Jackson: University Press of Mississippi, 2022. | Includes bibliographical references and index.
Identifiers: LCCN 2021026462 (print) | LCCN 2021026463 (ebook) | ISBN 978-1-4968-3700-4 (hardback) | ISBN 978-1-4968-3701-1 (paperback) | ISBN 978-1-4968-3702-8 (epub) | ISBN 978-1-4968-3703-5 (epub) | ISBN 978-1-4968-3704-2 (pdf) | ISBN 978-1-4968-3699-1 (pdf)
Subjects: LCSH: Guadeloupe, Francio, 1971– | Anthropologists—Biography. | Racism—Netherlands. | Blacks—Netherlands. | Ethnology—Netherlands. | Ethnicity—Netherlands. | Multiculturalism—Netherlands. | Anthropology—Netherlands. | Netherlands—Race relations. | Netherlands—Ethnic relations.
Classification: LCC GN308.3.N4 G83 2022 (print) | LCC GN308.3.N4 (ebook) | DDC 301.092 [B]—dc23
LC record available at https://lccn.loc.gov/2021026462
LC ebook record available at https://lccn.loc.gov/2021026463

British Library Cataloging-in-Publication Data available

This book is dedicated to Peter Geschiere, a friend and mentor.

CONTENTS

**PART 1: MY WORLD:
ON URBAN POPULAR CULTURE AND CONVIVIALITY**

**PART 2: THE OUTSIDE WORLD:
DEALING WITH ANTI-BLACK RACISM**

**PART 3: MY WORLD EMERGING IN THE OUTSIDE WORLD:
URBAN POPULAR CULTURE AND THE QUESTION OF RACE**

ACKNOWLEDGMENTS

The act of acknowledgment is perhaps more than anything else a confession of communal belonging. I belong to at least six such communities. As a senior researcher at the Royal Netherlands Institute of Southeast Asian and Caribbean Studies, I have the distinct pleasure of working with Gert Oostindie, Corinne Hofman, Rosemarijn Hoefte, Esther Captain, David Kloos, Alex van Stipriaan, Marieke Bloembergen, Sony Jean, Alana Osbourne, Stacey MacDonald, Sanne Rotmeijer, and Tibisay Sankatsing Nava, who are opening up area studies to global flows and therewith critically rethinking the afterlife of colonialism. This book is a contribution to our necessary endeavor.

My second intellectual home is the Anthropology Department of the University of Amsterdam. Thank you Julie McBrien, Rachel Spronk, Annelies Moors, Muriel Kiesel, Vincent de Rooij, Oskar Verkaaik, Annemarie Mol, Mattijs van de Port, Amade M'charek, Luisa Steur, Marieke Brand, Rivke Jaffe, Robert Pool, Yolanda van Ede, Eileen Moyer, Milena Veenis, Rob van Ginkel, Tina Harris, Nico Besnier, Peter van Rooden, Sarah Bracke-Grieder, Erella Grassiani, Sruti Bala, Laurens Bakker, Anne de Jong, Alex Strating, Lieve Connick, and Noelle Steneker for making my academic home a place that strives to hold the cardinal virtue of a Marxist dedication to praxis, which opens up scholarship to hidden voices, feminist, postcolonial, and otherwise.

I have witnessed that such an ethos fosters students who appreciate that pursuing scholarly excellence can go hand in hand with a rejection of prejudice and injustice. Of the many promising minds

I have had the privilege of engaging, Dastan Abdali deserves honorable mention. From the moment we met, Dastan has been willing to extend a helping hand gratis with this book project. I am sure, Dastan, that you will make a great scholar if that route chooses you and you accept the invitation. The fourth community of interest that I call home are scholars who are writing postcolonial and decolonial studies into academic existence in the Kingdom of the Netherlands: Miriyam Aouragh, Sharelly Emanuelson, Birgit Meyer, Wayne Modest, Yvon van der Pijl, Markus Balkenhol, Gloria Wekker, Donya Alinejad, Nancy Jouwe, Karwan Fatah Black, Jasmijn Rana, Anouk de Koning, Wigbertson Isenia, Pepijn Brandon, Pooyan Talbi, Marleen de Witte, Hebe Verrest, Naomi van Stapele, Charissa Granger, Rachel Gillet, Wim Manuhutu, Rosalba Icaza, Aminata Cairo, Lucia Nankoe, Eugene Clemencia, Jordi Halfman, Gregory Richardson, Lydia Emerencia, Melissa Weiner, Antonio Carmona Baez, Rose Mary Allen, Inchi Witteveen, Pedro de Weever, Nawal Mustafa, Angela Roe, Ellen van Beuren, Patricia Schor, Egbert Martina, Teresa Leslie, Richenel Ansano, Adnan Hossain, Zuleika Sheik, Markha Valenta, Irene Stengs, Rolando Vázquez, and Khadija Al-Mourabit. Let us remain in conversation as we do our work in our various locales.

While I grew up academically reading Caribbean classics such as *The Black Jacobins* by C. L. R. James and *Discourse on Colonialism* by Aimé Césaire, my schooling was based on personal exchanges with the brilliant writers who came after: Anton Allahar, Linden Lewis, Ivette Romero, Hilbourne Watson, Rhonda Frederick, Deborah Thomas, Brian Meeks, Dave Ramsaran, Rex Nettleford, Lisa Outar, Rhoda Reddock, Paul Gilroy, Patricia Mohammed, Ifeona Fulani, Patricia Saunders, Gaby Hosein, Samuel Furé Davis, Jocelyne Guibault, Patricia van Leeuwaarde Moonsammy, Tim Rommen, and Yarimar Bonilla. Your work exemplifies twenty-first-century Caribbean studies.

My most intimate community is my family. I would like to thank my wife Esmee and my fantastic four—Arum, Enzo, Nala, and Zora—for their unconditional love. When I look in their eyes, I see

my deceased maternal grandmother, Elza, my first and most enduring teacher. In remembering her, I recognize my mother and father,
Angela and Justin, and my in-laws, Jose and Herman. Academics you
may not be, but your commitment to nonracialism and economic
justice for all is the spirit that animates this book.

PREFACE

If I had been born and currently lived in a country that needed academic odes to remind its complacent inhabitants of the racial oppression of people who look like me, this essay would have been a Negro spiritual.

If I had been born and currently lived in a country where, after the official abolition of slavery, people who look like me faced Jim Crow, the new Jim Crow, and post-1960s forms of White supremacy, this essay would have been a blues.

If I had been born and currently lived in a country where the presidential election of a person who looks like me was succeeded by a president who refuses to acknowledge anti-black racism, this essay would have been a sorrow song.

Now, because none of this is my reality,

And,

Because I was born in the Dutch Caribbean, where today anti-black racism is nowhere comparable to what takes place in the United States,

Because I was born in the Dutch Caribbean, where today White normativity is nowhere comparable to what takes place in Latin America,

Because I was born in the Dutch Caribbean, where today abject poverty is nowhere comparable to countries that directly challenged Eurocentered colonialism like Haiti,

Now, because this is my reality,

And,

Because today I live in a country where most try not to practice anti-black racism, even though many often still do,

Because today I live in a country where, when people who look like me are racially discriminated against, they can appeal to the rule of law,

Because today I live in a country where people who look like me can make use of a substantive welfare state that allows them to live a decent life,

Now, because this is my reality today,

And,

Because I cultivate the virtue of ungrounded hope, this essay can only be what it is: a sweet and sour urban tune heralding an antiracist future.

What you encounter within the many, many details of this essay are:

1. An explanation of how I and many who look like me survive and thrive in the Netherlands despite the plague of racism.

2. An ethnographic account of a Netherlands that refuses to reduce that world to White versus Black conceptualizations.

3. An alternative to the dominant approach on how to combat anti-black racism that has become commonplace in antiracist scholarship.

People who only see black men in general being oppressed by white men in general, and are unable to trace the historical dialectic, do not understand anything.

—C. L. R. James, *On the "Negro Question"*

INTRODUCTION, OR RATHER, THE QUESTION

As someone who has dedicated his academic career to dismantling the world that racism created, I can just about recite these opening lines of *The Souls of Black Folk*, one of the United States' greatest sociological works of art:

> Between me and the other world there is ever an unasked question: unasked by some through feelings of delicacy; by others through the difficulty of rightly framing it. All, nevertheless, flutter round it. They approach me in a half-hesitant sort of way, eye me curiously or compassionately, and then, instead of saying directly, How does it feel to be a problem? they say, I know an excellent colored man in my town; or, I fought at Mechanicsville; or, Do not these Southern outrages make your blood boil? At these I smile, or am interested, or reduce the boiling to a simmer, as the occasion may require. To the real question, How does it feel to be a problem? I answer seldom a word. (Du Bois [1903] 2007, 1)

The author, W. E. B. Du Bois, was referring to his pink-skinned US compatriots of a liberal bent who take the naturalness of race and thus of racial hierarchies for granted. Now here is the irony: today, many brown- and pink-skinned scholars from his country who are well versed in critical race theory and postcolonial theorizations, eyeing me curiously and compassionately, to paraphrase Du Bois, find numerous ways to ask me how it feels to be a racial problem living in the Netherlands.

I take that the motives of these academic colleagues of mine are different from those of the Americans Du Bois was critically addressing in *The Souls of Black Folk*. Unlike his liberal interrogators, my colleagues are actually critically building on his antiracist legacy. As critical race scholars, they surely appreciate the global assemblage involving the fields of governance, art, religion, sports, the entertainment industry, economics, mass media, digital technology, warfare, science, and the humanities that continuously forges the naturalization of humans into racial groups. I trust that they, too, interpret race as the powerful effect and fiction created by racism.

Charitably, I interpret the call of these American colleagues that I give a racial account of being black in the Netherlands as similar though not the same as that which overcame Du Bois throughout his lifetime. The similarity is that they, too, seek to hail me into the colonially derived category of black people, which, when written in lower case, signifies the global commonsense way of referring to brown-skinned persons who are visibly of sub-Saharan descent. These are erudite women and men, committed to social justice, who have read Gloria Wekker's *White Innocence* (2016) and studied other critical works addressing the continuing blight of anti-black racism in the Dutch world (Balkenhol 2011; Blakely 1993; Botman, Jouwe, and Wekker 2001; Essed 1991; Essed and Hoving 2014; Essed and Trienekens 2008; Essed and Nimako 2006; Hira 2009; Hondius 2009; Jones 2007). Being hailed into race and thus being confronted with this question, posed with varying degrees of insistence, is unavoidable as part of the problematic of being black in a Europe that is still decolonizing.

African Americans I meet outside of the academic circuit ask me the very same question. In those encounters, which are free from the fashions of academia, and where being of Afro-Antillean extraction and being born a Dutch citizen are not mutually exclusive positions or a combination that is always conceived as a problem to be theorized, I find it easier to exchange experiences. Theirs is what I perceive to be a genuine curiosity; a sincere wanting to know. I am at ease with their initial premise, which is that my belonging to the Netherlands is somewhat similar to their belonging to the United States. North Atlantic imperialisms were entangled, mutually influencing iterations of racial logics that dehumanized persons who look like us. I am Dutch as they are American in our own particular ways. What founds our belonging are the specific narratives of struggle as well as joy that we tell ourselves and others. Our personal views are appreciated by each other as legitimate expressions of a sense of historical "situatedness" in, respectively, the United States and the Kingdom of the Netherlands. We come to the conclusion that ours is a contested belonging, but a belonging nevertheless; an agonistic love for the specific yet interrelated colonial histories that have formed us, which we would not trade for the world.

Admittedly, the same happens with most of my fellow American scholars. We are able to engage in fruitful exchanges about the merits and shortcomings of our academic inspirations. We discuss Anthony Appiah's liberal universalist approach to dismantling racism, the antiracist theories of the Black Radical Tradition forwarded by the likes of Cedric Robinson (1983), the liberation theology preached by Cornel West (1993), or, say, Paul Gilroy's radical humanism (2000, 2004, 2010), and compare these to Gloria Wekker's (2016) more psychoanalytically informed theorizations of the structures of white supremacy. I explain that in much more profound ways than Du Bois, my views on race have mainly been informed by the scholarship of his Caribbean contemporary C. L. R. James ([1938] 1963) and a host of other Marxist-inflected scholars for whom anti-black racism is an important historical modality through which capitalist-driven oppression operates (e.g., Allahar 2004; Fanon 1967; Fields and Fields 2012; Hall and Back 2009; Lewis 2013; Mbembe 2017; Michaels 2006; Reed 1999; Watson 2001).

In my way of thinking, *proletariatization* can be fruitfully conceived as the Marxist understanding of the recurring historical operation of making some human beings *Black*, regardless of their hue or ethnicity, and therewith exploitable and at times expendable in the capitalist-dominated global order (which still privileges the West).[1] Note here the subtle distinction that Black is written with an uppercase *B*. All oppressed and exploited persons are Black in my Marxist scholarship, not only those known as black people. While the colonially derived name of the latter coincides with Blackness, most oppressed are also designated that way without carrying the label.[2] I take to heart, in other words, that "[w]ithin modernity, [B]lackness is functional and instrumental—it provides the permanent violation of Kant's categorical imperative; [B]lackness is pure means" (Warren 2017, 223). They understand that for me the destiny of black people is not to be free black people, but to be free in such a way that they can decide what and who they want to be.

With North American activist scholars who emphasize Afrocentric versions of critical race studies, the matter plays itself out differently. These are persons who are inspired by the Afro-pessimist thought of the likes of Frank B. Wilderson III (2003) and the black nationalism of Molefi Asante (2006), both of whom argue that most if not all theories produced by pink-skinned Europeans cannot adequately address the predicament of brown-skinned sub-Saharans and their descendants. For these critical race theory scholars, the world that colonialism built is inherently white supremacist and anti-black. It cannot be reformed in any shape or form. Every black man or woman in the West lives in a society that is de facto against them. I find the critique powerful, yet too totalizing and too sanitized in its reduction of life and the history of the people who look like me almost exclusively to recipients of violence (Hunter and Robinson 2016; Thomas 2018). Their quest to dismantle the world that racism created leaves the racial categories of black and white and brown intact (cf. Allahar 2004; Fields and Fields 2012; Gilroy 2000; Mbembe 2017; Reed 1999; Watson 2001).

Now in conversations with activist scholars who subscribe to black nationalism or Afro-pessimism, the question of how it feels to be black in the Netherlands is understandably not really a question. For them, "[B]lackness's distinction from a specific set of things [and people] that are called black remains largely unthought" (Moten 2008, 1745), or when acknowledged often lapses into exclusivity.[3] What is forgotten, in other words, is that the historical operation of making humans Black (i.e., global anti-Blackness) did not only happen to brown-skinned sub-Saharans. For these activist scholars following Asante (2006) and Wilderson (2003), however, Blackness is solely the condition of black people, and it is one of utter abjection. So, before I can answer, a dynamic yet implicitly static oppressor versus oppressed frame is erected, in which I am expected to solely present a narrative of the struggle for ethnoracial recognition.

Besides the intellectual disagreement, which I can live with, it is the obligatory ritual that gets under my skin. I find it quite annoying to have to exclusively embody the role of the racially hurt outsider of the Dutch world. Why can I not just be an Afro-Antillean man going about the business of doing life, whereby racism is one of the major ills I must also successfully contend with? I find myself hesitating when asked to exclusively reduce my life to a story of racial sleight.

These academic colleagues are not in any way close friends among whom I can let off steam about Dutch racism and who would recognize this as simply an expression of temporary frustration. After all, among kin and friends who love you, one always experiences moments of loving kindness that feed a positive sense of self, which can act as a buffer against inhumanities that abound. In contrast, these visiting scholars expect those temporary blues to be "structural"; to be, in other words, expressions of eternal senses of nonbelonging that overshadow my whole existence.

I sense that I am expected to rehearse in my own words something they seemingly already know about me—namely that my comfortable "corporeal schema" is shattered when reduced to the *n-word* due to the White racist gaze and actions. "My body given back to me sprawled out, distorted . . . clad in mourning" (Fanon 1967, 112), the mandatory corroboration of pop versions of Frantz Fanon's psycho-analytic theorizing.[4] Moreover, since they know that I was born and partially raised in the Dutch Caribbean islands, which are still constitutionally part of the Kingdom of the Netherlands, and having read critical academic literature on the colonial relations of the French Caribbean islands, which share a similar political status, and organic works by independence activists living in the Dutch

Antilles, I am supposed to present myself as a colonized subject seeking national independence for my people due to such daily social and economic humiliations (for academic works focusing on the French islands, see, e.g., Price 2017; Vété-Congolo 2014; for the Dutch Caribbean, see Arrindell 2014).

In tandem with European academic superstars with Caribbean roots, such as Barnor Hesse, they await my echo of "It's their world and we're just living in it" (1997, 375). They expect me to say that I do not belong and do not want to belong to the Kingdom of the Netherlands. Wanting to belong is *assimilationism*, which is disreputable. So, what I should say is something like, "*What I want is for pharaoh to set my people free!*" I am expected in other words to endorse a very superficial reading of the embattled politics of redemption that Hesse (1997), Kobena Mercer (1994), Claire Alexander (2018, 2002), and Paul Gilroy (2004, 2006) present us with. The latter avers that the ultimate goal is not only liberation from "white supremacy alone, however urgent that is required, but from all racializing and raciological thought, from racialized seeing, racialized thinking, and racialized thinking about thinking" (2000, 40).

These authors, like their mentor Stuart Hall (1992a, 1992b, 1999), remind us that boundaries are constantly being breached and that Afro-Europeans are not passive victims undone of class and other kinds of diversity. Work must continuously be done to uphold the racial myth of a white versus black Manichean world, one whereby the so-called proper natural boundary of the *white Kingdom of the Netherlands* ought to stop at the North Sea; while in the Caribbean begins *the authentic black world*. Given the reality that so many brown-skinned Dutch citizens like me either were born in or are living in the Netherlands, and given the exemplary writings on Black Brits embracing a "Britishness" whereby their Caribbean belonging is also integral to their sense of self (think of the Jamaican-born Stuart Hall critically positioning himself as a British intellectual marked by the colonial difference), why not radically rethink geography by analytically presupposing that today the Caribbean ethnically and ethically extends into Europe?[5] Why not generously presuppose that this may be part of a daring decolonial project that many Caribbean Dutch are implicitly engaged in? All it takes is a set of nonassuming conversations and the perusal of government reports to recognize that for most this is the case (Huijnk and Andriessen 2016, 300).[6] While the Windrush generation and their descendants became Black Brits as their countries became independent, most "Dutch Caribbeans" from the islands do not want full political sovereignty.[7] They want a decolonized kingdom consisting of a federation of constituent states *somewhat* as it functions today, in which their historical mode of becoming Dutch will be equally acknowledged (Guadeloupe 2013a; de Jong 2009; Oostindie 2010; Oostindie and Verton 1998).

I qualify this longing with the term *somewhat*, for currently, the kingdom consists of the constituent states of Aruba, Curaçao, Sint Maarten, and the Netherlands. The latter also includes the three Caribbean islands of Bonaire, Sint Eustatius, and Saba as overseas public entities. This is all that remains of the Dutch empire that until the Second World War also consisted of Oost Indië (now Indonesia) and Surinam. All citizens of the constituent states of the kingdom have their own prime minister and Parliament, although they all are bearers of the same Dutch EU passport. There is a democratic deficit as, above these separate apparatuses, one finds the kingdom government. In this supranational administrative unit, one encounters all the ministers of the Netherlands, with one representative of each of the other three constituent states, presiding over kingdom affairs such as defense, foreign affairs, and the safeguarding of the civil and political rights of all the citizens of the polity. The Netherlands decides, as it is politically overrepresented, much to the chagrin of political elites on the islands.

The current makeup is the outcome a long, contingent colonial history, whereby constitutional developments during and after the Second World War mark a decisive turning point. While the Netherlands was occupied by the Germans and Japan came to rule over the Dutch East Indies, "[o]nly the Caribbean territories remained 'free,' that is, colonial possessions ruled by the government in exile," as the historian and don of Dutch Caribbean studies Gert Oostindie puts it. While it took a "full four years of bitter warfare and thorny negotiations before the transfer of sovereignty was accomplished by the end of 1949," the first phase of decolonization of the Dutch Caribbean went about quietly.

> In the 1954 "Statuut" or Charter of the Kingdom, both Suriname and the Netherlands Antilles attained autonomy within the Kingdom of the Netherlands. This constitutional status would prevail for Suriname until the full transfer of sovereignty in 1975. The Statuut still holds the six islands to the Netherlands in an ambivalent postcolonial imbroglio—not because the Dutch wanted to retain their former colonies in the Caribbean sea, but rather because they found no valid arguments and effective means to impose independence on populations consistently refusing the "gift" of sovereignty. (Oostindie 2008, 4)

Nowadays you can of course find some activist intellectuals and politicians who gladly welcome the gift of full sovereignty, but for many of them more power within the kingdom will suffice. In the various conversations I have had and overheard, and the anthropological research I have conducted, I recognize that this sentiment holds less so for the vast majority of the citizens on the islands as well as the Dutch Antillean communities living in the Netherlands. They are content with being legally Dutch citizens, as it brings benefits in a world where, especially in the North Atlantic part of the kingdom, boundaries are often erected when one's skin is brown and/or one's wallet insufficiently filled. What most want, however, is more justice and equal recognition of belonging for the brown skins and the working poor; yet this need not necessarily come about via reforms that give the political elites on the islands more discretionary power—many feel they are abusing the constitutional autonomy they already have (Guadeloupe 2013a; Oostindie 2010, 2008; Oostindie and Verton 1998).[8]

TEXT BOX 1: TERMINOLOGY

1. Blackness in this book denotes the historical racist operations (political, economic, culture, scientific, and social) of naming or implicitly designating a group of people Black and therewith making it legitimate that they be treated as means rather than ends in themselves.

2. Global anti-Black racism refers to the way, since the horror of transatlantic slavery (part of the operation of Blackness), that brown-skinned people of sub-Saharan African descent became known as Black people. In being given this name, they have been symbolically and materially disenfranchised on the basis of the idea of racial difference.

3. Global anti-Blackness speaks to a wider operation. The concept accommodates all historically constituted groups from North African Amazigh to Australian Aboriginals to Native Americans to the Rohingya in Myanmar, the latter facing genocidal racism.

4. Urban Blackness is a concept coined to analyze the way in which popular cultural expressions and styles mostly attributed to Black people are being commodified by capitalism and marketed as a hip meta-identity that anyone can don.

5. In contradistinction to this commoditization process, political Blackness, a term borrowed from Stuart Hall, designates those people who resignify and transform Blackness into a political identity similar to that of the proletariat. In doing so, they seek to dismantle the racial and unjust economic order.

6. Nonracialism designates the dismantling of the idea of racial difference in governance and other institutional arrangements and practices. Contesting antiracism in one's scholarship, politics, and everyday routine is a means of combating all forms of global anti-Blackness to arrive at a place in which nonracialism is the rule rather than the exception. We get there when humankind as a whole becomes Black. In other words, when the materially and phenotypically privileged also acknowledge and accept the accursed Blacks (descendants of enslaved persons like me, Aboriginals, Rohingya, etc.) and their histories of subjugation as part of who we as an expression of life are.

Isn't this nonracist desire of most Antilleans premised on staying within the kingdom and transforming it into a nonracial polity, whereby there is no one specific way a Dutch citizen should ideally look, a project that can help further dismantle the anti-black racism and global anti-Blackness that most socially engaged scholars struggle against? (see text box 1).

I think it can be and is, and as such I have come to subscribe to it. What's more, it troubles—to employ the terms of the anthropologist Michel-Rolph Trouillot—our implicit scholastic adherence to the colonially produced *geography of management* and *of imagination*. Trouillot coined those terms to refer to "those aspects of the development of world capitalism" that reordered the world into the West and the non-West with the accompanying realized fictions of hermetically closed-off continents, civilizations, peoples, heritages, cultures, and identities—in short, hegemonic racialized conceptualizations of self and other that we today take for granted (Trouillot 2003, 37).[9] The deconstruction of these myths of separation and ethnic incommensurability, through the desire and work of most Afro-Antilleans toward a higher synthesis within the kingdom, is a *counter gift* (following the metaphor of Oostindie) with which many in the Netherlands still have to come to terms. They understand that racism is a Dutch problem, not something solely related to them. So what do I say to my academic peers who ask me about being a black man living in the Netherlands?

I begin by reminding them about what they already know, that "there is no whole body" (Lyotard 1993, 112) except in the mind of a theorist or policy maker. Belonging to a society is a matter of context, degree, structure, agency, and choice. No individual living in a society and bearing equal citizenship rights can ever be totally outside of that society. One is always inside in a particular way, at particular times and places, with particular others. We are embodied beings, as the anthropologist Michael Jackson reminds us, always grounded in particular environments with objects and others through which we move and with whom we interact (2013, 70). It is this continuous shifting mix, with all the cooperation and struggle it implies, that makes itself felt when one is asked how one imagines and appreciates society. I choose to see it as a political act to imagine myself as an agent actively integrating with multiple others and therewith co-constructing the ever-changing open collective called Dutch society. Moreover, thinking of the Netherlands as outside the constitutional reality of the kingdom where we all carry the same passport and have equal rights as citizens is a strange fiction to me. I tell my academic peers that I am beginning to realize that this way of claiming the kingdom and the wider North Atlantic is one of the underacknowledged visions that luminaries like the political theorist C. L. R. James hinted at, when he provocatively called himself a black European and made that magnificent speech entitled "Black Studies and the Contemporary Student" in 1969 (see text box 2).

For James, the dream of a just, planet-wide politics and ethics of interhuman recognition is only possible when the hidden faces of all those who have contributed ideationally and materially to the wealth and power of Western civilization—so also those of my brown-skinned great-grandparents—are fully acknowledged:

The wealth which enabled the bourgeoisie to challenge those who were in charge of society and institute the power-building industrial regime came from slavery, the slave trade, and the industries that were based upon that. . . . And secondly, in the struggle by which the bourgeoisie established the political and social structure of this new form in the very front line, fighting as anybody else and better than most in France in the French revolutionary war, and in the American Civil War, were slaves. . . . This is the history of Western civilization. (James 1992b, 396–97)[10]

If this is the history of Western civilization, which has impacted the world, everyone in the world will have to acknowledge the enslaved sub-Saharans as part of their modern heritage; part of the acknowledgment that our ancestry is, to willfully use an outmoded term, creole and universal. And, thus Black! Only then will racism as an ideology be no more. The human diversities of the world will

TEXT BOX 2: C. L. R. JAMES

C. L. R. James (January 4, 1901—May 31, 1989) was one of the foremost Marxist intellectuals of the twentieth century. Born in Trinidad and Tobago into a middle-class family, James's stature in Caribbean studies is perhaps only equaled by that of Frantz Fanon. His discussions with Trotsky and E. P. Thompson, as well as his influence on academics such as Stuart Hall, have earned him international acclaim in theorizing the interrelation between racism and capitalist exploitation. It is not too much of an overstatement to claim that there are many readings of C. L. R. James. He is known among other things as a pan-Africanist, a Marxist theorist, a cricket commentator, a Caribbean revolutionary, a Europhile, and more. The spirit of C. L. R. James that animates this book is the same that highlights the possibility of cooperation between working-class oldcomers and newcomers in Europe, due to their everyday psychological jolts of awareness that they and others occupying a similarly deprived station are not being given a fair share of the riches of the world. Europeans of different hues could come together and seek to dismantle their prison of racism and capitalism. Their goal would be to institute a global economic and social order that benefits all. I contend that this nonracist and humanist spirit of a planetary revolt runs through the differing politics and scholarship of C. L. R. James. The spirit can of course be critiqued for particular analytical shortcomings, for instance that it is not intersectional enough, that it is too easy on race, too Eurocentric, too dependent on Leninist Marxism. As this book is not an exegesis on the thought of James, I do not directly engage with these shortcomings here. What remains useful for me is James's unflinching hope. Now to be clear: my take is that James was not a naïve idealist but someone who was always offering radical re/descriptions that made his peers and readers see and act on liberating possibilities in the midst of structural symbolic and material injustice.

remain; however, their meaning will not be tied to the hierarchical colonial understandings that we have inherited. With a nonracialist frame of mind, we might be more effective in creating a transnational force geared toward dismantling the global economic power structure suffocating most of humanity. As Bob Marley phrased it at his most nonracialist: "Until that day the dream of lasting peace, world citizenship, rule of international morality will remain but a fleeting illusion to be pursued but never attained."[11]

This way of being in the world, this way of making the abstract universal of a world where all belong, equally concrete for the Netherlands, is not what my academic interlocutors primarily engaged in black nationalism and Afro-pessimism want to hear. My presupposition of the denigrated black subjectivity that I am hailed to perform usually turns out to be factual, because whenever I begin with an upbeat story of my agency and that of other Afro-Antilleans in re/making the Netherlands, I am told something to the effect of, "Yes, but tell us about your experiences with racism even though you are legally Dutch." I am expected as I mentioned above to renounce my specific bodily experiences, and my political act of working toward a more just Dutch kingdom, for an abstract, negated black body. I should solely talk about being or feeling myself exclusively a legal alien, maligned by the populist and racist winds they rightfully read so much about (Geschiere 2009; de Jong 2010; Jones 2007; Wekker 2016).

I startle them when I push back that the Netherlands is my home, for it is a Dutch Caribbean island. I live in it and think about it *as though* it were a Caribbean isle; just one of the island countries that make up the Kingdom of the Netherlands that thinks too much of itself. And even if they think of the Netherlands as European, they must reckon with the fact that "Europe is no longer white and never will be again. . . . All of us are faced with a stark choice: we can rail against European evolution, or we can help to smooth its process. And if we choose the latter, the first thing we must remind ourselves of is the lesson that great fiction teaches us as we sink into character

and plot and suspend our disbelief: for a moment 'they' are 'us'"
(Phillips 2013, 16). Most find all this interesting, in an amusing kind
of way; however, after the amusement comes the reproach.
Did I forget how The Hague belittles the Dutch Caribbean isles
where I was born? Did I forget about the Middle Passage? Did I
forget about the Kala Pani? Did I forget about the hundreds of thou-
sands of African and Asian men and women and children worked to
death? Did I forget about what was done to my great-grandmothers
and great-grandfathers? All at the hands of the native (read: white)
Dutch! And did I wish to be blind to the struggles of the Afro-Dutch
residing in the Netherlands today? Did the Europhilia of C. L. R.
James and a steady diet of supposedly radical French dead men, like
the philosophers Jean-François Lyotard and Jean Baudrillard, lead
me to a postmodern false consciousness, whereby an incredulity toward metanarratives translates itself into a disbelief in the symbolic
and material power of anti-black racism? For the record, I am not,
and I did not. I concur with much that has been written about racism in the Dutch world. It is an undeniable everyday phenomenon.
There are, indeed, historically constituted repertoires and institutional practices than many native Dutch and the state itself resort
to, often unthinkingly, but my project is an essential complement
to those necessary insights. Mine is a politics of re/description, of
unlikely interpretations, highlighting undervalued causal relations
and reasons for actions that challenge all inhabitants of the Dutch
kingdom to dwell and act in decolonial ways. Where Philomena
Essed (1991) focuses on the experience that Afro-Dutch women have
regarding everyday racism, and Gloria Wekker (2016) undertakes
a "psychoanalysis" of white people as she phrases it, mine is one
that brings to the fore the ways brown-skinned women and men of
Antillean descent in the Netherlands contest their *secondarization*
and together with other Dutch construct a more inclusive belonging.
    I take seriously C. L. R. James's words: "Always, always, always, the
task is to develop the consciousness, the independence, the sense
of destiny, the sense of responsibility, among the masses of people"
(1992d, 150).[12] Let me put it differently. What I do is to contribute

to that branch of anthropology, similar in style to the essayistic writings of the likes of Patrick Chamoiseau (2018), Edwidge Danticat (2011), Caryl Phillips (2013), Maryse Condé (2004), Édouard Glissant (2000), Derek Walcott (1998), James Baldwin (1998), Alice Walker (1983), and Wilson Harris (1970)—think in anthropology of the work of Karin Willemse (2014), Tine Davids (2014), Michael Jackson (2013), and Nigel Rapport (2008)—that seeks to critically complement the important political abstractions concretized in varied forms of strategic identity politics and aligned academic productions. As useful as these interventions may be, in the wrong hands they may inadvertently reproduce the racial and ethnic camp thinking that is being combated (the strategic and socially constructed nature of ethnoracial identities being easily forgotten). And in my quest to write against race, while acknowledging the force of racism, C. L. R. James and, yes, even the insights of the Jean-François Lyotards of Europe as appreciated by that old Caribbean master have been indispensable to me.[13]

I cannot forget that "people who only see black men in general being oppressed by white men in general, and are unable to trace the historical dialectic, do not understand anything" (James 1996, 96). The same goes for critical race scholars who read these words of Du Bois, again taken from *The Souls of Black Folk*, in racially exclusive ways: "One ever feels his two-ness,—an American, a Negro; two souls, two thoughts, two unreconciled strivings; two warring ideals in one dark body, whose dogged strength alone keeps it from being torn asunder" ([1903] 2007, 8–9).

Du Bois was presenting his readers with an interpretation of the inner conflict faced by African Americans that nevertheless could be reconciled once the United States' racial order was dismantled. I find it more profitable to somewhat unmoor Du Bois's theory of double consciousness from its African American specificity, by interpreting it as very powerful local iteration of his recognition of the creole constitution of the world: capitalist-driven imperialism entails that all the peoples of the world are in each other, for they co-constitute each other.

In presenting the mental effect of this co-constitution in terms of double consciousness, Du Bois was attempting to break the intellectual vice grip that led pink-skinned Americans to misrecognize him and others who looked like him in racially and culturally exclusive terms. To be effective in his circumstances, he nationalized and exclusively circumscribed the potentiality of the creole consciousness of all modern subjects in the racial terms of the United States. We need not follow him.[14]

The sociology of the likes of Orlando Patterson demonstrates that an updating of Du Bois is necessary, given the Oprah Winfreys in the United States, but also that Afro-Caribbeans and Afro-Latinos usually do not feel the war of twoness that Du Bois describes (Patterson 1977, 1980, 2000, 2005, 2006; Williams 1995). Just think how odd it would sound for an Afro-Jamaican like, say, Usain Bolt, part of the Afro-Caribbean world, to claim that his "Negro-ness" and Jamaican-ness are warring ideals in his dark body! Context matters.

C. L. R. James exemplified the understanding that critically inheriting the past means exclusively appreciating Black and White as conceptual categories instead of so-called facts of nature. To repeat, in my Marxist way of thinking, Black and White are concepts I employ to hierarchically categorize a person's station in the capitalist order. Skin complexion is of little relevance here. I categorize wealthy blacks like Jay-Z or Oprah Winfrey as White, while pink-skinned Poles who migrate to the Netherlands to work for next to nothing are best described as Black. My categorization coincides with the implicit common sense of the economic sphere. In addition, since the economic sphere cannot be fully divorced from that of politics, Black and White are also implicitly operative as categories of governance. Here, however, a repetition with a difference occurs. While benefiting from tax breaks for the rich and other policy perks accorded the wealthy few, most censuses in the North Atlantic would classify Jay-Z and Oprah Winfrey as black billionaires. I read the adjective "black" as a qualification within the more general category of rich (read White). Then, there is the sphere populated among others by those who contest this racialized political economy: universities, think tanks, social movements. In constructing their theoretical edifices against race, many operatives in this sphere also employ Black and White as analytical concepts. Usually, however, they do not sufficiently discriminate Black and White from blacks and whites. Skin complexion and phenotype remain implicitly leading in their productions. I am not implying that the work of the latter is equitable with the racial essentialisms of many of those involved in capitalist-mediated modes of governance; however, the two often meet and merge temporarily in activism and engaged scholarship—think of the many scholars who are avowed black nationalists or who espouse the ideology's positive effects (e.g., Irele 2005; Asante 2006; Eaton, Livingston, and McAdoo 2010). That temporary merger often becomes a matter of fact leading to the naturalization of racial identities while combating racism. To avoid this pitfall, I categorically distinguish black and white (people)—the common sense of the West that has gone global—written fully in lowercase, from Black and White, which deconstructs that habit of thought. I take my cues from James, who foregrounded the fact that all peoples are marked by the transcultural inheritance of colonialism and resistance thereto, even if disproportionally benefiting those pink-skinned folks who act and are structurally positioned as White.

We, born after the tragic conquest of the earth by European superpowers, are the inheritors of the varied logics and cultures of the *Conquistadores* (conquerors) and the *Nativos* (downtrodden natives), my terms for the historical products and producers of what Trouillot (2003) described as the geography of the imagination and its contestations. As these two logics emerged together, and often merged in the heat of battle informing the subjectivity of all peoples, the great decolonial work on an interindividual and institutional level is balancing the symbolic cleansing of both inheritances in a mutually transformative way, a way that allows us to recognize our plural historical becoming as we seek to demolish global anti-Blackness, in its varied local expressions (see text box 3).[15]

As such, what follows is the kind of extensively *penned* answer I would give to the brown- and pink-skinned scholars from the

TEXT BOX 3: *NATIVO* AND *CONQUISTADOR*

While in first instance the terms *Nativo* and *Conquistador* allude to the West and the formally colonized peoples and lands, as analytical categories they signal more complicated relations. Within the category of the colonized *Nativos*, there were those who fell into the camp of the *Conquistadores*—namely, groups who were imperial prior to the Western conquest, or groups who gained power and economic might through various modes of indirect rule instituted after colonization. So, too, in the geographic camp of the *Conquistadores*, one has to acknowledge that there were those who lived and were treated as *Nativos* (designated Black). Still, regardless of whichever camp our ancestors belonged to, by virtue of their position within the colonial orders, they were impacted by the relations between the empires and their colonies. The work of racism was and continues to be that of having us understand ourselves as belonging to separate so-called races and ethnic groups. Philosophical accounts of world history are at their best when they go against that common sense and present these complications, thereby revealing the mechanisms that conceal the global creolization from which we emerged.

United States, and their followers in the Netherlands, whom I only fleetingly encounter, who ask me to speak about my personal experience as a segue into a discussion on anti-black racism in the Netherlands. It is a response based upon my radical, bodily subjectivity born of inter- and intrasubjective encounters in the Netherlands that were shaped by and that retroactively shape my reflections on life in the Dutch Caribbean isles, where I spent most of my childhood. As it is my contention following Lyotard that we are born in the middle of things, always write and reflect in the middle of things, and that what we understand as the past and present are abstractions we employ to manage and make sense of the ungovernable unfolding of life in the middle of things, I do not make any sharp distinction between fieldwork and life. There is no beginning and end of reflection. For me, anthropology is a discipline of infinitely rehearsing life experiences with others on and off the job, behind and in front of the computer, whereby academic and nonacademic interpretations and ways of doing life are inspirations to make sense of the objective of tackling injustice; the ultimate moral and social task being that one renders a contribution to bringing about what Paul Gilroy (2000), inspired by the likes of C. L. R. James, termed a planetary humanism—modes of interhuman recognition that explicitly seek to demolish global anti-Blackness. I call this mode of living "dwelling in life with decolonial eyes": a fully visceral politics of seeing that appreciates and brings to the fore the small acts of ordinary men and women of all hues who despite their prejudices are perpetually deconstructing in their own ways the continuing relevance of assessing self and other in the colonial categories of racial superiors and inferiors or as cultural incompatibles.

This collective work can only be done and have effect due to the cultures of conviviality, the modes of living together, which emerged in various neighborhoods in the Netherlands. Paul Gilroy (2004, 2006) was again one of the first theorists who called on us to be attentive to this dynamic that had made the unruly multiculture a fact of life, despite the highly mediatized pronouncements of political pundits to the contrary.[16] These convivial cultures meet and merge and are sometimes taken up in commerce.

The product of this unfinished synthesis, as we know, is popular culture in Stuart Hall's understanding of the term. Popular culture, artistic-aesthetic renditions of life, is not the exclusive property of oldcomers or newcomers in the Netherlands. Neither is it fully free or fully co-opted by commerce and formal politics. Most of the commercially successful popular culture in my part of the world, and the culture I have made the focus of my scholarship, is Black Atlantic—meaning those super-creolized cultural products that are primarily produced by the descendants of those who survived the Middle Passage (Gilroy 1993).

"Urban popular culture" is the term I use to refer to this varied collection of cultural expressions. This is also the way these cultural expressions are referred to by most who produce and who partake of them in the Netherlands. It harks back to the name given to these cultural products by Frankie Crocker, the legendary American radio disc jockey.[17] Urban popular culture is the culture of hip with a cosmopolitan city attitude.[18]

I grew up with and was nourished intellectually by urban popular culture. It is one of the reasons why I identify and refer to persons who look like me as brown rather than black. I learned that from the hip-hop MC KRS-One (1993) when he rapped: "STILL, with no name, with no fight, with no fuss / We just, take on the name, that MASSA give us / That name is NIGGA, the correct is NEGRO / It's Spanish for BLACK, white mahn call us DAT / There is also NEGROID, also NEGRO / Now, all nigga pon the corner playin cee-lo / Man you're not a ne-gro, cause your skin is not black / Take a look at yourself, you're brown and that's a fact."

I follow KRS-One in recognizing that brown-skinned individuals and pinkish-skinned individuals are what exists on a visually informed phenomenological level. Nonetheless, every minute of the day brown-skinned people and pink-skinned people are continuously enticed to naturalize the idea of being black or white, and equating these with Black and White. In so doing, they help animate and reinforce the categories created to alienate and desensitize them from recognizing commonalities. White as a conceptual category may not be rescuable (as it is bound up with exclusive power in the aforementioned hierarchy). Black, as I mentioned earlier, can be reconceived in a way similar to, say, the Marxist notion of the proletariat, that is, political Blackness. Black then would be a signifier that unites people of sub-Saharan African descent, or brown-skinned people of various ethnicities facing oppression, and can be extended to include pinkish people undergoing the same faith. At its most expansive, Black would include all those who wish and struggle to live in a nonracialized world where racial and class oppression is a thing of the past. The 1805 constitution of the Caribbean nation of Haiti is an early example of this possibility, in which all inhabitants regardless of hue or ethnicity became Black (Saucier and Woods 2016).[19]

Now this dream and work at inhabiting a nonracist future, expressed in the key of political Blackness, did not disappear. It is just that the dream and work to make it concrete are increasingly manifested in ways that are not immediately recognized. This brings me to the main argument of this book, which is: in the Netherlands, one can discern the transposition of political Blackness into urban popular culture. Dutch of all hues and ethnicities who are into this culture are embracing the urban Black performances of the, for the most part, brown-skinned heroes and heroines that they emulate. They actually desire to be and to look like them. Antiracist activists and intellectuals invested in strategic essentialisms would do well to recognize the antiracist transfigurations at play in urban popular culture. Within the structures and everyday understandings of "race" in the Netherlands, alternative modes of being are implicit in urban popular culture that do not fully adhere to the well-known colonially derived categorizations of people into black, brown, and white.

Capitalism figures front and center in the transposition of Blackness from the explicitly political to the cultural. As such, urban popular culture is contradictory. It is pregnant with this possibility of resignifying Blackness—making it cool and therewith removing the stigma attached to brown-skinned sub-Saharans and everyone else historically and contextually positioned as racially lesser—but it is also ridden with opposing forces.[20] In the expressions of urban popular culture, the quest for a world undone of anti-black racism sits untidily with a longing for status and wealth. They are expressions of agonistic encounters that loop back in unexpected ways into the cultures of conviviality. As such, progress is not linear. In the cultures of conviviality and their contextual expressions, in urban popular culture, one encounters decoloniality threatened and seduced by reactionary ways of being. Both do not necessarily produce the clear-cut progressive politics or mass mobilization that impatient and hyperwoke intellectuals desire. Yet it is important to bear in mind what C. L. R. James perceived and never ceased reminding us of: "The history of man is his effort to make the abstract universal concrete. He constantly seeks to destroy, to move aside, that is to say, to negate what impedes his movement towards freedom and happiness. Man is the subject of history" (James 1980b, 84). To see with decolonial eyes is to acknowledge and promote this Jamesian dynamic or rather redescription of human history within the cultures of conviviality and urban popular culture that seem and are somewhat contrary or conflicted. James's "Man," meaning here human beings in a world based on anti-black racism and other forms of oppression (class, gendered, and religious), may not always be aware that they cannot be free and treated equally without everyone else also being free and treated equally, too. It is therefore imperative to explicitly take up the position of Barrymore Anthony Bogues, a heretical intellectual championed in scholarship attending to anti-Blackness. He argues:

> Black radical intellectual production engages in a double opera-
> tion—an engagement with Western radical theory and then a cri-
> tique of this theory.... We are now well aware of the disciplinary
> dimension of orthodoxy, which fashions subjects into a specific
> set of social practices and customs—in the Spanish Inquisition,
> making the Muslim a Christian. For the black radical intellectual,
> "heresy" means becoming human, not white nor imitative of the
> colonial, but overrunning white/European normativity—in the
> words of Robert Marley, refusing "what you wanted us to be."
> (Bogues 2003, 13)

A "heretical intellectual" distinguishes himself from Antonio Gramsci's organic (people-oriented) and traditional (professional-oriented) intellectual in that he is both and explicitly cognizant of the power of anti-black racism as that which has shaped the way humans conceive of self and other. He employs the scholastics of the academic establishment, mixing these with the wisdom of the subalterns to produce texts that contribute to demolishing anti-black racism and accompanying modes of subjugation. Bogues, the political theorist who coined the term, refers to C. L. R. James and W. E. B. Du Bois as heretical intellectuals par excellence. In keeping with the spirit of James's planetary humanism and thus avoiding to unwittingly mark the heretical intellectual in exclusively racial terms, it is important to recognize that the work of any engaged antiracist anthropologist ought to be indistinguishable from that of those donning the former label. At their best, anthropologists are heretical intellectuals in that their nonracial epistemological premise is the psychic unity and interrelated existence of humankind. They are in the business to employ Bogues's terms of *discursive representation* of the under- or unpresented, and in doing so they critically *rewrite history* and therewith challenge common sense by establishing *different values* for doing politics and more widely fostering interhuman recognition (on these points, see Bogues 2003, 91–92). My anthropology is such that squeamishness or implicit reluctance toward fully tackling anti-black racism and intraclass discrimination among everyday brown-skinned and pink-skinned people is not denied. Rather, they are placed in perspective and redescribed using theory and urban popular culture in ways that nevertheless foreground positive forays within the cultures of conviviality toward decoloniality. I am not a good Friday anthropologist, one who specializes in solely reminding readers of the dread of Western imperialism; rather, I am one who focuses on the convivial rays of sunlight within the dark night of racism and class oppression. Here follows a set of reworked musings that first saw light in edited volumes and journals. This book is my way of critically giving something back to the cultures of conviviality and the insights from urban popular cultures that have shaped me, while also giving a worthwhile answer to those who have asked me, How does it feel to be a black man living in the Netherlands?

PART 1

MY WORLD

ON URBAN POPULAR CULTURE AND CONVIVIALITY

CHAPTER 1

THE BEGINNING OF AN ANSWER

Nowadays, it goes against the grain to get critical interlocutors to see the Netherlands as I see it. To appreciate my political project in solidarity with those Afro-Antilleans and others whose act of decoloniality is to go against the grain and acknowledge that *les Pays-Bas* is part of the Dutch kingdom and belongs to the unruly multiculture that currently resides here, I begin by offering a clearing by way of a seemingly unrelated letter I wrote several years ago:

Dear Alyah,
Your aunties Sabah and Naima, with whom I have been best friends for years, asked me to write a eulogy to commemorate the passing of your father Yusef. I started doing so, but with every line I wrote, I recognized that I should actually be addressing you. Yes, you, a five-month-old infant. It is in you that his hopes and dreams live on. If your father did not have faith in love and life, he would not have conceived you. No matter how bleak a moment you will face when you grow up, and those moments will surely come, you must always remember that you are a symbol of his faith.

I address this letter to you not as an academic to a child, nor as the learned man to the novice. Such is the foolishness of those who take their social status far too seriously. I am writing to you because I realize that one of the most important aspects of human life is the passing on of advice. What I offer is advice. Sift through it, and you can use what you like.

I cannot offer you a credible explanation as to why your father was murdered. All I can say to you is that God, the beautiful name men and women of all cultures have given to Universal Justice, does not sleep. And God was not asleep the day your father died. So why did God then let such a terrible crime happen, you may ask yourself when you are old enough to fathom what happened. I advise you to never contemplate such thoughts. Such a question is not worth asking. It leads to madness and what's more, it is actually not the right question to ask.

You should be addressing your question to humankind, for it is we who constantly show disregard for each other's lives. Your father's death, and I do not mean to trivialize it by saying this, is an echo of one of the consistent sounds our species has been making. When you realize this, despair disappears, and hope appears. For anything that we have created, we can re-create differently. God can lend a helping hand in these endeavors, for goodness comes to those who struggle and fight for their goodness and the goodness of others. I/We, meaning I am because We are, and We are what We are because of how each and every individual acts and thinks, is the simplest and truest philosophical formula. You will do well to remember this formula.

All this means that when you grow up, you will have to decide what role you will play as a co-creator of the kingdom of humankind. In the Netherlands, this little hamlet of that global kingdom, persons of Moroccan descent have a bad name. From my fellow academics who earn their bread and butter researching the so-called marokkaanse probleem, the Moroccan issue, you can get all the statistics about the felonies committed by Moroccan problem youth and the rise of Islamic fundamentalism among this sector of the Dutch population. From the mouthpieces of popularized barbarism, and by that I mean populist politicians and columnists, you can get a sense of the current sentiment that lives in the hearts of too many Dutch citizens.

From defenders of the Moroccan "community"—academics, liberal politicians, and columnists—you can get counterarguments to demolish the equating of the term "Moroccan" with crime and religious fanaticism. I refuse to offer you that.

I refuse to use your father's death as a social cause, whether it is a liberal cause or a conservative one. Your father did not die for a cause. He died so that many of us can reduce ourselves solely to passion-driven beings because we are socially reduced to unthinking beings. Your father's killer was such a being. You have every right to be angry with him. You do not have any right to hate him. Anger and hatred must not be confused. My way of not confusing them is to always remember that the person I am angry with is also somebody's child. Hating him or her is dehumanizing that person and therefore indirectly doing violence to the mother and father of the perpetrator of the offence. Moreover, it makes the hater a passion-driven being, a being that does not combine passion with thought.

You must never let that happen to you, and we who love you must do our utmost best that this does not happen to you. And if we do our best and you do yours, when you are a grown woman, the Moroccan issue will be but a distant memory. You will be able to climb into trams, walk in the parks, and go to job interviews, without the sneers and the fears. You will also be aware of the new scapegoat (a recently arrived group). If you remember that I/We philosophy, you will not participate in that latest hysteria. You will combine passion with rigorous thought, which when done well breeds morality.

I promised your aunties Sabah and Naima to write a eulogy. I wrote a letter to you. I hope that one day you too will write a letter to someone who needs to hear words of hope in the storm that we call life. Yours Truly, Francio[1]

CHAPTER 2

THE SECURE DUTCH WORLD
OF MY TEENAGE YEARS

Let me offer some background information before I explain how this letter relates to thinking about the Netherlands as though it were a Caribbean island—by which I mean, a place where living with difference is a fact of life. I arrived in the Netherlands when I was eighteen years of age. It was 1989. I went to live in the south of the Netherlands. The city of Helmond to be exact. The neighborhood where I settled was working class and multiethnic. I moved there because the apartments were cheap and affordable for a Dutch Caribbean student like myself attending university. For the most part, working-class Dutch of Surinamese, Moroccan, Turkish, Indonesian, Sinti, Roma, native Dutch, Antillean, Moluccan, West African, and East African descent and mixtures of all these groups lived there, sometimes side by side, sometimes indifferent to each other, sometimes fighting each other, sometimes with each other, but always cognizant that cultural difference was an inescapable fact of life. In this way it was like the West Indies, where people cannot experientially or conceptually live a life of cultural homogeneity (Benítez-Rojo 1992; Mintz 1996).

Sabah and Naima, born in Morocco but having moved to the Netherlands at the ages of eight and eleven, respectively, were some of the first persons I met there. Both parents had died. One after the other. A tragedy. Naima, just turned twenty-one, was charged with taking care of eighteen-year-old Sabah and Sulaima, her younger sister, who was ten at the time. Naima's older brothers in turn supervised her, but they had their own families, and this meant that

6

she had an enormous amount of freedom and responsibility. We immediately hit it off based on our love for urban popular culture. Shabba Ranks, Bell Biv DeVoe, Joe, New Edition, Michael and Janet Jackson, Keith Sweat, En Vogue, Kassav', Juan Luis Guerra, Toni Braxton, Romario, Michael Jordan, Chaka Demus and Pliers, UB40, and Karyn White were our idols.

These forms of urban popular culture were primarily identified with the style of the Afro-Antilleans and Afro-Surinamese—Caribbean modes of being—and it was we who acted as the major cultural brokers.[1] What must be mentioned is that these expressions had a wider impact than more localized music/cultures such as Raï music identified with North Africa; the same holds for West African Azonto. Today, the latter is fully part of the urban scene in the Netherlands. Being urban and being hip means being *Afro-Caribbean like.* I was not aware back then that "urban" was becoming a cultural identity marker that can encompass the various ethnic groups who live on this Caribbean island called the Netherlands (to stick with the metaphor with which I began this chapter). The evolution of this encompassing identity will be discussed in part 3 of this book.

Sabah and Naima were forerunners. They were *Afro-Caribbean like* without relinquishing what they most cherished about their Dutch Moroccan ways. Sabah and Naima professed Islam while I did not profess any faith really, but contrary to what most people might think, this distinction did not create a barrier. Being into the urban was already in the early 1990s implicitly our encompassing identity. With them, I shared those vital years of transitioning from teenager to young adult. To me, they were like sisters. Their older brothers trusted me. We were family, so Yusef, the eldest son of Naima and Sabah's brother Appie, was my family too.

Yusef my *nefi,* Sranan Tongo for "my cousin," as I used to call him, was shot in the head when he sought to intervene in a conflict between two rival gangs. This happened in the southern Dutch city of 's-Hertogenbosch, where he lived. Yusef was always trying to show renegade Moroccans another way of living. Trying to do a good deed proved fatal.

Sabah immediately called me when she heard the news. We cried together. I soon realized, however, that Sabah's tears were not only about what had happened; they were also about the way the murder was immediately being framed. Once again, it became an ethnic issue: Moroccan gangs. Once again, it was being forgotten that Dutch Moroccans are Dutch too! I understood her.

The hegemonic message in the media and policy documents is that there are the truer Dutch and then there are us, the others; the newcomers (Essed and Nimako 2006; Geschiere 2009; Guadeloupe and de Rooij 2007). No matter that the others were born in the Netherlands, are of mixed ethnic parentage, or have lived here for years, they remain the "Others." This unfortunately is also unwittingly conveyed in many historical and sociological publications bent on keeping it real—giving truthful accounts of what people often think and sometimes do. This is what the American scholars I seek to answer in this book read and hear about in conferences. There is much to commend in highlighting the "othering" of newcomers. There is rampant ethnic discrimination and institutional, everyday racism; there is no denying it. Yet it is my contention that we need to develop a language that does not unwittingly reinforce these divides. It goes without saying that university-based intellectuals are not the only ones in need of a new language. Some organic intellectual spokespersons of newcomers also frame the matter in exclusivist Us and Them terms. Ethnic and religious specificity and the figment of pigment become their badge of honor. Hegemony would not be what we conceptualize it to be, if it did not include the spokespersons of those deemed lesser humans. This habitual exclusionary Us versus Them framing is part of what contributed to Sabah's grief.

Knowing that I write essays and give talks on multicultural conviviality and racism, Sabah and Naima asked me to write a eulogy for Yusef. They wanted a description that reflected their multicultural becoming, the mix of cultures that had shaped Yusef and them. Not a media representation that reduced them to being only *Marokkanen afkomstig van het Rif* (Moroccans from the Rif area of North Africa).

As I sat back and reflected on what I had put on paper, I realized that it was a poetic exultation of my teenage years in the Netherlands. All those whom I was closest to—who had no real institutional power back then—implicitly worked on what we had some control of, namely our embodied senses of personhood. Looking back, I realize that as an implicit act of decoloniality, we were collectively busy balancing the *Conquistador* and *Nativo* logics of being in ourselves.

The "us" I am referring to are not only Sabah, Naima, and myself but also Geertje, Mike, Dragana, Hassan, Martijn, Sonja, Mercus, and Wincho. We were Dutch citizens belonging to various ethnic formations—Surinamese, Moroccan, Yugoslavian, Moluccan, Antillean, and native; expressions of the unruly multiculture that had emerged primarily in the urban centers of the Netherlands. This was what "Dutchness," or Dutch people, symbolized to me; it was us, too.

None of us denied our cultural roots. In fact, we were proud of our ancestry. Yet to limit the possibility of the erection of walls of cultural incompatibility that ethnic and religious pride can cause, we practiced our version of what in urban popular culture is called "the dozens" (Wald 2012).

We involved ourselves in contests of verbal dueling, whereby two or more of us cast aspersions on each other as others cheered on. You had to think on your feet and be quick with your tongue. You lost if you (1) began to curse, (2) got angry, or (3) could not respond quickly enough. We made harsh stereotypical jokes about each other's background.

Outsiders would call some of these pranks downright sexist or racist. For us, it was all so outlandish that we knew it was really just a joke. In our play of the dozens, we never sought to totally humiliate each other. And we were milder in the presence of outsiders—family members or friends of friends—who we felt would not understand. A fight never broke out, because the cardinal rule of the game was that we would also make jokes about our own background. For instance, my mimicry of the speech of Hassan's uncles trying to make themselves understood in Dutch would earn me a curse-out by

Hassan, even if I also made fun of older Antilleans' speech patterns. Yet he, too, would be the first to be critical of Dutch Moroccans who sneered at anything Dutch—those who were in our estimation too religious or ethnic centered. He would make jokes that they were much too enamored with the idea of cultural incompatibility. And whenever I began to excessively exalt my "Arubaness," I would be on the receiving end—Naima would tell stereotypical jokes about the laziness of Dutch Antilleans. When Wincho, one of our Antillean friends, did not show up on the block on time, she would say something to the effect of: "hullie Antillianen kennen wel het goeie leven; Wincho die doet net als de mensen op Curaçao, de hele dag uitrusten zodat hij s'nachts beter kan slapen" (You Antilleans know about the good life; Wincho behaves like the people on Curaçao, he rests the whole day so he can sleep better in the evening). I, too, had to acknowledge that not all that was Antillean or specifically Aruban was good. There was a lot of complacency and in my estimation suspect use of facile arguments among Afro-Antilleans to excuse immoral behavior, such as, "Our ancestors worked hard, so we are entitled to work less and have a right to collect unemployment benefits" (I imagined our great-grandparents, who did not want handouts but respect and a fair share, turning over in their graves). No one was excluded from this process. For instance, Sonja and Geertje, whose grandparents were both born in Helmond, had to admit that, behind a lot of the talk, *buitenlanders* (foreigners) weren't hired not because they lacked the so-called *Nederlandse normen van punctualiteit en arbeidsethos* (Dutch norms of punctuality and an untiring work ethic); there was also the cold, hard fact of racial and class prejudice. So, our version of "the dozens" was a way of teaching and helping each other to be open to other cultural ways by being critical of our own. Looking back, I realize that, every day while hanging out on the block, we built a common world through transcultural play that allowed for difference while deconstructing the walls of coloniality that kept us from truly seeing each other.

What was equally remarkable was the manner in which we positively embodied all the cultural material that was at our disposal.

Knowing and being able to imitate cultural types was an asset. A way of crossing seemingly ethnic-specific lines until what mattered most was the quality of one's crossing, not the ethnic group to which one belonged. This was our decolonial work; it wasn't driven by extensive knowledge of critical race theory or related academic wisdom. Yet making the crossing of ethnic boundaries habitual—and thereby rendering ideas of racial essence an ineffective banality—is a powerful everyday expression of decoloniality at work.

CHAPTER 3

APPRECIATING DUTCH CARIBBEAN WAYS OF BEING IN THE NETHERLANDS

I am smiling as I listen to and watch "Money Like We," an urban hit featuring the rappers Sevn Alias, Kevin, Josylvio, and Kempi. It is part of a Dutch tribute album to the American rapper Tupac Shakur. The ethnicities of the rappers—Surinamese Dutch, native Dutch, Egyptian Dutch, and Antillean Dutch, respectively—don't matter to most lovers of the music I speak to about the tune. It's about how convincingly all of them perform the urban, namely being at ease and embracing life come what may. To be urban is to have artistic skills, a cool demeanor, material goods, and enough money to live a happy life. When you perform the urban well enough, you believe you are what you enact, and others do so as well, regardless of what takes place after the lights and cameras go out or after you are no longer in the gaze of those you are trying to impress. The clip and soundtrack of "Money We Like" remind me of summer days on the block in Helmond when my friends and I were playing at being urban; when, to use Tracy Chapman's phrase, we dreamed of having "mountains o' things," when the world seemed just right.

My smile signals an emerging insight about how multicultural conviviality comes into existence. I am beginning to dimly comprehend that it has to do with mastering the art of *becoming the other* and allowing the other to become *you*. Such is only possible because *you* and *the other* conceived as group identities are continuously shifting and changing. Conviviality undoes the tendency toward ethnic absolutism. As Paul Gilroy argues, it "is a social pattern in which different metropolitan groups dwell in close proximity but where racial, linguistic and religious particularities do not—as the logic of ethnic absolutism suggests they must—add up to discontinuities of experience or insuperable problems of communication" (2006, 40). Communication remains possible because all groups contain persons who are versed in the ethnic register of others and thereby bridge divides and suture wounds. In Helmond, the Moroccan baker whose shop I would frequent would speak a few words of broken Papiamento to create familiarity with me and his other Antillean clients. Although he wasn't versed in our language and had never been to the islands, his effort did create amicable relations. And the fact that one of his daughters, Jamila, who was a few years younger than I, was better at the language added to the luster of his bakery and made his gestures seem more sincere. She had Antillean Dutch girlfriends with whom she usually hung out. It was as if she, too, were Antillean, which made her father's broken Papiamento seem less of a trick to lure us into buying bread. It is code switchers like Jamila who make conviviality durable; they become the other while remaining themselves in other circumstances.

To fully appreciate the implications of what I am intuiting, I'll elicit an earlier, seemingly unrelated recollection. It draws on the wisdom of my grandmother, who once explained to me that anyone could be anyone else, and convince everyone else including themselves, as long as they played the role well enough. This wisdom was applied to a neighbor who had a child who absolutely did not look like him or his wife. Rumor had it that his wife had fooled around with one of the Americans she worked for as a domestic. The wife of the duped man had, however, been able to convince him that the child was his. She explained that the child's light brown complexion and "classic" European features were a throwback to one of her ancestors. It was a plausible story, given the mixed-up ancestry of all Caribbean folk. But it wasn't likely, as the child was the spitting image of one of her employers. Still, the husband believed her so much that many began to also believe him. The child grew up being considered his son biologically and socially. I only knew the son as an adult and had not known his father, who had died before

I was born. I also, for a long while, was not privy to the rumor. I questioned my grandmother, as the boy (then a grown man) looked nothing like his mother, and that is when she explained this wisdom to me. What mattered, she said, was that as a son he was good to his father and mother. That was the truth. I took from her that a belief, meaning a habit of action that one repeats with conviction and sincerity, becomes true.

As I mentioned above, the baker did not play Antillean well enough, but his daughter Jamila was an ace. When she wanted to, she sounded and seemed Antillean by the way she moved. Her performance acted as a deterrent to those Antillean Dutch men who wanted to create a ruckus. Their friends told them that Jamila was fully immersed in the Antillean network. And her bossy demeanor often drew a smile, which eased the tensions that occasionally emerged between her father and certain Antillean Dutch clients. Persons like Jamila strengthen the multicultural conviviality that Gilroy theorizes. Moroccan Dutch ceased to be a totally separate ethnic other when I entered that bakery, as there was Jamila, who was kind of Antillean like me.

Like Jamila, Sevn Alias, one of the rappers featured in the "Money Like We" clip,[1] is a living example that connects Gilroy's insight to my grandmother's wisdom. Being an artist, Sevn Alias's reach is wider. He is also the ultimate code switcher. Sevn is, according to our habitual way of classifying people, an artist of Afro-Antillean and Afro-Surinamese descent. He is a lyrical virtuoso, fluent in Dutch, English, Arabic, Papiamento, and Sranan Tongo. He also mixes various types of urban music, from trap to house to dancehall to hardcore rap. His name already reveals as much. The "Sevn" is related to his favorite number, which is the uneven numeral 7, and "Alias" has to do with the fact that, given that he had so many nicknames growing up, he was considered to have many different persona. Alias, alias, alias … Still there is a more basic sound to which Sevn returns in interviews and his raps, and that is Dutch with a stereotypical Moroccan accent. It's not a gimmick, as he explains that, growing up, most of his friends were Moroccan Dutch:

I am from [Amsterdam] West; I only had *mocros* [Moroccan Dutch] around me. Then I ended up in Almere, and there too were only Moroccans. That was just the way it was. See it like this—every day I'm with Moroccans. Every year they would go back home and come back and tell me how beautiful it is there. That made me desire to be there. I haven't even been in Surinam, even though I'm half Surinamese [here he is relating that he wasn't as interested in going to Surinam as vacationing in Morocco]. But the stories I hear about Morocco, the pictures and videos I see . . . I can relate to that more. (De Keijzer 2015)[2]

In terms of the dominant conventions, whereby ethnic identities are considered essentially linked to primordial racialized groupings, Sevn is fooling himself. He is not a *mocro*. But that is only in terms of the dominant conventions. Indeed, if you code switch as frequently as Sevn, what will matter most is the quality of the crossing, not the ethnic group to which one supposedly naturally belongs. Sevn Alias is also a *mocro* rapper because that is the way he is seen by others. Especially in the neighborhood he grew up in, he is a Surinamese-Antillean who is also *mocro*. As was the case with Jamila, Sevn has been instrumental in strengthening conviviality. Moreover, I take seriously that one needs to take identities as being contextually essential when emerging within a field of interactions.

In the neighborhood where I grew up in Helmond, no group actually dominated. My group of friends was ethnically diverse. So, a dominant accent connected to a particular ethnic group did not emerge. There were Jamilas in the neighborhood who were truly experts in code switching, but they did not have to play a particular ethnic group most of the time.

What was dominant for us was a way of being urban, which also holds for Sevn and connects him to other rappers such as Kevin and Kempi. The practice of artistically code switching, as we imitated urban pop icons' way of dressing and carrying themselves while we also played "the dozens" with our ethnic inheritance, is the wider point of connection between the clip I am watching, the wisdom of my grandmother, and my teenage years.

Code switching was also part of my history. This ability to cross and code switch in terms of cultural expressions and ethnicity seemed very Dutch Caribbean to me. It was what I was accustomed to. Doing multiple ethnicities was the norm on Aruba, where I was born. Let me elaborate by recalling my youth on Aruba.

In my childhood years, I would exchange some Spanish words with my grandmother from the Dominican Republic and other recently arrived immigrants from Latin America, speak Dutch in school or with expats from the Netherlands (or with my mom, who loved the language), rhyme and reason in Papiamento and Aruban English with my family and friends, and employ the standard variety of English when engaging with tourists or having to perform at official community functions. Every language switch was accompanied by an adjustment in my behavior and mode of being (which could be labeled "temporarily essential"). I would be proud of Aruban and other Antillean teams whenever there were pan-Caribbean sporting events. Then it was "Aruba ariba! (Aruba at the top)—We are the best baseball players in the entire hemisphere." In a dance of méringue or bachata, I would be enamored with my *Dominicanidad* (Dominicanness). *La Republica* (the Republic; an endearing name for the Dominican Republic) was in me via my grandmother. When engaging with persons from the politically independent former British islands, I would be adamant that the "Dutch" in my Dutch Caribbean status was not simply an accidental adjective. We weren't a colonized people; we were part of the Dutch kingdom (thus one sees that the strategy of Dutch Antilleans I mentioned at the beginning of this book, namely claiming Dutch citizenship by foregrounding the federation, is not *new* at all). At other times, when West Indian cricket was lauded, or the intellectual prowess of British and French Caribbean musicians and thinkers such as Bob Marley and Aimé Césaire was taught at school, I would be the first to foreground my British and French roots. My identity was contextual and relational.

But there was also an accumulative process at work, for at my most encompassing moments I would come to the deep realization that what I shared with the rest of the people living in the Caribbean basin was that we all came by boat or plane and mixed with the few remaining indigenous peoples who had arrived earlier on foot or via canoes (in history lessons, we were taught that the Amerindians arrived via the Bering Strait or the Pacific coast). So, they too were immigrants. We were one big family. Color, hair, and bone faded to the background as we established kinship beyond the maleficent construct of "race." For instance, Cabeza, my pinkish-skinned Venezuelan neighbor, who bore no visible traces of black Africa as I did, had to be called *tio* (uncle). In fact, he was my uncle correcting me, when I had to be corrected. Likewise, he displayed absolute deference to my grandmother, calling her *mai* (mother). Like a mother, she would scold Cabeza, who had a predilection for weed, throwing dice, and engaging in fistfights. My grandmother was a *mai* for most in the multiethnic neighborhood I grew up in. This was my Caribbean. Ridden with unresolved racial and class and gender conflict, but still my Caribbean. We were all the offspring of the conquistadores, the Native Americans, the Africans, the Asians, and the rest who contributed to the work of belonging to these lands (Harney 1996). As such, all heritages were our heritage. Nowhere was that more clear than during the carnival season and at parties where all Arubans danced and sang along to various urban music—salsa, méringue, hip-hop, R&B, reggae, zouk, *kompa*, *tumba*, dancehall, bachata, soca, and so on—because they were all ours. These cultural expressions were the products of the *Nativo* and *Conquistador* logics of dwelling, living unsteadily and therefore creatively in one body. As is the case in urban music, our task in seeking to live ethically, doing what I call decolonial work, was to critically examine and correct these inheritances as they structure our current world. This decolonial work was, in the terms of a philosopher of the Caribbean experience, Éduoard Glissant (2000, 2002), becoming creole in practice, which for some was also an explicit and well-articulated consciousness (see text box 4).

TEXT BOX 4: ÉDOUARD GLISSANT

After C. L. R. James and Frantz Fanon, Édouard Glissant (September 21, 1928–February 3, 2011) is the most acclaimed decolonial theorist arguing for a nonracial future. Glissant merged poetic intuition with philosophical speculation and therewith produced a body of work foregrounding the creolization of the world. For him, all thought and politics of self and other ought to commence with the recognition of mutual imbrication, where the idea of racial distinctiveness has no place.

Such distinctiveness is part and parcel of the West, which Glissant theorized was more fruitfully understood as a project rather than as a place. As such, one also encounters the West (Western thought) among those for whom colonialism and anti-Blackness has been a damnation. Glissant took the understanding of creolization furthest when he argued: "To assert [that] peoples are creolized, that creolization has value, is to deconstruct in this way the category of 'creolized' that is considered halfway between two 'pure' extremes. Creolization as an idea means the negation of creolization as a category . . . , which the human imagination has always wished to deny or disguise (in Western tradition)" (Glissant 1989, 140–41).

What I later came to realize was that Glissant, implicitly, I would say, echoing the insight of C. L. R. James, also made the argument that the whole world was becoming creole in its consciousness. The "Caribbean experience" could be perceived in many places. The multicultural neighborhoods in the Netherlands were beginning to resemble my Dutch Caribbean experience. It was *as if* the Netherlands, too, was a Caribbean island. That is why Sabah and Naima were my sisters, too, regardless of sociological or genealogical notions of ethnic distance. We belonged agonistically, like all the descendants of the other peoples of the earth who populate the Caribbean belong, to a just world to come. And the soundtrack that heralds that to come is urban music with the lifestyle that comes with it . . . But what about the question of money, the question of the relation between capital and performing the urban? And what about the harsh winds of anti-black racism in the Netherlands? It is to the latter I turn now and in so doing must highlight the small acts of decoloniality against that evil. The question of capital, about which I follow C. L. R. James in recognizing as fundamental, will be addressed afterward.

PART 2

THE
OUTSIDE
WORLD

DEALING WITH
ANTI-BLACK RACISM

CHAPTER 4

THE HOSTILE OUTSIDE WORLD IN THE NETHERLANDS

Conviviality and our immersion in urban popular culture did not shield my friends and me in Helmond from Dutch racism. As teenagers in a world where we constantly encountered grown-ups who made us feel that we weren't as Dutch as those of us who were native, or that there were unbridgeable differences between us because of our ethnic heritages, we drew sustenance from towering figures who were doing the decolonial work in their own way. But before referring to these figures, most of whom were females, I will use this chapter to highlight my experiences with racism in the Netherlands. In this chapter, I convey some of the ways I was addressed outside of my neighborhood in the 1990s.

On many occasions, as soon as I left my home to attend school, shop in one of the malls, or seek a summer job, I was made to feel as though I did not fully belong to the Netherlands. I was not alone. Habitually, security guards would walk behind my friends and me (all of us bearing a darker hue) when we entered a store that sold expensive clothing. Similarly, in certain clubs, we, the brown skins, would always miraculously just happen to be the ones who were asked to show membership cards. Parents of native Dutch girls I dated would be amazed that I was attending university. Later, attending a course taught by the foremost Dutch scholar on racism, Philomena Essed, I learned to recognize this as *everyday racism*:

Everyday racism is racism, but not all racism is everyday racism. The concept of everyday racism counters the view, prevalent in particular in the Netherlands, that racism is an individual problem, a question of "to be or not to be racist." The crucial criterion distinguishing racism from everyday racism is that the latter involves only systematic, recurrent, familiar practices. . . . Because everyday racism is infused into familiar practices, it involves socialized attitudes and behavior. Finally, its systematic nature indicates that everyday racism includes cumulative instantiation. These arguments make clear that the notion of everyday racism is defined in terms of practices prevalent in a given system. Note that practices are not just "acts" but also include complex relations of acts and (attributed) attitudes. (Essed 1991, 3)

Essed's emphasis is less to point fingers at who is or isn't a racist. Instead, she highlights the systemic nature of racial sleight and injustice, and rightfully so. However, as a teenager I did not feel the need to choose between the structure and the actors. There were moments you had to call native Dutch out: wake them up and let them know that you knew that they were applying double standards in vigilance or hiring practices, so that they would know more clearly that engaging in anti-black racism was unacceptable.

Admittedly, it was always much easier to deal with persons who were explicitly xenophobic or racist. You could curse them out as they had violated you and cursed you out, and then forget about them. They had power. But I reasoned that I had power as well, as I knew that I carried the same passport they did. I was secure, as many of my peers were, and hence I did not immediately lash out when persons in everyday life sought to treat me as being lesser Dutch. I encountered marginalization, but I did not feel myself marginal. I was simply one of those Afro-Antilleans who knew that growing up in a Netherlands that was *multiculturalizing* and decolonizing meant having to fight race-based ignorance from time to time. Yet racism, everyday and at times blatant, did not marginalize me existentially. I can relate to Stuart Hall's insight that "young black people today are marginalized, fragmented, disenfranchised, disadvantaged and dispersed. And yet, they look as if they own the territory. Somehow, they too, in spite of everything, are centered, in place" (1996, 114).

Hall's point is that in a multiculturalizing Europe where newcomers are here to stay, and where old ideas of authentic belonging are constantly being challenged in explicit and implicit ways, they, too, can begin to feel as centered as oldcomers. Despite the racism I encountered, I never doubted my Dutch citizenship as an Afro-Antillean man. The secure world of my neighborhood strengthened my Dutch Caribbean sense of personhood. I had no problem with being a human born in a brown skin. I was proud to have descended from people who, I had learned from my grandmother, had successfully fought against their "thingification" during the time of plantations and the transatlantic slave trade. I loved my grandmother, and thus I loved her mother and her mother's mother who had come from Africa. Because I belonged in the Dutch Caribbean, I belonged in the Netherlands, too.

I had seen the movie *Roots*. I had also read Alex Haley's *Queen: The Story of an American Family* (Haley and Stevens 1993) and his *Autobiography of Malcolm X* ([1965] 2010). I had grown up dancing and listening to the Wailers and other urban stars like Public Enemy who presented a redemptive history in their music, so I knew that I was part of women and men who had performed an amazing feat: we survived and thrived, and most of us weren't bogged down by hate (self-hate and hate of others). We weren't perfect, but neither was anyone else, and the great work of decoloniality was unfinished (Fanon 2004, 1967).[1] This was part of my enculturation in the Dutch Caribbean before I made my way to the Netherlands when I turned eighteen.

In the Netherlands, there were several reputable municipally funded NGOs in the 1990s run by professionals with an ethnic background like mine, community centers like Srefi Jepi and Stanvaste in the city of Eindhoven, a commercial hub near Helmond, that catered to primarily Surinamese and Dutch Antillean youngsters. They offered safe places and legally defended brown-skinned Dutch persons like me against everyday racism and other forms of negative discrimination. I had institutional backup to fight the system and those I considered *vuile racisten* (filthy racists).

My first career, after obtaining a bachelor's degree in social and cultural development in the early 1990s, was in the field of community development and youth work. I worked in the cities of Helmond, Utrecht, and Eindhoven. I was employed in neighborhoods serving people whose experience was similar to mine. I got to see how the Netherlands was changing and beginning to grudgingly accept that those who looked like me were here to stay.

I worked with all generations and ethnicities. I even held a job as a social therapist in the city of Hilvarenbeek working with pink-skinned elderly women who suffered from various forms of dementia. I learned through those experiences that, even in the days prior to mass immigration from the Global South to the Netherlands, views on anti-black racism were quite diverse. As is the case in all European countries that fully participated in the Western imperial enterprise, "racial imaginations [can be considered] to be part of the [native] Dutch psychological and cultural makeup; these imaginations [being] intertwined with the deepest desires and anxieties of many Dutch people" (Wekker 2016, 31). The key is, however, not to confuse the qualification "many" in this quotation for terms such as "most" or, worse, "all" native Dutch. Some of the Alzheimer patients clearly had racial prejudices, which their illness did not permit them to hide, while others simply found my brown skin a curiosity to which they did not immediately attach negative labels.

In Hilvarenbeek, I was simply the male nurse from the *ABC eilanden* (ABC islands, meaning Aruba, Bonaire, and Curaçao), which was the way these old folks had learned to memorize the names of the Dutch Antillean islands in school. Their children came to know me as the male nurse who would spice up their parents' afternoons by playing tunes of old-time greats like Louis Armstrong, Billie Holiday, and Ella Fitzgerald. Mrs. Knol, one of these patients, a woman whose family had owned several small businesses in earlier days, would consider it a delight to dance with me as many others watched.

She would talk about how jazz and blues were musical forms that when she was younger had been considered the quite rambunctious music of *negers* (Negroes), but that she and her friends would listen to unbeknown to members of her society who she knew would not approve. Even among these elderly native Dutch, music produced primarily by the descendants of those who survived transatlantic slavery and its aftermath could bridge differences.[2]

I used urban music in my career as a youth worker. It allowed me to connect with youngsters, as I knew what drove and motivated them. I could speak to them, for instance, about Public Enemy's records on anti-black racism in the United States and employ them as a way to start a discussion about what they experienced in school and in their neighborhoods. I had their acceptance, as I had had a stint as a member of the boy band Positive Vibes, with whom I performed and toured in various cities in the Netherlands, Germany, Belgium, and Luxembourg. I had even composed music for internationally renowned Dutch artists such as 2 Unlimited and TV celebrities like Bart de Graaff. My background gave me clout and a network that enabled me as a youth worker to invite artists such as the famous Dutch rapper Def Rhymz to speak and perform during events.

I was part of the Dutch government–funded institutional matrix of the 1990s that was seeking to integrate newcomers by supporting some of their cultural activities. It did not lead to a sense of homogeneous Dutchness but instead inadvertently contributed to multicultural conviviality by providing official bulwarks against anti-black racism and other forms of injustice. It was by no means perfect, as municipal officers also displayed racial bias, but it existed, and we made good use of it. It allowed persons who look like me to feel at home. Since the late 1990s, however, the Netherlands has experienced major cutbacks in community development programs. As elsewhere, neoliberalism has hit Dutch shores, although the welfare state is still quite substantial.

I am both gladdened and saddened by the fact that, today, youngsters who look like me can still count on social provisions that allow them to be even more centered than I was, and feel more at home than I did in my teenage years, even though they still experience anti-black racism. I am speaking about the generation that was born in the Netherlands, some of whom also have at least one parent who was also born here. One memorable case I recorded doing fieldwork from 2007 to 2013, in the city of Rotterdam, was that of Afro-Dutch youngsters who had found ways to test whether their sense of experiencing everyday racism was correct.

Two fifteen-year old boys, Jairzinho and Clyde, fully into urban popular culture, who attended HAVO and VWO, the highest forms of secondary education, and who came from well-to-do liberal families, confided in me why they and their friends made it their business to be a nuisance hanging out in front of the Albert Heijn supermarket after they had experienced racism; moreover, they would only buy stuff at the competitor's, the supermarket chain Jumbo, and encourage their families and friends to do so as well. Their actions were prompted by the fact that they had been refused part-time jobs at Albert Heijn because of their surnames and faces. They knew this because they had created a made-up person a week after they had been turned down: a fictional native Dutch boy judging from his surname with otherwise the same address and educational background as theirs. This nonexistent person received a positive email stating that he was welcome, as there were several vacancies at Albert Heijn. When I asked the boys why they didn't confront the manager, a native Dutch man somewhere in his mid-fifties, they claimed that it was a matter of pride. They weren't going to stoop so low as to beg a racist for a job. Jairzinho told me that he was not surprised, as his mother, who was a native Dutch businesswoman (an accountant), had made him aware that such racists were still around. The other boy, Clyde, was the son of a Surinamese Antillean woman born in the Netherlands who had a successful career in Dutch politics. He did not tell her what had happened, knowing that his mother would immediately call the manager or someone higher up, and the usual apology would have followed with him being awarded a job. The fathers of the boys were professionals, too, Jairzinho's father a certified nurse and Clyde's a schoolteacher, born in Surinam and Curaçao, respectively; Jairzinho and Clyde had overheard them speak about the implicit racism they sometimes experienced on the job. Still, as their parents were secure and comfortable and given that they had been born and raised in Rotterdam, where they knew that native Dutch came in various political flavors from the openly racist to those fully accepting of the unruly multiculture, the boys reasoned that the Netherlands was their country, too. Their families consisted of a mix of Antillean, Surinamese, Spanish, Romanian, native Dutch, and Cape Verdean Dutch. Moreover, as various shades and subethnicities was their daily reality, they could not existentially be against the multicultural country they were living in. They had other ways of making the Albert Heijn's manager's life miserable; that their loud behavior hanging out in front of his store may have reinforced his racist views did not matter one bit to them. Furthermore, they found employment at the competitor's, the Jumbo supermarket, where the manager, likewise a native Dutch man in his fifties, treated them right.

I have kept contact with Jairzinho and Clyde, even during my three years of sabbatical during 2014–2017 when I held the post of president of the University of St. Martin on the island of Sint Maarten in the Dutch Caribbean.[3] The extension of my relationship with Jairzinho and Clyde was facilitated by my acquaintance with their parents; the boys' insights have been valuable in my writing this book, as they are still fully engaged in urban popular culture, while they've left high school to attend Erasmus University in Rotterdam. These boys and others have kept me focused and aware that the unruly multiculture of the Netherlands, and the permanent revolution against anti-black racism and anti-Blackness in general, is alive and well.

Still, discerning racism turned out to be more complicated for Jairzinho and Clyde when they interacted with native Dutch of a liberal bent. I am referring here to liberal-minded oldcomers who are convinced that civil and political rights should hold for all who carry a Dutch passport. They also welcome socioeconomic rights for newcomers, meaning welfare state provisions that are specifically related to sustaining the cultural practices of the new Dutch, and champion international human rights. Their progressivism does not, however, prevent them from engaging in the racial logic of a clear-cut division of the world into the West and the non-West whereby the latter is implicitly considered less civilized. In their reasoning, the future of the world will be secured when Western values become hegemonic. Native Dutch with this truncated form of liberal sensibility are more sophisticated in their everyday racism. Jairzinho and Clyde told me that it isn't easy to recognize when such figures implicitly place them on a lower rung of belonging. They gave me countless examples of liberal-minded teachers who would subtly presuppose that they weren't necessarily the ones who had come up with the brilliant idea in a group assignment. Or, an insight that they had presented was only heralded when it was also put forth by a pink-skinned student: only then was their original contribution duly considered.

Jairzinho and Clyde had a clear sense that they weren't treated equally by many liberal-minded teachers who made an implicitly hierarchical distinction between native Dutch and newcomers, but they found it hard to usher critique, as such persons were also positive about the multiculturalizing of the Netherlands. So, while *minoritized*, Jairzinho and Clyde were simultaneously seen as an enrichment, a welcome dose of diversity in what their liberal teachers said was a dull and gray country. The boys found the differential treatment difficult to deal with and usually tried to ignore it. They were not really engaged, as an academic would be, in seeking out racial structures or discerning who was and who was not implicitly behaving in racist ways (or had explicit racist intent). They only responded when they experienced unambiguous forms of racism of the everyday kind, and of the rougher kind, as when someone openly called them names.

I understood Jairzinho's and Clyde's predicament. Grossly simplifying, I would say that, with respect to anti-black racism, liberal-minded oldcomers come in two flavors. I had experienced persons embodying both positions studying at the university in the 1990s.

There are those who acknowledge the prevalence of everyday racism and their own possible complicity. As such, they seek to undo themselves of it. I call these "conscientious liberals." While I was attending Radboud University in Nijmegen, some professors encouraged their students to take an elective course on racism at the University of Amsterdam with Philomena Essed; this is how I came to take Essed's course. One of my professors at Radboud, the feminist anthropologist Tine Davids, included the work of intersectional and womanist feminists in her courses. It was in her classes that I first heard of and read pieces by bell hooks and Alice Walker.[4] Davids continuously reiterated that, as a liberal, she had blind spots when it came to racism, and with a wink she told us male students that, similarly, most men have implicit biases when it comes to gender. Like class divisions, gender inequality and racism are alive and well in the Netherlands. As we were all implicated, Davids would stress, it was a matter of remembering that we are a work in progress.

The flip side consists of liberal-minded oldcomers who reason that racism is a negligible part of Dutch life. For them, racism is the practice of a stubbornly dying breed. In their reasoning, most native Dutch are prejudiced, not racist. I call these the "self-congratulatory liberals." They stand for a Netherlands where sooner or later the majority will supposedly be liberal minded in a self-congratulatory manner like they already are. These women and men, whom I also encountered in university life, preach the gospel of tolerance for the multiculturalizing of the Netherlands to those *vuile racisten* and unthinking folk whom they identify as lower class or less intelligent. I knew that this approach was based on a myth, as in my neighborhood native Dutch came in all flavors. You did not need to have a university degree, be well traveled, and work as a middle-class professional to be an avowed anti-racist. But you can know something and still also partially believe in its opposite. Such was the case with me.

At the time, I did not critique self-congratulatory liberals. They may have had their blind spots that their vanity would not allow them to see, as Tine Davids would say, but for the most part they were respectful. Looking back, I would say that they wanted change without truly tackling the presence of anti-black racism, a presence that is tied to the whole edifice of a conception of the Netherlands in which the history of colonialism is presented as a minor note. Incidents that my fellow brown-skinned students would categorize as racism or Islamophobia, such as when they felt they'd received negative differential treatment because of their skin color or ethnic background, were hardly ever acknowledged. The R-word (racism) in settings and classes where self-congratulatory liberals held sway was taboo, as it was a notion that belonged to the riffraff. They reasoned that racism wasn't habitual among the educated European middle class, and the Netherlands was a predominantly middle-class country.

Liberal native Dutch of the self-congratulatory kind tolerated persons of my ethnicity as long as I behaved civilly according to their standards, and in their estimation sought to become like them—evincing moderately toned laughter and speech in public places; no sagging pants; no deep commitment to religiosities that did not at least resemble liberal versions of Christendom; no positive sense of personhood that did not directly relate to climbing the economic ladder and holding a steady, well-paying job; and no doubts when it came to the acceptance of gender equality and the rights of homosexuals. Today, this ethic of encouraging newcomers to integrate affectively and cognitively into this racially blind middle-class liberal imaginary of the Netherlands is termed "the culturalization of citizenship"—the attempt to render citizenship into an exclusively cultural trait (see Duyvendak, Geschiere, and Tonkens 2016).

Like Jairzinho and Clyde, I knew that something wasn't correct with this type of liberal tolerance, but back then I wasn't the explicit and politically aware decolonial academic I now reason myself to be.[5] I could not refer to insights of Alice Walker (1983) or Caryl Phillips (2013), or present the work of the philosophers Charles

Mills (2006) and Achille Mbembe (2017), which argue that racial logic is also part of the architecture of liberalism's condensation in Western polities.

Moreover, as decoloniality in my estimation presupposes an ethic of generosity, it is my political belief that those native Dutch liberals who implicitly *secondarize* me and persons who look like me are alienated, too. I truly appreciate that, prior to the 1950s, when the Netherlands became multicolored leading to its current multicultural state, it was a country that consisted almost exclusively of pink-skinned persons. Many native liberals, too, those who do not take anti-black racism seriously enough, are trying to find their way in this new, emerging world; they, too, are seeking to come to terms with a Netherlands that the children of the formerly colonized, like Jairzinho, Clyde, Sabah, Naima, and me, also call their home. Their dream seems to be to culturalize (integrate) everyone into their norms without explicitly conceding and tackling existing power inequalities, without a thorough nonracist reconception of the Netherlands.

My reservations vis-à-vis self-congratulatory liberals should not be read as a full-blown criticism of their ideas of being cultured. Much of their ethic I shared and still share, as it is part of my colonial inheritance, but again due to my historical location I sense the racism in their rhetoric whenever liberalism is presented as an ideology without any roots in the colonial enterprise. There is nothing of C. L. R. James's insight in their argument (or the updated understanding of that outlook by thinkers such as the philosopher Achille Mbembe who write on the manner in which anti-black racism was instituted after the imperial conquests of Europe; I will discuss this in chapter 10). Unlike James and Mbembe, they did not explicitly acknowledge that liberation must be a nonracist liberation beyond the colonially derived myth of a lily-white version of the West being the place that offers the best, politically and socially, to the rest of the world.

The most memorable of my encounters with native Dutch of a liberal bent was the day I was called Tarzan and invited to join the tribe of the liberal-minded. For the record, let me state that I employ the terms "self-congratulatory" and "conscientious" liberals as ideal types. Most native Dutch exhibit both tendencies, as becomes clear in the following chapter.

CHAPTER 5

WILL YOU JOIN TARZAN IN SAVING US FROM THE UNRULY MULTICULTURE?

I found myself saying to myself, "He didn't just called me that!" Yes, he had. He called me what North Americans refer to as the n-word and what was far worse for me, "Tarzan," and expected me to consider it a compliment. I was appalled by being likened to that wild man from the jungle. Well, he hadn't exactly used the term "Tarzan," but the association of me and those who look like me with the tropics was clear (first in my own mind, and subsequently corroborated by other experiences I had with this individual). I have to admit that he was not talking to me directly but to his sister on the telephone when he enthusiastically blurted out that his daughter had brought home "een neger, een echte, eentje uit de tropen" (a Negro, a real one from the tropics!).

Back then, the late 1990s, I sported a well-kept high top and was into Conscious Hip-Hop. The latter was our term for the politics of emancipation, a contestation of anti-black racism embedded in the feel-good, danceable rhythms of that creole musical formation that came of age in the United States. The bands Public Enemy, Poor Righteous Teachers, X Clan, Digable Planets, De La Soul, and a Tribe Called Quest were all following and updating George Clinton and P-Funk's creed that in striving to free one's mind, one's ass surely follows.

Academic musings about the mind's strange relationship with the body made little sense to me, as the political philosophy I encountered dancing and singing along to that music, as with many

others such as roots reggae, political calypso, and salsa, and writings
on Black Atlantic musical traditions, led me to appreciate that our
minds are part of the alienated body of we who are the descendants
of those who survived the social death-inducing regimes that were
the New World plantations (Berrios-Miranda 2004; DeCosmo 1995;
Gilroy 2005; Gosa 2011; Guadeloupe and de Rooij 2014; Perry 2008).
Total decolonization and reparation of the Wrong that was Western
imperialism was the agenda.[1]

This is not a cheap criticism of academics or scholarly life, which I
define as a worthy endeavor, in which the mind-body problematic is
part of a wider conversation about the relationship between matter,
information, self-consciousness, and consciousness. Scholarly life
is a place where insightful discussions take place about the origin
of life, the meaning of meaning, and the possible meaning of our
meanings. After all, while I was listening to Public Enemy and Bunny
Wailer, I was attending college and indulging in the works of Ton
Lemaire, C. L. R. James, Frantz Fanon, Ivan Illich, Pierre Teilhard de
Chardin, Gerrit Huizer, Karl Marx, Francisco Varela, Donna Har-
away, bell hooks, and Paulo Freire. Back then, and it still remains the
case for me today, it is a question of what you prioritize. My stance
and practice are that once full de-alienation has taken place—once
we live in a fully decolonized world where character matters more
than pigmentation, sexual orientation, the size of one's wallet, or
the diplomas acquired—we will see what remains of the academic
inquiry into the mind-body problematic. Such is nicely captured in
the pragmatist axiom of the philosopher Richard Rorty in a book of
interviews (2006), who wages that if we take care of freedom and
safeguard that all live a dignified life—which, C. L. R. James would
have added, means fully eradicating global anti-Blackness—truth
will take care of itself.

It would be a lie to claim that when that man, the father of Ans—
the girl I was dating, who came from an upper middle-class neighborhood—called me the n-word, I was the academic I am today. It
would be equally fictitious to present myself as a figure who only

listened to Public Enemy's "Fight the Power" (1990). I was in my late teens when the episode took place. Yes, I played "the dozens" and implicitly did decolonial work with my friends, but I saw no wider meaning in it back then, and the politics of combatting anti-black racism did not occupy me all of the time.

Like most youngsters in the Netherlands, I was down with that latest fad in urban popular culture and therefore deeply into all that hip-hop had to offer: the rap and R&B music, graffiti, dance, style, and myriad politics including that deemed politically suspect. I was also a big fan of gangsta rappers of the likes of NWA (Niggaz Wit Attitudes) and Lil' Kim. In the club, I, too, shouted "fuck the police!" and regularly employed the words "bitches" and "hoes." Gangsta rap was sweet rebellion.

If you employ the language of the Frankfurt school of critical theory, you could say that the carefully crafted rebels of the culture industry's version of ghetto life articulated well with my emergence from puberty and the invasion of testosterone (Adorno and Horkheimer 1997; Marcuse 1964). I, too, it could be argued, was under the spell of capitalism's sale of popular mass culture (in this case, commercialized urban popular culture). I, too, was supposedly mistaking my life for the constructions presented by rappers. Such arguments, however, do not sufficiently take my agency into account. My enduring sense of self was born from moments of enculturation that are not reducible to narrow economics. My grandmother, parents, relatives, and friends weren't simply automatons that reproduced oppressive global dynamics when they engaged with me. Also, it is odd not to recognize that urban popular culture enables while undoubtedly repressing possible routes that desire can take. This is an insight that did not escape C. L. R. James (1992a), who was equally critical of popular culture while recognizing that it could never produce the dupes Theodor Adorno, that foremost Frankfurt school don, argued that it could.[2] The specificities of the wider processes of my socialization and enculturation, the secure world of my teenage years in the Netherlands, drove a wedge into any one-on-one identification with either the legacy of Jim Crow USA or the ghettoes of Los Angeles or New York. I knew I wasn't a "black boy" from Compton.

I was from the Dutch Caribbean. Although there were prejudice and stubborn traces of the colonial order in my neck of the woods, rampant poverty and apartheid-like anti-black racism was not my reality. *Mississippi Burning* and *Malcolm X* were Hollywood, not Aruba, where I spent most of childhood.

As I made clear in the previous chapter, I grew up in a multicultural and polyethnic world. In the Netherlands, I was back into the same, albeit that there were more pink skins in the creole mix of Helmond. I was a college kid from a respectable liberal-minded family that believed in an antiracism that in time would fully undo the excesses of color-coded identity politics. My girlfriends resembled the colors of the rainbow, and therein I wasn't exceptional, as in the Dutch hip-hop world so-called interracial dating was the norm rather than the exception.

Eazy-E, Ice Cube, and even Chuck D might have been what the marketing magicians promoted most, but for me they could not beat Big Daddy Kane or Father MC or their crooner version, Johnny Gill. In fact, Johnny Gill—most of my friends felt I had Gill's look with the voice of Ralph Tresvant—was my nickname back then, as I did my utmost to keep that smooth New Edition demeanor. Every Friday, I was at the barber, and dressing up like an urban crooner mattered most.

I met Ans in Srefi Jepi, a community center that regularly organized parties for youngsters where urban music was played. If some of the more renowned clubs made it difficult for brown-skinned young men like me to enter because of our ethnicity, or would not regularly play the urban hits we loved, at places like Srefi Jepi and other community centers, we had a world where the multiculturalizing Netherlands was an acceptable reality. These were extensions of my secure world outside of my Helmond neighborhood.

After a few dances, Ans and I hit it off, as we both recognized that besides our love for urban music, we were college students into social studies. Our ambition was to change the world, while pursuing our goal of becoming established professionals. We wanted to inhabit a planet undone of anti-Blackness, where we could dance and sing along to Bell Biv DeVoe and Chaka Demus and Pliers.

As it was not bon ton on the Dutch Caribbean isles, I never really used the n-word, but since it was frequently used in the Dutch hip-hop scene and in my neighborhood, I did not immediately think "OOH YOU RACIST" when I heard Ans's father describing me in this way to his sister. It was a matter of how you said the n-word and in what context.

Neger (Negro) could be *neger* (nigga) or *nikker* (nigger), but it wasn't the second or the third variety in this case. Ans's was a liberal family that did their utmost best not to wantonly practice anti-black racism. Her father was simply giving what he felt was an innocent description of me. I did not feel the need to school him by quoting lyrics from the likes of Conscious Hip-Hop artists such as Poor Righteous Teachers to enable him to see me as celestial divinity incarnate rather than the oppressed racist caricature handed down since colonial times; to see that my politics was to dismantle Babylon, the world that created first- and second-class humans. As Wise Intelligent put it: "I'm infinite, I'm yesterday, today, tonight / Tomorrow morning, you see this is your future talking / Babylon is fallen" (Poor Righteous Teachers 1996).

Getting into a deep discussion with him wasn't worth my while. I was searching for conceptions of self that were decolonial, and thus I was cherry picking from here and there through my immersion in urban popular culture. I took from mystical strands of Rastafari that humans were specific incarnations of the celestial, and thus both finite and infinite. This was the meaning I privileged in the Rastafari philosophy of *I and I*. And it was through this nonracialist lens, combined with what I was learning of human evolution, that I took on some of the tenets of US hip-hop artists that presented brown-skinned people of African descent as the planet's original inhabitants.[3] I will discuss how these have shaped my conception of racism and the way to combat it in the last chapter of this book.

Back then, I found the articulating of my position too complicated, and furthermore no reason to engage. After all, Ans was back for the weekend in Geertruidenberg and had brought the guy she was dating and had spoken so much about to meet her parents. Her parents extended a warm welcome to me.

There was of course what today I refer to as "exotic racism" going on. More than once, Ans's mother hinted at the fact that she found *halfbloedjes* (half-castes) so beautiful, intimating that she and her husband hoped for mocha-colored grandchildren. As I had no dreams of marrying their daughter or having children, I considered the fact that Ans's parents had already bought my wedding suit and made provisions for their progeny, perhaps more problematic than their exoticizing version of racism.

What got to me was being implicitly likened to Tarzan by locating me in *de tropen*, a Dutch translation for the tropics, which carries with it exotic racialism. The tropics, in the Dutch sense of the word, were not the way I referred to the Dutch Caribbean isles. That they are located close to the equator and blessed with warm weather are facts, but so is more than half of the world. What should I call their daughter, "eentje van het gematigde klimaat" (one from the temperate climate)? It made no sense. The only time I had heard anyone referred to as "tropical" was a particular cross section of the people who lived on Aruba, namely the pink-skinned children of the Dutch expats. In the more distant past, in the early days of Dutch colonialism, people who look like me and the natives of the East Indies were seen as "tropical," meaning uncouth (Michielsen 2019; Oomen 2019).

This was an example of the strange life of colonial racism, as when I was growing up on the islands the term was only used to refer to certain pink-skinned Arubans, the children of Dutch expats. Pink-skinned children whose ancestors had been in the Caribbean perhaps longer than most of mine weren't called "tropical," and neither as a matter of nuance were those children of Dutch expats who kept more to themselves and seemed to emulate what many saw as the social stiffness of their parents. It was only those relative newcomers who were rambunctious and spoke and acted like the "bad Johns" among us oldcomers who could be described in that way.

These expat children in fact made the way of being of the "bad Johns" and "bad Janes" (there were female versions) look totally immoral (Besson 2002; Wilson 1969). That way of being, based on acquiring personal worth by any means, was in fact a survival tactic of those without the right family connections or education who were looked down upon; those who hustled, used their fists and verbal wits in an effort to gain the respect of the notables. A middle-class person could exhibit this ethic but would always match it with the respectable norms of her or his social station. That dual performance was considered being truly Caribbean. In fact, the bad Johns and Janes also did their best to mix their bravado reputation with some adherence to middle-class respectability. In solely performing reputation, my friends and most persons I knew reasoned, these *tropical Arubans* were not being sincere. They resembled caricatured versions of that Caribbean way of being; a slick, happy-go-lucky fellow, quick with his tongue, sexually lewd, and good with his knuckles, whose lack of respectability was more than compensated for by his reputation. A bad John or bad Jane was not tropical in the Dutch Caribbean, as being tropical was to be acculturated in an excessive way, as some children of Dutch expats were—the wild ones.

I had a friend called Pjotr who was exactly that way. His parents were from the Netherlands and worked as technical assistants in the Aruban government. Pjotr's swagger, demeanor, and way of speaking Aruban Papiamento and English were just so over the top. He overdid it, trying to fit in. His longing to go native made him less native than those who behaved as though they were living in the Netherlands. His overseas relatives, whom I met once or twice while they were vacationing, would refer to him as a *tropisch kind* (child from the tropics), meaning a Dutch boy who had become wild like their imaginary "natives." They meant it in an endearing way. They saw Pjotr as being like them and also in his tropical wildness supposedly like us. Civilized and wild.

No one in Aruba was like that. Being wild and civilized in the way that Pjotr's relatives and others visiting from the Netherlands described children like him, was their fantasy. There was in fact only one person we knew who was like that: Tarzan.

So, we simply gave Pjotr that nickname. For us, the Hollywood king of the jungle, raised by apes and living with wild animals, was a dangerous lunatic. The Tarzan figure was of course revered when we were younger, as every self-assured child identifies with that hero, but the older we got, the more we were exposed to American sitcoms such as *The Jeffersons*, *Good Times*, and *Sanford and Son*, with their implicit and ironic critiques of pink-skinned overlords from the North Atlantic going native. Tarzan became a figure of ridicule (I cannot help musing that Frantz Fanon, who wrote of Antillean children categorically identifying with racist personages like Tarzan, would have come to a more ambivalent conclusion if he had lived in a Caribbean more saturated by the aesthetic politics in urban popular culture). Tarzan's domain was the jungle, the Western version of the world that was colonized, and we did not live in a Warner Bros. rainforest. Being called a tropical man, a Tarzan for us, was being seen as someone without measure or morals.

Not so for Pjotr's liberal-minded relatives in the Netherlands. The tropical boy had an edge. He was Dutch like them but with the supposed mannerisms of the imaginary natives who lived in the parts of the world I was from. For them, I reckoned that those who resembled Tarzan remained heroes.

For Ans's parents, who were sometimes conscientious and sometimes self-congratulatory liberals, I could only be *Tarzanesque*, as I wasn't the son of Dutch expats born in the tropics but was something akin to that wild yet surprisingly cultured man. Had I been the anthropologist I am today, I would have elicited their views on Tarzan (and his host of filmic avatars such as Rambo) and his connection with the tropics. I can only rely on the implicit connections, using the Tarzan symbol as a simile. The weekend I spent with them, and the other times we interacted, I understood that they made a distinction between (1) those who looked like me but were born and lived most of their lives in the Netherlands, (2) those who had just arrived in the country but lacked the proper cultural capital, and (3) those like me who had just arrived and seemed to have a middle-class educational and social resourcefulness. It was to us that they felt closest, and it was to us that they would confess their disappointments concerning newcomers who were abusing the system and were for them symbols of the multicultural drama that was unfolding. They were also quite critical of native Dutch elites whom they deemed exploitative and condescending, who were scatting about the native working classes who in their estimation were useless. Like Tarzan but with a difference, people like me interacting or falling in love with their offspring would culturally or biologically breed progeny who would save their way of life in a world growing more culturally diverse and less graspable for them; or, as Ans's father once put it when he had had too much to drink, "onze toekomst ligt in jouw handen" (our future is in your hands).

For them, persons like me were so much more real, authentic, and in touch with life in a way that would not irredeemably threaten their way of life. Neither did we resemble them so much as those newcomers (Antilleans and others) born or raised in the Netherlands; those that they feared would take their place and sooner or later demand radical equality. Culturally, I was close to them, having been brought up in a liberal household, but since I was in their estimation originally from the tropics, I was also different from them. I was kind of like Pjotr. I supposedly had that liberal, controlled tropical wildness they desired, and, maybe through my relationship with Ans, they could generate new Tarzans in the Netherlands: Me-chocolate-version-of-Tarzan with Ans as Jane, and our offspring inculcated with liberal values that would gain strength due to their inborn wildness—the new tribe of saviors of the Western world.

Admittedly, back then I had not yet come to such a fantastic provisional conclusion; the fact of the matter is that most of the time I did not know what to make of their outlook and behavior. I would simply tease Ans, saying, "Me Tarzan, you Jane," but I left it at that. I knew, however, that there was something odd, but before I could figure it out, I broke up with Ans and did not see her parents again. Looking back on the experience, I can recount similar encounters whereby "tropical" was always a term of endearment uttered by persons who did not fully embrace the multicultural drift of the Netherlands. I am now beginning to discern a particularly frightening picture. It makes little sense; it might simply be informed by the wave of xenophobia and resentment against the unruly multiculture of my teenage years that is currently (around 2020) rampant in political circles, but let me share it. The romanticism of the tropics and desire for a wild man who embodies the best of "the West" and the supposedly coveted traits of "the Rest" is definitely not an antiracist or decolonial stance.

Returning to the dichotomy between mind and body, I more fully appreciate that, as a translation of that academic problematic into mass culture and politics, Tarzan and his modern-day avatars are symbolic of attractive beings whose wild impulses are controlled. Tarzan's natural habitat is the jungle, a trope that is increasingly heard and employed in liberal circles as a metaphor for the places within and without the Netherlands where the so-called frightening newcomers primarily doing working-class labor hail or reside. Dutch leftist public intellectual Maarten van Rossem has argued that the idea of society as a life-threatening and dysfunctional system emerges because we are barraged with negative news of all sorts, every single day, just watching television: "Most citizens apparently do not have an eye for the strange discrepancy between their own mundane, safe life and the gruesome jungle, that according to the media is just around the corner of their amiable street" (van Rossem 2009).[4]

Yet for all the anxiety he summons as a wild body, Tarzan makes the threatening jungle and its other inhabitants a place that can be managed, as he also possesses something of the mind and moderate temperament of the supposedly North Atlantic home of liberalism. Tarzan is, despite his impressive though frightening body, still a child of the West; And so was I, the child of the colonized who had benefited from Western culture, reasoned the parents of Ans.

Based on the experience I have just related, three insights about liberal native Dutch emerge. First, there are many liberal native Dutch like Ans's parents who both embrace the multiculturalization of the Netherlands and simultaneously find it a difficult reality to live with. With the latter, I am referring to the norms of some newcomers as they relate to unequal gender relations, the dream of theocracies, and intolerance for LGBTQI relationships and ways of being. I think that this worry of conscientious and self-congratulatory liberals should be deemed important and critically engaged. In doing so, one should not, however, negate the fact that one also encounters these antiliberal tendencies among oldcomers, as Ans's parents also acknowledge. They implicitly recognize, in other words, that the issue is not per se an ethnoracial one, even if their kneejerk reaction is to racialize their worries.

This occurs as they still deem liberalism and other progressive ideals as exclusively stemming from Europe. In their quest to counter their anxieties, liberals like Ans's parents desire a Tarzan-like figure. Someone whose wildness is tempered by liberal sensibilities.

They hope that such a person will be able to defend the liberal tradition of the indubitable right of individuals to be self-governing agents of their own life, while taming the so-called jungle folk with their illiberal ways who supposedly threaten to tear down the whole moral edifice.

Now this figure of Tarzan as the savior of the liberal project in the Netherlands also has a much darker incarnation, which brings me to my second insight. There are self-congratulatory liberals who squarely place the blame for the supposedly growing illiberalism displayed by some newcomers squarely in the lap of what they despairingly refer to as *de linkse kerk* (the social democratic political Left, whom they equate with the established elites who are actually calling the shots in The Hague). The *linkse kerk* has been far too accommodating, in the estimation of these self-congratulatory liberals. The latter find that the *linkse kerk*'s growing displays of penance for the wrongs of Dutch colonialism are unacceptable.[5] The same goes for the categorical siding with the calls of self-proclaimed black activist intellectuals like Quinsy Gario, Kno'Ledge Cesare, and Mitchell Esajas for the reform or scrapping of native Dutch traditions deemed implicitly racist or xenophobic. I will elaborate on the views of these activists later. Now this group of self-congratulatory liberals also desires a Tarzan-like savior. They appeal to the side of the king of the jungle who is against the decadence of Western elites as well as that of the so-called wild savages. They are willing to support a Tarzan-like figure, who is allowed to be temporarily wild and illiberal like the jungle people. His wildness is warranted to paradoxically salvage the liberal tradition. Now I think of the *unheimlich* support among self-congratulatory liberals for Dutch politicians who exhibit populist traits, such as the member of Parliament Geert Wilders and even Prime Minister Mark Rutte. These politicians can be productively analyzed via the Tarzan metaphor.

A third group of native Dutch with liberal sensibilities exists, however, who do not exhibit the two aforementioned longings for a Tarzan. I am referring to persons like Ans, Tine Davids, and Jairzinho's mother who wholeheartedly embrace the new Netherlands in the making. They are fully committed to combatting anti-black racism. These are persons who hold the same convictions I do. They desire a nonracial world. It is people like these who strengthen my resolve that an antiracist scholarship has to be developed that does not conceptually reintroduce our colonially inherited racial divisions of white people versus black people in researching current multicultural dynamics in the Dutch world.

With these three insights I have begun to discern two routes that can be employed to respond to the idea that the multiculturalizing of the Netherlands is leading to the country becoming a jungle.

ROUTE 1

If I follow the dynamics in urban popular culture exemplified by artists like the successful Dutch rap formation Broederliefde, the jungle should be fully embraced, for it is actually the Netherlands as it is today. To girls like Ans, they sing about the jungle.[6] Even if it all starts with an exotic attraction coupled to gender-based stereotyping—the brown-skinned boy from the jungle meets the pink-skinned girl from the civilized world who is attracted to him—the relationship can grow into one in which the sharing of cultural expressions without senses of exclusive ethnic ownership can emerge. I take this to be possible, as did C. L. R. James, Frantz Fanon, Maryse Condé, and Édouard Glissant, living in a time when fewer brown-skinned women and men in Europe experienced romantic love across ethnoracial lines (even if Fanon explicitly argued in *Black Skin, White Masks* that it was not easy to attain) (see text box 5).

More than half a century later in a decolonizing Netherlands, where one encounters boys teaching their pink-skinned lovers the Krio of the Cape Verde islands, Fanon's and James's vision of nonracist love is rendered a future in the present in this song. And what happens in song echoes real life. Jairzinho told me how his mother's choice had made her family come more to terms with the current multicultural mix in the Netherlands. His mother told me that, although her father was weary of her choice of brown-skinned partners, Jairzinho became his favorite grandson. He even claimed that he resembled him most in terms of intelligence and good looks. Like his best friend Clyde, Jairzinho, too, dated girls who were native Dutch, and in the hip-hop scene these girls learned to confront the racism of their parents and check their own prejudices. In fact, truth be told, I became aware of Broederliefde and other artists signaling the current tensions and possibilities in the Netherlands via Jairzinho and Clyde. I could see the similarities of this mode of resolution to the ones I sought together with my working-class friends in Helmond way back in the 1990s. Also, Ans and I were forerunners.

TEXT BOX 5: FRANTZ FANON

Frantz Fanon (July 20, 1925–December 6, 1961) was born on the French Caribbean island of Martinique. He is known as a psychiatrist, philosopher, and anticolonial freedom fighter. Postcolonial and decolonial theorists both claim him as an intellectual precursor. In addition, no serious discussion of French existentialism and the workings of anti-Black racism in psychoanalysis can avoid contending with Fanon. Despite these accolades, within the academic and activist worlds, Fanon's name is also connected to the unpleasant realities of being homophobic, an apostle of violence against pink-skinned people, and an advocate of Black power. A careful reading of his work reveals that while there are troubling heteronormative passages, the latter two accusations do not stand up to sustained scrutiny.

Fully involved in the anticolonial struggle in Algeria, Fanon described the importance of violence in combatting the extremely brutal oppression of the French state in that colony. His description of the counter use of violence by the colonized should not be read as an endorsement. His hope was to canalize that violence into the recognition of the mutual vulnerability of humankind, thereby instituting a nonracist, just global order.

Jairzinho and Clyde, though, were born in the Netherlands and belong to the upper middle class, as do most of their girlfriends. There is a difference that these distinctions create that I will discuss in chapter 10. Suffice it to say that what is shared is the understanding that there was no need for a Tarzan (politically), for the jungle is not a place to fear. It is to reiterate one of the unacknowledged realities of the Netherlands.

ROUTE 2

The second route centers Tarzan with xenophobic results. Since the king of the jungle is ambiguously neither friend nor foe of the natives of the jungle or of the white man, once this desire is fully transposed into the political realm as it is currently structured, it can set in motion a process whereby a perpetual fresh batch of enemies has to be produced!

Tomorrow, as I wrote in my letter to Yusef's child, Dutch Moroccans and people who look like me might be fully accepted as Dutch citizens; however, a new category of undesirables will emerge. After all, the savior must continue to save. And, therewith, even native Dutch can be rendered suspect—those belonging to the so-called *linkse kerk* and the working classes whose behavior is considered unbecoming.

Moreover, those newcomers who belie the liberal native Dutch imaginary of them as Tarzan and other newcomers as jungle inhabitants, can still unthinkingly and paradoxically play the role of being Tarzanesque saviors implicitly constructing racialized solidarities as they seek to combat racism—implicitly thinking of themselves as brown-skinned Tarzan-like figures, for instance Caribbean with a Dutch flavor, who join their lower-class brothers and sisters to fight for justice in ethnically absolutist social movements supported by their white allies (pink-skinned Dutch). The outcome: a kind of semiprogressive, elite-driven, multicolored and polyethnic Dutchness in which we accept each other's ethnically owned particularities in the form of stereotypical racialized identities and folklore, even making provisions for interracial mixtures, based on the perpetual existence of lower- and working-class jungle people of all hues needing to be tamed; a serious parody that emulates in a more benign way the colonial construction of self and other.

I call this second route *decoloniality tamed through an updated colonially derived racial settlement*: the ideology that, before colonialism, the world was already divided into black, white, and brown peoples. Emancipation only entails equal recognition of these primordial identities, with each getting a fair share of the national and global economic pie. It's a dead-end route, with in the worst-case scenarios the Netherlands and the wider Dutch kingdom transformed into a collection of race-based nationalist groups where the elites of each find each other. In this book's last chapter, I present the views of antiracist activists who claim exclusive ownership of black identity and flirt with this idea.

Luckily, it is not the only way. There is the first route with its challenges, which I will return to later. And . . . as I recall the secure neighborhood of my teenage years and my equally secure fieldwork experiences in the Netherlands, I come across another worthy alternative. I present it in the following chapter before returning to the first route.

CHAPTER 6

ANOTHER ROUTE: MULTICULTURAL SOCIAL PARENTING

As effective as it might seem, the formal political realm is not the only possible place to strive for a Dutch world sanitized of anti-Blackness. I learnt this from Elza, my grandmother, to whom in the past I dedicated an academic article or two (Guadeloupe 2006, 2009). As a child during election time on Aruba, *mai* would often say that the realm of politics was the house of the *mentirosos* (liars).

Politics was dominated by the big men with the right networks and credentials who operated as though they could singlehandedly change the world. Among those big men, she would say one also encountered some *man-womans*, her term for women who, with a slight femininity for good taste, displayed the same masculine bravado and authoritarian ways. Most politicians were in her estimation self-enrichers who craved status and power. My grandmother's take was not exceptional. It was the rule. Common knowledge had it that political leaders on our small Caribbean islands were in the pockets of wealthy families and big businesses from primarily the North Atlantic. They never made a drastic move to better the position of the small people outside of the whims of these powers. There was also the influence of The Hague, which Antillean politicians accused of neocolonialism whenever edicts from that center of power went against their self-enrichment schemes or those of their sponsors.

Real change happened, my grandmother would say, when the small people could not take the injustice anymore and were willing to take blows. At those times, those who enjoyed some education

51

among the small people would be bought by the big men, and thus only a fraction of the possible change would be realized. That was the way of the world, my grandmother's philosophy of history. Her outlook was in many ways similar to C. L. R. James's, even though he primarily focused on the men among the small people.

I later learned to further universalize my grandmother's insights in terms of gendered anti-black racism through the work of Alice Walker, Edwidge Danticat, bell hooks, and Maryse Condé. Reading them taught me that, globally, the realm of official politics and its formal contestations is usually a masculine realm where male figures, or masculinity, dominates. If we only focus on the mighty men and women in politics, we miss much of the transformative history that allows women and men who look like me to inhabit the world as we do.

The social realm, understood as spaces and moments that weren't fully colonized by formal political concerns or the dictates of economic forces, was where most of the ordinary decolonial work was conducted. Coming of age in the Netherlands, I experienced the social realm as places of conviviality where I usually saw ordinary brown-skinned and pink-skinned women seeking to concretize the abstract universal of equality and liberty for all. Like my grandmother, the women I am about to present were mothers for all who lived in the multicultural neighborhoods where they operated. This book would not be complete if I did not mention Annette Slijngaard. *Juffrouw* Annette (she insisted that we call her "Miss") is the Surinamese-born mother of my friend Mike. She inspired so many newcomers and working-class children in Helmond to aim for the stars.

Mike's house was always filled with children, which we would tease him about, calling his house a *crèche*. Having finished the Mulo (the equivalent of high school in the former Dutch educational system), and being good with numbers, Miss Annette was employed as a part-time administrative secretary in a factory. Later, she went to work as a nurse in an elderly home. Her common-law husband was a welder. In the afternoons, she would invite school kids of various hues, ethnicities, and religious persuasions into her home to do schoolwork.

There were always cookies and the loving strictness of Miss Annette heartening them to do their best. These sessions meant the world to many of these kids whose parents' proficiency in the Dutch language was limited, or who disbelieved in the possibility of social and economic ascent. She taught them to be critical of the ethnic enculturation of their parents and other community leaders. Annette was the first to tell them that a nickel could become a dime and then a dollar. As such, they went to her to show her their school report cards. She was truly loved.

Looking back, I interpret her as someone who was teaching them to balance the *Conquistador* and *Nativo* logics of being that animated their individual becoming. Being critical of the hypocrisy and superiority complexes of the well-to-do native Dutch should not amount to a tout court rejection of all knowledge or advice for living from the West. Without having read C. L. R. James, Miss Annette in many ways was enacting his view that the best of the accomplishments of the West belonged to her, too.

Years later, I spoke to Miss Annette while conducting fieldwork on the politics of belonging in multicultural neighborhoods. She told me that she was simply putting into practice what she had learned in Surinam: It was not solely biological mothers and fathers who raised their children, it was those in the community who were older and had time on their hands. Besides biological parentage, there were *buurtmoeders* (mothers of the neighborhood) practicing multicultural social parenting. And those who took up that function beyond ethnic exclusivity had to be culturally ambidextrous.

Buurtmoeders had to be able to do multiple cultural expressions, speak to the sensitivities of specific ethnic groups, and know what young people liked. When Miss Annette arrived in the Netherlands in the late 1960s, there was little understanding that in multicultural settings assimilation or implicit segregation had to give way to integration with each other into an open commonwealth that did not seek to erase differences. She deemed the implicit segregation of the

12,500 Moluccans who arrived in the Netherlands in 1951 a violent travesty. After they had supported the Netherlands in its struggle against the independence of East Indies, these Moluccan immigrants were placed in camps removed from the rest of country. They had not chosen to migrate to the Netherlands, but after opposing Sukarno's struggle to make Indonesia an independent country, they were temporarily brought to the Netherlands for their own safety. They were promised that would only be there until the Dutch government had negotiated with Sukarno that the Maluku Islands would become their free homeland. The promise never materialized. Miss Annette was equally scathing about the assimilation policies begun in the 1950s that forced 300,000 Indo-Dutch—the descendants of native Dutch and Chinese who had been born in Indonesia, as well as those of mixed Indonesian parentage—to relinquish cultural expressions not deemed "Dutch" enough (Jones 2007). Facing similar forms of misrecognition, Miss Annette informed me that newcomers joined hands to contest the racism they experienced. Yet besides addressing formal powers, Miss Annette made it her business to educate her neighborhood in the ethics of conviviality and antiracism. Recognition of ethnic specificity had to go hand in hand with a rejection of ethnic absolutism and the creation of transcultural ways of being. It all began with the small acts of making the existing multiculture unremarkable. In my talks with her, I realized that my letter to Yusef's daughter was about practicing this mode of becoming and being together. We—Mike, Dragana, Naima, Sabah, Geertje, and I—even though we weren't the children Miss Annette catered to, were the offspring of multicultural social parenting. This mode of enculturation is alive and well, as I would later find out when I conducted fieldwork from 2007 to 2013 in Rotterdam.

What Miss Annette did yesterday is being done today by Bea, or I should say *Oma* Bea, and Ingrid, a mother and daughter I met in the overwhelmingly working-class district of Feyenoord in Rotterdam. *Oma* is the Dutch word for grandma. It is used as an endearing term of respect in working-class neighborhoods. Both Oma Bea and Ingrid were born in Rotterdam. They considered themselves *rasechte Rotterdammers* (authentic Rotterdammers).

When I questioned her on her implicit politics of authenticity, Oma Bea remarked rather dryly that being a firstcomer with roots in the city meant very little these days. Today, Rotterdam is *multicultureel*. Oma Bea, in her sixties, had witnessed the change.

She could still remember how the neighborhood of Kruiskade had become *Kroes*kade (*kroes* in Dutch is the word for the tightly coiled hair of many Afro-Dutch; so here it relates to the concentration of persons with that kind of hair). She could recall how this development had become the talk of the town. The so-called *messentrekkende* (knife-toting) Surinamers, a stereotype about the aggressive behavior of these newcomers, both repelled and appealed to young women like her.

In time, Oma Bea got to know some Surinamese women who were working in the old folks' home where she, too, was employed. They were strong, "no nonsense" women who invited her into their homes. There, she learned about the multicultural social parenting that Miss Annette practiced; about how a kitchen and living room could be a *buurthuis* (community center), a *kantoor voor maatschappelijk werk* (office for social work), and a temple for a Winti *pre* (the practice of Afro-Surinamese spirit possession).

Oma Bea marveled at first at how Surinamese had so many relatives. Everyone was each other's cousins and sisters and uncles and aunts. Well, at least some of the time. When they wanted a favor, everyone became an *oomu* (uncle) or *nefi* (cousin) or *tante* (aunt). Biology and ethnicity were trumped by social relatedness. It is not that biology or ethnic specificity did not matter. It is just that it didn't matter all the time, and so Oma Bea became family.[1]

She credits these women with teaching her to be a strong woman when she was reeling from a husband who was unfaithful and who was bullying her. These women taught her that there was nothing wrong with being a single parent; that there was no shame that her husband did not find satisfaction with her; that that was how men were. They told her things such as "straathonden zijn ze, trouw tot een andere slet voorbij komt" (they are street hounds who remain faithful until another bitch arrives on the scene). She was advised that if she could not take it anymore, she should leave her husband. There were many other fish in the sea, and beautiful brown ones to boot, but no less unfaithful. Yes, men would be men. When she finally did decide to leave her husband, her new—Surinamese—family was there when some of her biological kin did not look at her. She and her little Ingrid, fourteen at the time, visited their houses without scorn. Without their support, she would never have been able to follow through with the divorce and the life of a single mother.

Eventually, Oma Bea became active in the *bewonersorganisatie* (volunteer organization of tenants) and other welfare-related activities. She was quite something, as she was a native Dutch who could talk to the Surinamers. One who, as the gossip goes, enjoyed sleeping with *negers* (Negroes). In the end, she decided that that was not her route, as, like her ex, Ingrid's father, these men were indeed "straathonden, trouw tot een andere slet voorbijkomt" (street dogs, faithful until another bitch shows up). In love she was unlucky. She invested her libidinal energy in doing volunteer work for the neighborhood.

Bea's daughter, Ingrid, had better luck. She followed her mother and was active as a concierge in a *speeltuin* (a municipally funded and run community center with an extensive playground) and had a steady boyfriend, Robert. Oma Bea, who was Ingrid's number one volunteer and confidant, did not think much of Robert, as he had so many *schulden* (debts) and was unemployed for some time. All that mattered to him was beer and the Rotterdam football club Feyenoord (which carried the same name as the district), but also Bea's Ingrid and the two daughters he had with her. And though he protested, he eventually accepted that Oma Bea would permanently reside with them. Ingrid had told him that if he did not concede to this, she would leave. He loved Ingrid and so he accepted. For Oma Bea, Robert wasn't much, but he was good as far as men could be good.

When I met Oma Bea, she was helping out her daughter at the *speeltuin,* and her Ingrid was a hit because she spoke Sranan Tongo (a creole language spoken by Surinamese Dutch) and could communicate with the *antis* (Antillean Dutch) and *mocros* (Moroccan Dutch), along with the rest of the *nieuwe Rotterdammers* (newcomers in Rotterdam). The *speeltuin* was a place where *Surinaamse feestjes* (Surinamese parties) and *Antilliaanse bruiloft recepties* (Antillean wedding receptions) were held. But Ingrid also remained true to tradition, as whenever there was a Feyenoord match, or in the evenings, the *speeltuin* was transformed into a *bruin café* (working-class pub) where *smartlappen* (traditional working-class native Dutch music with a blues theme) and *top 40* (primarily North Atlantic–oriented popular music) could be heard. Oma Bea made sure that this *tata* (Surinamese for native Dutch) heritage was passed down to her Ingrid and that Robert cemented it. The municipality tolerated the antics of Oma Bea and Ingrid, for they had one of the best running *speeltuinen.*

I got to know Oma Bea and Ingrid while following up on the work of an Aruba-born youth worker, Wendell, in the wealthier district of IJsselmonde, which is adjacent to Feyenoord. He had developed quite a reputation as a youth worker who could work with the most difficult youngsters of all ethnic backgrounds, and his services were in demand. There was a group of youngsters, primarily Antillean Dutch, who were supposedly terrorizing an upper middle-class neighborhood in IJsselmonde called the Verandah. These boys were from a different class than Jairzinho and Clyde, who knew not to make a ruckus in their own middle-class neighborhood in Rotterdam Oost (IJsselmonde is in Rotterdam Zuid). Their community center was open to them, given the networks to which their parents belonged; they would never be called *straatterroristen* (street terrorists), like the boys hanging out in the Verandah were.

Terroriseren (terrorizing) is a heavy word of course, top heavy even, ludicrous. But then who am I to judge? It might be more important to try to understand why people speak the way they do. Contextualization is just as important as making intertextual leaps to argue that, on a discursive level, anti-black racism was at play. The hanging out of these youngsters on street corners, talking loudly and cranking their mopeds, constituted a terrorist act, I was told by some of the middle-class residents living in the Verandah. They used the word "terrorism" unthinkingly. To them, it was just a word. When I asked them about it, they said that they meant nothing by it. No racial discrimination intended, for in the same neighborhood one also found well-to-do Surinamese Dutch families who also found the behavior of the youngsters undesirable. Most if not all residents of the Verandah were really annoyed by what for the boys was simply a question of having fun. Still, their reaction reminded me of the fashion of referring to newcomers as jungle people. Was Wendell then somehow a Tarzan? I am sure he would not agree. Be that as it may, they wanted someone who spoke the youngsters' language and could make them attentive to bourgeois norms of always taking the auditory tolerance of others into consideration; and, of course, the working schedules of those who paid the most taxes. The liberals among the middle-class residents of the Verandah tried to do so themselves. They believed in dialogue and reason. It had little effect. What's more, the style of these youngsters was beginning to attract the decent girls of the neighborhood. Something had to be done.

So, the most concerned of these well-to-do IJsselmondse residents complained to the aldermen, who complained to the neighborhood police, who complained to the welfare foundation, whose director charged Wendell, their best youth worker, to take care of the issue. Being an athletic basketball player and knowing how to combine street lingo with welfare methods allowed Wendell to reach these renegade youths. He gained their trust and that of the frustrated middle-class residents.

The trouble was that these youths wanted a hangout spot. One in which they could do their do, which means hanging out without having to engage in any productive activity if they did not wish to, and one where there were beautiful *chickies* (Dutch street lingo for girls) around. It was not an impossible request, had it not been for the fact that these youths had caused so much ruckus in *buurthuizen* (community centers) that the social workers there weren't happy welcoming them in their establishments.

Wendell had to be creative. Perhaps he could find a solution outside of IJsselmonde, as these youths were mobile. They did not spend their whole day in the district. They would just come and hang out in the middle-class neighborhood of the Verandah when there was nothing else to do. It was then that he remembered Ingrid and Oma Bea.

He had been to an Antillean wedding at the *speeltuin*. He liked Oma Bea's style: multicultural to the bone, as he put it. The *speeltuin* was in Feyenoord, another district, but that issue could be resolved, since the new informal policy among welfare organizations in the city was to recognize and accommodate the mobility of renegade youths.

Wendell contacted Oma Bea and Ingrid and explained the issue. Oma Bea responded that the youngsters were welcome, but she first had to have a talk with them. She had to know what *voor vis ze in de kuip had* (what kind of fish she would be letting into her basin), a Dutch saying illustrating that a person needed to know who they were dealing with before they made any serious decisions; and the youngsters had to know that Ingrid and she were not walkovers. He then told the youngsters that he had found them a place where they could hang out unimpeded and where they were welcome.

After a period of getting to know each other, the youngsters were given one evening in the week to hang out at the *speeltuin*. Wendell used that day to do *ambulante jongerenwerk* (street corner youth work) in Feyenoord, supposedly following the youths in their per-egrinations. He needed to be there, for there were the occasional struggles, tensions, and fights in which Oma Bea and Ingrid and the youngsters had it out; no weed on the premises meant no weed for Oma Bea. But these falling-outs were exceptional. All in all, the youngsters liked Oma Bea, and she liked them.

She called them *haar jongens* (her boys), and, like Miss Annette, she heartened them to stay in school, find a job, or keep the job they had. She was even up to the business of giving them and their girlfriends unsolicited advice on love matters.

Many of the youngsters took so much to Oma Bea and Ingrid that they came to the *speeltuin* on other days than the one allotted. They even became friends with Robert, with whom they shared a love for football, beer, and Feyenoord. The ultimate symbol of their respect for Oma Bea was that, when they heard that Ingrid and Robert were finally getting married, some of them who played in a brass band (these are primarily percussion and horn–based ensembles that play during festivals and street festivities; brass bands have become enormously popular among urban youngsters) did a free performance. It was quite a sight to see Oma Bea jamming to the brass band and the boys *hossend* (dancing in a train-like formation) to *smartlappen*. As exponents of multicultural social parenting, Oma Bea and Ingrid reminded me of Miss Annette. Yes, this was the Netherlands. Yes, this was just like the Caribbean.

CHAPTER 7

AN UNFINISHED PROJECT

In resembling the islands from where I come, the multiculturalizing Netherlands is also a work in progress. Anti-black racism isn't as virulent and violent as it is in the United States, but it still is an enduring and pervasive factor. I saw clearly how Oma Bea and her boys embodied this about five years ago, when antiracist movements emerged in the public sphere contesting the colonial underpinnings of the yearly Sinterklaas en Zwarte Piet (Saint Nicholas and Black Peter) children's fest.

According to lore, on the fifth of December, Sinterklaas, helped by his Black Peters, arrives from Spain bringing gifts for well-behaving Dutch children. Sinterklaas is depicted as an old, wise, pink-skinned man, while his Peters are his Moorish servants, whose faces are blackened as they go down chimneys to place gifts in the shoes of the children. The problem arises when one considers that the faces of the Peters are always black, and they often speak with a stereotypical Surinamese Dutch accent. They are Black Peters! Moreover, they act as childish and happy-go-lucky servants; this is somewhat of an improvement, as in the past Black Peters were depicted as scary devils who would abduct naughty children and take them to Spain.

Quinsy Gario and Kno'Ledge Cesare, both antiracist activists, the first of Antillean Dutch extraction and the second a Ghanaian Dutch, revitalized the growing sentiment that there was something anachronistic about the Sinterklaas en Zwarte Piet fest. Citing and popularizing existing academic and activist research on the racist character of Black Peter, the two men revealed that, in its current incarnation, the tradition could be traced back to the transatlantic slave trade. In 1850, Jan Schenkman, a Dutch educator and author, transformed Sinterklaas's demonic helpers, depicted sometimes as ravens, into dark-skinned African pages (Helsloot 2012; McGrane 2013; Weiner 2014, 334–35; Wekker 2016, 139–67).

The violent arrest by the Dutch police in 2011 of Gario and Cesare for wearing T-shirts with the slogan "Zwarte Piet is racisme" (Black Peter is racism) during a peaceful protest sparked international outrage (Helsloot 2012; McGrane 2013). The incident was massively shared on social media and commented on in prominent international media outlets like CNN, propelling the struggle around Black Peter into the Dutch mainstream. Every Dutch person had to contend with the matter.

Oma Bea's daughter and grandchildren would traditionally paint their faces black and dress up like Black Peter. The festivity brought back childhood memories. It was their thing; a moment to look forward to. Still, given the commotion surrounding the arrest of Gario and Cesare, they, too, had to form an opinion.

Ingrid and Oma Bea could not understand why activists like Gario, and social movements like Reason against Racism and Kick Out Zwarte Piet, likened their cherished tradition to the racist blackface practices of pink-skinned North Americans. While she could not condone the death threats delivered to the addresses of these activists, and while she accepted their argument that brown children were being teased and likened to Black Peter, she would have nothing of their contestation that the figure as such was a manifestation of anti-black racism. She reasoned that it was only the behavior of a few pink-skinned *klootzakken* (assholes) that was being blown out of proportion by the savvy media performances of articulate brown-skinned anti–Black Peter activists.

Oma Bea became irate when I asked her what she thought about the support these brown-skinned activists received from famous native Dutch celebrities like Sunny Bergman and Doutzen Kroes. For her, it was a case of upper-class native Dutch seeking to once again make the cultural ways of her class look bad. She told me that she always knew that those uppity folks despised her kind.

Bea and the rest of her family were strengthened by the fact that many Antillean Dutch, Surinamese Dutch, and Somali Dutch would bring their children to the celebrations that they organized in the *speeltuin*. These gifts for the neighborhood children were sponsored by local businesses and the municipality. Her boys, too, were not very interested in the movement of Quinsy Gario and the rest. "Lekker boeien" (I can't be bothered), they would say to me. They knew Oma Bea, and they knew that her intentions were sincere. Quinsy Gario was someone they only vaguely knew from TV.

An additional factor was that many of their parents and grandparents had grown up celebrating Sinterklaas and Zwarte Piet on Curaçao. There, brown-skinned and pink-skinned persons had to whiten or blacken their faces during the festivity—for Saint Nicholas and Black Peter could not be likened to mere mortals. What this meant is that brown-skinned persons whitened their faces to play Sinterklaas or put on black tar in their Black Peter performance. Their pink-skinned compatriots did the same (Broere 2017).[1] On Curaçao, as on Aruba and Bonaire, Sinterklaas en Zwarte Piet is strictly a children's celebration. It takes place primarily in schools, community centers, and clubs where grown-ups and parents aren't allowed. Grown-ups do it for the children and thus do not entertain conversations as to whether it is similar to the American blackface tradition. A brown-skinned child being identified with Black Peter happens only rarely. There is also far more innovation; while often sporting a jet-black face, Peter also comes in the various colors of the rainbow (Broek 2017). I celebrated the festivity as a child and never once thought of Black Peter as being similar to me. He was like Santa Claus, fairies, and Peter Pan. A creature from beyond.

I began to interpret him differently when I moved to Sint Maarten in my teens, where Sinterklaas en Zwarte Piet was not celebrated. Few knew about the tradition. It was blackface, I was told, or it was something "you Arubans" do, and that was the end of the conversation. I paid this no mind, since as a teen, Black Peter was the furthest thing from my attention. Today, given what I now know, and given

the way many racist Dutch in the Netherlands identify Black Peter
with people who look like me, I recognize the colonial provenance
of the festivity. It is important to note that, before migrating to the
Netherlands, Quinsy Gario also lived on Sint Maarten. Antillean
Dutch with roots in Aruba, Curaçao, or Bonaire are far less prominent in the anti–Black Peter protests. Moreover, antiracist activists
on Curaçao and Aruba seeking to identify Black Peter with blackface
have been far less successful than their counterparts in the Netherlands. They cannot argue that on these Antillean islands, as is the
case in the Netherlands, brown-skinned people should not darken
their faces, or only pink-skinned individuals can play Sinterklaas.
Another important difference with the Netherlands is that on these
islands parents rarely accompany their children to clubs and schools
to relive their childhood memories of Sinterklaas en Zwarte Piet. It
is not a grown-up affair. I say all this to explain that Oma Bea's boys
have little cousins on the islands who, like their little brothers and
sisters, also celebrate Sinterklaas en Zwarte Piet. The transnationality
of their experience makes it hard for them to make the connection
that Quinsy, Kno'Ledge, and I made.

What Oma Bea's boys detested about the whole affair was the
police, who, by arresting Gario and Cesare, had behaved, they said,
like "the pigs they are." But that is as far as their solidarity with the
anti–Zwarte Piet activists went. That they, too, faced racism on a
structural basis was one thing; that the party where their little brothers and cousins received free gifts from Oma Bea and Ingrid was
a racist festivity was quite another. They followed Oma Bea in her
reasoning that it was a question of respecting each other's traditions.

Oma Bea felt that integration was becoming a one-way street.
Everything of the working-class native Dutch was being taken away,
because they had a colonially derived racist provenance. At the same
time, people who look like her had to embrace the festivities of the
newcomers. She was beginning to feel like a minority in her own
country.

To explain what she meant, Oma Bea likened the growing acceptance of Eid al-Fitr to the commotion surrounding the *negerzoenen*

(Negro kisses). *Negerzoenen* are what is known in the English world as chocolate teacakes. After protests that the name was a colonial racist leftover, it was changed to *zoenen* (kisses) in 2006 (Hondius 2009, 30–31). Now, as far as the Eid is concerned, some municipal officers have sought to resignify this festivity marking the end of Ramadan into a multicultural occasion for non-Muslim Dutch to get better acquainted with their fellow citizens who practice Islam.

Given these social facts, one cannot but conclude that the comparison between the *negerzoenen* and the Eid celebration is a non-starter. There are cultural ways of speaking and doing that we have to decolonize, meaning update to fit current standards. There is no one-size-fits-all solution.

Now on a broader level I realized that I could also not endorse Oma Bea's general idea that most cultural expressions identified with native Dutch belonging to her social station are being curtailed. I have come across this sentiment often. I sympathize, for the sentiment is real to those involved. The multiculturalizing of the Netherlands is creating anxieties for some native Dutch, even as they embrace it. I cannot, however, endorse the idea of cultural loss, because I do not think of culture as a thing or as property.

Still, this is anthropological speak. It was easy to get Oma Bea to concede that cultures change. So, too, that culture always contains elements from near and far. Matters got more complicated when it came to being specific with respect to the struggle around Zwarte Piet. I found it hard to engage in an academic argument with people like Oma Bea and her daughter for whom terms like *coloniality and decoloniality of Being, neoliberal racism, blackface, White supremacy,* and *microaggressions* are part of a strange language.

My own struggle has led me to recognize that when Dutch social activists borrow too much from the international hip speech emerging on US campuses, they become unable to engage wide cross sections of the Dutch public. "Whitesplaining," "intersectionality," "white privilege," and other such borrowings aren't prevalent in Dutch popular discourse or mass media. "Man Piaba," that classic 1956 hit of Harry Belafonte, comes to mind.[2] The song is about a man who thinks he can find wisdom in the books of renowned scholars. However, he becomes frustrated with the works of the Einsteins and Freuds of this world, as they do not help him truly understand what he considers fundamental: what brings men and women together to reproduce the species. To me, this classic is an early artistic reminder in urban popular culture that lessons for living well are not necessarily found in the musings of academics.

I take from this song—read in less heteropatriarchal and reproductively centered ways—that if antiracist activists want to reach people like Oma Bea in their quest to eradicate anti-black racism, they have to reach them where they are. What that entails is doing the work of establishing common ground. Antiracist activists should not expect the Oma Beas of the Netherlands to immediately convert to their way of understanding the impact of anti-black racism—or the colonial traces in figures like Zwarte Piet and what used to be called *negerzoenen*. What they should actually hope for is acceptable temporary compromises that allow the Oma Beas to maintain a sense of dignity. These temporary compromises are the newly acquired common ground from which activists can continue their political work. In all of this, they have to critically examine themselves as they critically seek to win over others to their antiracist cause. This is an understanding that Belafonte never ceased promoting (Belafonte and Shnayerson 2012). Magic formulas won't work.

For the theoretical critique of Black Peter to immediately make sense—as a cultural icon of anti-black structures of feeling and action that encourages the infantilization of brown-skinned people of sub-Saharan descent—a person has to have had a prior introduction to the hip vocabulary of the Dutch activist world, where a term like "White supremacy" or "blackface" resonates. And this fact is linked to cosmopolitan-oriented Dutch middle-class ways of being. It is thus understandable that Jairzinho and Clyde, having grown up in privilege with more exposure to how racialization functions in the United States—their parents had traveled to that country and spoken about these matters—did consider Black Peter a racist stereotype.

Knowledge of the global entanglement of anti-black racism, however, does not make one act. Jairzinho and Clyde, like their parents,
weren't antiracist activists. They supported the social movements
against the Zwarte Piet tradition from afar: a "like" here and there
on Facebook. When I asked Clyde and Jairzinho about their relative
(in)action, they explained that they could not always successfully
articulate their misgivings to equally economically privileged family members who still upheld the celebration of Black Peter in its
classic form. The truce I understood from the parents of Clyde and
Jairzinho was that, in family affairs, those who did not celebrate
Zwarte Piet would not bother those who did, and vice versa.

Having economic capital without proper initiation into the terminology and interpretative ways of North American critical race
studies would not do.

Wendell, who understood the struggle and backed Quinsy Gario,
took his time in schooling the youths he worked with on the impact of anti-black racism. He helped me appreciate the gains that
had already been made. The boys took note of Gario and Cesare's
plight and recognized that the force of the state was unjust. Also, he
begged me to realize that Oma Bea was vehement about the racism
her boys faced, openly spoke out against native Dutch who were
denigrating toward the asylum seekers whose the children visited
the *speeltuin*, and acknowledged that global solidarity between the
workers of the world was a must. That is quite a lot. Sooner or later,
he reasoned, Oma Bea would connect these realities to her cherished
Black Peter tradition. She would first have to experience far more
brown-skinned youngsters she cared for claiming racial abuse due
to the tradition, or things had to radically change in politics and
the world of commerce. Wendell was convinced that if the classes
with money and political power stopped supporting the festivity,
and more persons began to connect Black Peter to racism, Oma Bea
would come around.[3]

I know what Wendell meant. I also think that he is right. I am
strengthened by the fact that there has been some movement, as
many teenagers and young adults primarily in the cities agree that

the Black Peter figure has to be stripped of its racist characteristics. Some prominent politicians have also publicly stated that the figure would need to lose characteristics that the protesters find hurtful. There was more, however.

What Wendell did not highlight was that the popular antiracist activists who have gained national fame have had some work to do, too. To repeat, many people would not have made the connection between Black Peter and anti-black racism if these activists continued to employ the North American–derived academic vocabulary that they had grown accustomed to.

Asking native Dutch like Oma Bea to learn that language, and to instantaneously feel interpellated by categories such as her having "white privilege" and her having to make space for POC (People of Color) as a "white ally," was asking a lot.

I usually bump up against a wall when asking antiracist activists against Zwarte Piet to appreciate why the Oma Beas of the Netherlands—who are embracing the unruly multiculture—still want to keep celebrating the Sinterklaas en Zwarte Piet tradition.[4] They will have nothing of it. For them, persons like Oma Bea are simply closet racists who need to stop performing "white innocence."

A rethinking of how anti-black racism operates in the Netherlands, especially in places where multicultural conviviality is a given, is in order. There is much to gain in doing so, as the polyethnic appeal of urban popular culture is becoming mainstream. The reality of my Helmond years is infiltrating the outside world, and the outside world is embracing the cultural styles of being that connected Sabah and me despite our differing ethnicities and cultures.

Oma Bea's granddaughters are fully into urban popular culture. They will have nothing of the *smartlappen*. She might one day have brown-skinned great-grandchildren. I say this, as her granddaughters are fans of brown-skinned artists like Rihanna and Gyptian. They drool over the actors of the movie *Black Panther* and date Afro-Dutch men who look like and emulate the style of Quincy Promes and Memphis Depay—revered Dutch football players. These factors may in time also impact how Oma Bea appreciates Black Peter.

Jairzinho and Clyde are growing up in a world where there is much greater acceptance of their skin color and physiognomy. They still face anti-black racism, but they do so in a way that is somewhat different from when I was a teenager. They are one generation removed from the shock and discomfort that native Dutch felt in relation to the transformation of the Netherlands. They, too, are becoming a norm, and this correlates with them feeling centered.

For Oma Bea's granddaughters, and in fact for many native Dutch who live middle-class lives, urban renditions of Blackness are an attractive mode of being. I call this "urban Blackness." It is commercially popular, a dominant new ethnicity that is beginning to extend beyond teenagers of all hues, a point I will elaborate on below. Dutch of all walks of life are beginning to embrace "the jungle," to employ Broederliefde's tune. Paying attention to this cultural change helps me to elaborate critically on the first route I hinted at when presenting the return of the Tarzan ideal in the Netherlands.

PART 3

MY WORLD EMERGING IN THE OUTSIDE WORLD

URBAN POPULAR CULTURE AND THE QUESTION OF RACE

THE COMING OF AGE OF
URBAN POPULAR CULTURE

After my brief career in the field of social and welfare work in the 1990s, I went back to the university and in 2006 obtained a PhD in social and cultural anthropology. I eventually found employment at the University of Amsterdam, where I am tenured.[1] It is from this position that I pen this book. As I mentioned in the introduction, I have become a thinker who focuses on the ways urban popular culture and everyday conviviality contribute to and complicate a wider acceptance of the multiculturalizing of the Kingdom of the Netherlands. More specifically, I have begun to systematically look with decolonial eyes at the evolution of the convivial culture in the Netherlands that gave me the tools to be the anthropologist I am today. I have done so in dialogue with my colleagues.[2]

I have come to appreciate that urban music, from hip-hop to R&B to soca to dancehall to salsa to bachata to reggae, is the soundtrack of the North Atlantic going global. At their most ethical and political, these sounds, still predominantly produced by descendants of the Africans forcefully brought to the New World, evoke ideal ways of inhabiting the now and dreaming the tomorrow. The promise of urban music as such lies in a non-place and non-time. It lies in one of those fantastic places and marvelous-real (Carpentier 1995) times that oppressed people, like the people I descend from, imagine in an effort to both assert their worth and will a nonoppressive world (Morant 2011; Shonekan 2011; Perry 2008; Dyson 1993). These people's freedom dreams, to paraphrase the historian Robin Kelley (2002), given musical form by artists, do not however appear out of thin air. These utopian visions are born of ordinary, everyday people's perception of the perpetual cracks in the wider structures of domination, as well as their appreciation of the possibilities inherent in convivial places that nurture their dreams. We do well to always keep in mind that urban music and the lifestyle that accompanies it have been

> formed by long and brutal experiences of racialized subordination through slavery and colonialism[,] and . . . against the odds amid the suffering and dispossession . . . [these] vernacular cultures and the social movements that were built upon their strengths and tactics have contributed important moral and political resources to modern struggles in pursuit of freedom, democracy, and justice. Their powerful influences have left their imprint on an increasingly globalized popular culture. (Gilroy 2000, 13)

Some social theorists of this experience, like Paul Gilroy whom I just quoted, alert us that these vernacular cultures might be losing their critical edge. They argue that these cultural expressions are being co-opted by capitalists and black nationalists. It is important to take note of this worry. I do so more extensively in the next chapter.

For now, I focus on the liberating potential still alive in urban music, as it is often the cultural glue that binds the convivial cultures that Gilroy specifically heralds in a follow-up publication (2004).

People like Miss Annette Slijngaard and Oma Bea, working with youths of various ethnic backgrounds in places like Helmond and Rotterdam as discussed in chapter 7, bolster my faith that a time will come when racist misrecognition will be a thing of the past. Struggle and strife will, of course, remain. However, more of the Netherlands and the wider Dutch kingdom will resemble the convivial places that fostered my political and ethical outlook. This provincial dream is part of a planet-wide desire. Sam Cooke's classic "A Change Is Gonna Come" offers a glimpse into this world, anticipating that the oppressed hope will ultimately emerge.

Willing this new world into existence also entails demolishing the hegemonic idea of the supposedly *White* West and the *Black* Rest—the racialized conception of Us and Them, born of Western imperialism and capitalism, which denies that we are all inheritors of *Conquistador* and *Nativo* logics of being. It means, as I mentioned in the introduction, working on and through our common inheritance. This wisdom is beautifully expressed in songs such as Aretha Franklin's "A Rose Is Still a Rose." In that song, she reveals that the even in the intimate relationships between brown-skinned men and women of sub-Saharan descent, the *Conquistador* logic of using women as disposable commodities often prevails. What Franklin also made clear in her immemorial rendition of "Respect," when that song became the anthem of the American civil rights movement, is that working interpersonally and on oneself cannot be divorced from seeking to dismantle the wider structures of oppression (Brown 2018).

C. L. R. James was attentive to how, at its best, urban popular culture, or as he termed it "the popular arts," brought the societal, interpersonal, and personal together. Recording his stay in the United States in the 1950s James already intuited that these arts "assumed a very intimate relation to the daily lives of the great masses of the people" (1980c, 9). As ordinary folk related to the personages and situations presented in urban popular culture, a possibility arose for them to reflect on their condition and seek more space to express their individuality beyond the strictures of hermetically sealed identity labels and groupthink. At its best, urban popular culture could incite collective action to forward the quest for a materially and symbolically just planetary humanism.

My grandmother inducted me into an appreciation that in their songs, videos, and live performances, some urban musical artists produced ethical and political philosophies of living in an effort to help bring about a better tomorrow. She taught me and her other grandchildren to love ourselves as we danced to Johnny Ventura, Celia Cruz, Juan Luis Guerra, and other artists whose music she enjoyed. Yes, we were somebody, and yes, we were beautiful.

This insight was reinforced later in Helmond, seeing Sabah, Naima, and other young women discover and love their bodies and themselves, dancing and singing along to hits such as Lucy Pearl's "Don't Mess with My Man." It did more, as it reinforced and reinvigorated their battle against racism and other accompanying forms of injustice. Sabah, whose style of dress and behavior always reminds me of the classy, powerful ladies of the 1990s R&B group En Vogue, actively promotes ethnic diversity in her work at the municipality. She is a policy maker who makes sure that funding arrives, and policies are supported, that allow Wendell and Oma Bea to do their social work. Sabah in her own way is being true to the legacy of Miss Slijngaard and therewith charting new ground. An example is her critique of men practicing Islam who wish to disconnect their battle against Islamophobia from modes of masculine domination. She told me that urban music and the lifestyle that goes with it was part of her informal education in assertive womanhood; it also kept her sane when she faced racism and implicit Islam bashing during her time at the university.

In the 1990s, I, too, was listening to urban music while studying the likes of C. L. R. James and Frantz Fanon at the university. When I became a university lecturer, I came to the understanding that this was a commonplace. Sabah and I weren't exceptions. Many students I interacted with were into hip-hop, salsa, and the latest urban-inflected Hollywood sitcoms and movies. In my anthropology classes, I began to introduce the work of Paul Gilroy and Stuart Hall, and the early pioneering work of C. L. R. James.

I felt that my culture, urban popular culture, mattered. I reasoned that discussing the work of theorists critically interrogating urban popular culture, in combination with analyses of the politics of pop artists like Bunny Wailer and Nina Simone, had to be part of academia. That is how I met Manu, the legendary Dutch rapper, DJ, producer, and radio talk-show host.

Manu had also studied anthropology at Utrecht. Through the grapevine, he had heard about what I was doing. I was invited a couple of times to his talk show on the urban radio station FunX

FM to talk about the role of education in combating anti-black racism. As we got to know each other better, Manu began to reveal that
he learned more about the importance of demolishing anti-black
racism from hip-hop and other styles of urban music than he did
from most social science literature.

Manu, in his mid-thirties during our conversations, explained
that he had been inducted into urban popular culture by his older
brother. At that time, the mid-1980s, hip-hop was firmly part of an
underground movement. It wasn't regularly played on the radio or
TV, but it was already the soundtrack of the convivial culture of
the polyethnic neighborhood in the city of Gouda, where he grew
up. At thirteen years of age, he used his monthly allowance to buy
a CD of the world-renowned hip-hop artist KRS-One. He did not
know KRS-One; he just liked the cover of the CD. After listening to
the music and seeking to imitate KRS's lyrical flow, he became an
immediate fan. One of the highlights of his life was when he had the
opportunity to perform with this pioneering rap philosopher. Manu
explained that his main identity, like that of KRS-One, is being a
hip-hopper against anti-black racism. As he put it, KRS-One taught
him the hip-hop creed: "It's not where you're from, it's where you're
at mentally and politically."

When we met to talk about this book in January 2018, Manu
and I agreed that KRS-One's "The World Is Mind," off the album
of the same title (2017), is as good as any theory explaining that
perception plays a pivotal role in how we dwell in life. In this song,
"the Blastmaster" depicts a scene of two patients lying in a hospital,
sharing a room. The first patient is jealous because the second patient's bed is next to the window and he can look outside, while he,
from the vantage point of his own bed, can't see anything at all. He
asks the second patient to relay what he is seeing outside. Although
he can only listen, it improves his health to hear these depictions
of the hustle and bustle of everyday life. The patient remains jealous, however, desiring the other patient's bed. When one day the
second patient is discharged, he immediately requests to be moved
to the bed next to the window, only to find himself staring at a brick

wall. There is no window. The patient feels bamboozled. Realization dawns on him, however, when the nurse explains to him that there was never a window and that the other patient is blind. KRS-One closes the song with the following line: "He realized right at that time, you create your reality, the world is mind" (2017).

In "Wat ik Zie" (What I See), Manu's 2010 musical collaboration with fellow rappers Amier Papier and Brakko, he puts forth a similar point. In our discussion, he agreed that "geloof niet wat je ziet, maar zie wat je in gelooft" (don't believe everything you see, but see [in the sense of realize] what you believe in). In that song and other productions, Manu champions a politics of seeing, of the mind interpreting the world through words, that is critical of anti-black racism and economic injustice.[3] Manu's songs usually emphasize the way class and racism make it impossible for the working classes in the Netherlands and the wider world to live a decent life.

Manu also revealed that in his youth he was part of an informal reading group. Listening to KRS-One brought him and his friends to read books such as Alex Haley's *The Autobiography of Malcolm X* and Frances Cress Welling's *The Isis Papers*. He told me that they would have deep conversations on what the texts exactly meant and how it related to the Netherlands. Together they came to the conclusion that a white-versus-black dichotomy promoted by Afrocentric thinkers from the United States such as Welling's was too narrow. This did not prevent him, like it didn't prevent me, from acknowledging the strong presence of anti-black racism in the Netherlands, and working to eradicate it.

I had heard about these informal reading groups before, although it was not part of my experience growing up in Helmond. My friends and I stuck primarily to urban music and the wider art scene associated with it (graffiti, breakdance, salsa contests, parties, etc.). This sufficed, as we found "the deep form and the deep structure of our cultural life," to paraphrase Stuart Hall (1992b, 27), in urban music and the styles of doing our bodies it promoted. Pigment became less consequential if you could move like Janet Jackson or if you were debonair like Keith Sweat. Through urban music, our awareness grew that our inherited ethnic differences did not have to matter that much for us to be friends. Listening and dancing to urban music, and working on our bodies as "canvases of representation" without engaging in logocentric criticism (book-based learning), to once again paraphrase Hall, led to our willing of a world where, as Bob Marley (1976) phrased it, "the color of a person's skin should be of no more significance than the color of his eyes."

But Manu's engagement with books was not exceptional. Wendell, the youth worker I introduced in chapter 7, had also spoken to me about informal reading groups in conversations I had with him in 2010 (at the time he was working with Oma Bea). Wendell, too, was a fan of KRS-One. Around the same time that Manu began reading the books of Alex Haley, Wendell and his friends, most of whom were brown-skinned students who had recently arrived from the Dutch Antillean islands, were becoming fed up with only reading books written by pink-skinned men. They began reading books and watching videos of Afrocentric authors like Yosef Ben-Jochannan, Marcus Garvey, Tony Martin, and Runoko Rashidi. He told me that attending college or watching TV in the 1980s was equivalent to being brainwashed into thinking that brown-skinned women and men of sub-Saharan descent were only good for dancing and sing-ing; that deep thinking and philosophizing about life in books was not something brown-skinned people did. If "his people," as he put it, could produce incisive critiques of the system in songs like Bob Marley's "War" or KRS-One's "My Philosophy," imagine, Wendell rhetorically reasoned, what they could do in their writings!

Wendell said that he had grown up in the Dutch Caribbean, so he knew that, as he put it, "my people wrote, too." Through fam-ily connections in the United States and England and during his vacations in the Dutch Caribbean, he and his friends were able to acquire books and documentaries by black nationalists. Remember, this was a time before the internet. He gravitated to those writers who specifically contested the superiority of Europe.

I questioned him about the explicitly segregationist and black supremacist tendencies of some of this literature. I had the worry of Paul Gilroy in mind. Wendell understood my concern but stuck to the importance of the literature of black nationalists. He went on to explain that, while he did not agree with everything that, say, Ben-Jochannan or Garvey taught, and most definitely not with their ideas of insurmountable differences between humans based on race, their writings did give him and his friends a sense of pride in their brown skin. Loving oneself and seeking to especially uplift disenfranchised Afro-Dutch did not entail hating pink-skinned native Dutch. This to him is what urban popular culture was about: creating a world where all peoples were respected. The awareness he gained via urban popular culture is what led him to choose to become a youth worker. Wendell further explained that he could work with everyone. As an example, he referred to Oma Bea, whom he appreciated. He had her back and she had his in negotiations with municipal officers to advance the cause of Antillean youngsters deemed renegade. He did, however, reason that he would never see eye to eye with Oma Bea on the issue of Black Peter. She was in his estimation simply wrong and had to come around. In fact, it was his full immersion in urban forms of popular culture that led him and his friends to their early awareness and call to deracialize the Sinterklaas en Zwarte Piet tradition.

It is important to note that the brown-skinned youngsters he worked with who visited Oma Bea's community center demonstrate that immersion in urban popular culture need not lead to an all-out rejection of the Black Peter phenomenon. Admittedly, while my teenage friends and I were staunch antiracists, the anti-black racism in Black Peter did not concern us. As long as no one likened us to that figure, we weren't bothered and did not campaign to abolish the festivity. I knew, in other words, from firsthand experience that there is no one-on-one relation between being into urban popular culture and vehemently wanting to change the Sinterklaas en Zwarte Piet tradition. Class, persons, and ideas one has been exposed to, situations one has experienced, and perhaps certain American critical race studies books one has read also matter; the exact details matter.

I came to this realization during my conversations with Manu. Having a similar class background and coming from a social milieu like Wendell's in that he, too, had parents who fostered intellectual curiosity and he, too, read Afrocentric books with his friends also led Manu to question the Sinterklaas en Zwarte Piet tradition. In fact, he was one of the first popular radio disc jockeys to address the topic of the racist roots of Zwarte Piet. Manu told me that as a teenager he and his brother had confronted their parents with their understanding that Black Peter was the Dutch version of the West's blackface tradition. He stopped celebrating the festivity, even though his mother could not fully go along. She reasoned like Oma Bea did that some people were racist, not the festivity as a whole. She did concede its racist roots but felt that the past did not determine the meaning that the majority might give to the festivity in the present time. Still, Manu's mother supported his decision and ceased to celebrate the feast. Aware that most native Dutch do not see things as he does, Manu has found a compromise. He and his wife, who happens to be brown skinned, allow their daughter to participate in the traditional Sinterklaas en Zwarte Piet celebration in school, but at home the blackface figure is not welcome. He was sure that the efforts of activists like Quinsy Gario and Kno'Ledge Cesare, and the small acts of women and men like him, would eventually lead to the full deracialization of the celebration (already there have been tremendous changes; in Amsterdam, the Black Peter figure has been replaced with Spanish servants who carry traces of soot on their faces).

I also spoke to Manu about the black nationalism of the Afrocentric writing he liked. How did he deal with it as a pink-skinned man, given that he holds some of these books in high esteem? He laughed and answered that long ago he sided with Malcolm X but later in life came to repudiate exclusive black nationalism, while recognizing the specificity of the impact of anti-black racism on brown-skinned people of sub-Saharan descent.

Moreover, he reasoned that in the Netherlands the lure of racial essentialism could not effectively work; it felt unreal. Totalizing forms of segregation found in the United States were unheard of in the Netherlands. He went on to argue that even in the worst-case scenario, say in attending schools or clubs that most native Dutch avoided, Afro-Dutch had to contend with Turkish, Moroccan, and Eastern European Dutch. He knew this from firsthand experience, as his childhood friends were of various hues and ethnicities. He might have often been the only native Dutch in the group, but he was there! He read and discussed with them the merits and faults of the texts of Afrocentric scholars and the ideas of hip-hop artists like Public Enemy. Immersion in the unruly multiculture of working-class neighborhoods, Manu stressed, is a matter of fact for most Afro-Dutch in the Netherlands. You need poverty and full stigmatization to feed and fully foster exclusivist black nationalism of the kind encountered in the United States. He gave the example of the Nation of Islam. The Netherlands for all its faults is a welfare state that guarantees some measure of decent living for all. Sooner rather than later, those professing exclusive black nationalism in the Netherlands would have to reckon with the fact that on their jobs, at school, in seeking subsidies for their antiracist awareness campaigns, and in making friends and accepting the friends of their friends, native Dutch and the polyethnic reality are an inescapable fact.

Manu was an optimist. I did not mind. So was I. We both marveled at how little of this conviviality was recorded in academic publications in the Netherlands. How different the country looks from a perspective conceding that the multicultural drift can easily be rolled back. Today, "cultures, histories, and structures of feeling previously separated by enormous distances could be found in the same place, the same time: school, bus, cafe, cell, waiting room, or traffic jam" (Gilroy 2004, iv).

And it goes even further, as there are women and men, actually too numerous to mention, who grew up in neighborhoods like the ones that formed Manu and myself, comedians like Howard Komproe, Najib Amhali, Jandino Asporaat, Jorgen Raymann, and Jetty Mathurin; sports stars like Ruud Gullit, Clarence Seedorf, Gregory van der Wiel, Virgil van Dijk, Nigel de Jong, Churandy Martina, Jerry

Morris, Nelli Cooman, and Letitia Vriesde; actors like Katja Schuur-
man, John Williams, Dolores Leeuwin, and Milouska Meulens; and
musicians and dancers like Edsilia Romney, Afrojack, Boef, Appa,
Reis Fernando, Kevin, Jayh, Sevn Alias, Fresku, Broederliefde, Strictly
Family Business, Jonna Fraser, Kempi, and Rotterdam Airport, who
have produced a vibrant urban cultural scene here in the Netherlands. As part of the Black Atlantic, as Gilroy would phrase it, expressions of urban popular culture in this country, too, are perpetually
emerging outcomes of creolization. They too are best characterized
as a particular mixing and remixing of cultural expressions from
across the globe (Gilroy 2010); in them too strict distinctions between intellectual, artistic, and spiritual work cannot be upheld;
with them too scholars *can* imagine rich, antiracist ways of making
abstract universals like equality and liberty concrete; and since these
cultures emerge in and feed spaces of conviviality, they bring forth
activists like Quinsy Gario, Kno'Ledge Cesare, Hélène Christelle,
and Mitchell Esajas, whose politics of fulfillment are beginning to
matter, too. The latter demand that the Dutch political establishment
fulfills, meaning fully lives up to, the idea enshrined in the law of
the land that all citizens ought to receive equal treatment and enjoy
a life free of racism and economic injustice. Unlike the artists who
are fully immersed in the world of commerce, where identities must
be fluid and negotiable, the group of activists I just mentioned are
dependent upon the Dutch government and NGOs, whose funding
criteria demands that they present their case and themselves in the
habitual ethnoracial categories of governance. I will elaborate on
this bind and the tactics of these activist intellectuals in chapter 12.

In my work, I have preferred to remain in close conversations
with the urban artists, and I have therefore focused less on the
politics of fulfillment promoted by the activists like the ones I just
mentioned. The latter often employ forms of essentialist identity
politics, using white and black as descriptive categories in line with
North American usages, to combat anti-black racism. Reification
and racialized camp thinking easily occur when this is the case.
Still, since this is their self-description, I will term them "black

activist-intellectuals." Most urban popular artists in the Netherlands, on the other hand, who aren't black activist-intellectuals sense that to be true to the conviviality that nurtures them and feeds their utopian dream of an antiracist tomorrow, a "complementary politics of transfiguration must be invoked by other, more deliberately opaque means. This politics exists on a lower frequency where it is played, danced, and acted, as well as sung and sung about" (Gilroy 1993, 37). They implicitly support the writerly urban intellectuals who do strategic essentialism, but choose another route. In doing so, they reach a wider audience and are often quite aware of their underground work.

I found this to be the case in my conversations with theater maker and comedian Howard Komproe. He led me to appreciate the full extent of the *intermediality* of urban popular culture—a complex whole consisting of CDs, books, videos, concerts, social media, You-Tube clips, poetry, stand-up comedy, and theater productions—that together are reshaping the Netherlands. Komproe is experienced in all of these. He is a gifted rapper, singer, dancer, composer, and filmmaker, besides the comedy and theater productions he is most famous for. He is also equally versed in articulating the politics of fulfillment based on black identity politics. Yet for him, he told me, it all started and always went back to urban music. Urban music is where he found inspiration, and where he found his deep identity. When I asked him about his identity, he said that of course he was an Afro-Dutch man, and proud of it, but most of all he was a man who had discovered his spiritual calling through music.

In urban music, Komproe found a template for a new Netherlands. He reasoned that the counterpoint of speaking while making music with words, for instance in the case of rap, undergirded and sometimes delicately disturbed by polyphonic rhythms and recurring melodies and harmonies, is democracy in action. Everyone, he told me, had to come together. Everyone had to become instruments and vocal chords, to produce a *swingbeat society*. Swingbeat is a particular genre in urban music that fuses hip-hop with soul and rhythm and blues. It was popularized by the producer and composer

Teddy Riley in the 1990s. The aforementioned distinct musical traditions are discernible in swingbeat, but their fusion produces a
specific sound that is not reducible to its individual components. A
Netherlands in swing beat would be one where the various cultures
would be respected and strong, while simultaneously being open
to each other due to the ever-emerging swing that belongs to none
of them exclusively.

The forerunners of this future swingbeat society, those who will
bring it about, are those fully into urban popular culture. Komproe defined U.R.B.A.N. in one of his shows thus: "U Respecteert
Buitenlanders Anders Nooit" (you would otherwise not respect
newcomers), meaning that without the impact of urban popular
culture, respect for newcomers would not quickly come about. The
"you" ("U" in Dutch) functions as a shifting signifier for Komproe.
It stands for the majority of the native Dutch who have come to an
understanding of equality and an acceptance of the multiculturalizing of the Netherlands through urban music. It also stands for
newcomers who have been cured of the malady of anti-Blackness
via this form of popular culture. Through their love for Bob Marley,
Komproe witnessed Moroccan Dutch youth become more sensitive
to the racial discriminations in their communities. Last, the "you"
stands for Afro-Dutch who have been able to fall in love with their
dark chocolate skin and their tightly coiled curls, therewith coming
to terms with the slavocratic history that bore them, by looking up
to Wesley Snipes and Aaron Hall. For Komproe, *without the popu-
larization of urban popular culture, there could be no mass agreement
on that anti-black racism.*

In my conversation with Komproe, he likened the emancipatory
work of the urban to Ice-T's 1993 CD *Home Invasion.* On the cover
of that CD, we see a young, pink-skinned boy, supposedly from
the suburbs, with earphones listening to rap music with a book by
Malcolm X. Ice-T, hovering like a spirit, is supposedly the musician
he is listening to. The boy is wearing a necklace with the Rasta colors
of red, green, and yellow and another with an emblem of Africa.
In the background, his mother is being sexually assaulted, and his

father is being gun whipped. He is oblivious to it all. Komproe explained that those who are established, those set in their ways, do not see that a new generation, via their consumption of urban popular culture, is emerging for whom the Netherlands without the unruly multiculture is unthinkable.

Komproe went on to qualify the comparison with Ice-T, as he does not wish urban popular culture to be seen as solely misogynistic and violent. He admitted that it contains those elements, too, but in his estimation those are not the major notes. He explained that he had two daughters and would not want them to be sexually objectified. And, laughingly, he said that his mother and father would not approve of Ice-T's lyrics or the *Home Invasion* CD cover. Komproe reiterated that the urban was for him primarily about the emerging swing of the swingbeat, a coming together, which is a positive thing.

Florid in the use of metaphors, Komproe went on to equate urban popular culture with the color gray. It makes the White and Black positions (he meant native Dutch and newcomers) inseparable. It has the potential to rectify the power differences between them.

Komproe sought to get this understanding across in his 2014 theater production *Grijs* (Gray). In that show, he recalls his youth and the power of urban popular culture. Those who grew up in that world can relate to the tales Komproe tells. Underneath all the sexism, profanity, and humor, one discerns how newcomers slowly acquire a sense of belonging to the Netherlands by being and dressing like the urban superstars. It is the story of Sabah and Wendell and me; it is also the story of Manu. In his play, Komproe describes urban popular culture, and its artists, as the gray of Dutch society. At the end of the show, he explains that while the people sitting in his audience might belong to different social classes and ethnicities, what brings them together is their love for the gray. Their love for him and urban popular culture.

Komproe and Manu signal that the small acts of decoloniality in convivial spaces, through urban popular culture, has had an effect on the Netherlands. Anti-black racism is still alive and well; however, there are more brown- and pink-skinned Dutch who are imagining and seeking to live in a world where nonracialism should be the norm. His swingbeat society is in the making. Many Dutch love the gray and inhabit the gray, but of course the gray has a price, and it is increasingly commodified. And implicitly sold with the imprint of "race." The other half of the story could not be ignored. Indeed, as C. L. R. James at his brightest remarked: "The race question is subsidiary to the class question in politics, and to think of imperialism in terms of race is disastrous. But to neglect the racial factor as merely incidental is an error only less grave than to make it fundamental" ([1938] 1963, 283).

I began to discern that capitalism was selling a hip version of Blackness. I am referring to the cherished identities and styles of being of brown-skinned people of sub-Saharan descent.

CHAPTER 9

ENTER URBAN BLACKNESS

My use of the term "urban Blackness" came about without my realizing that in the academic literature of the United States, the concept is used to designate the continuing hardships endured by African Americans who reside in urban areas (cf. Maharaj 1997). So, it is reserved for people who still experience the inhuman effects of the alignment of lower-class status and the racialization of dark-skinned Africans that began in the latter part of the seventeenth century. From then onward, they and their ancestors became known as black people. As Achille Mbembe put it: "To produce Blackness is to produce a social link of subjection and a *body of extraction*, that is, a body entirely exposed to the will of the master, a body from which great effort is made to extract maximum profit. An exploitable object" (2017, 18, 20).[1]

However, taking time and the diversity of histories of darker-skinned people of African descent into consideration, a case could be made that in five centuries much has changed. There are brown-skinned people labeled black such as Clyde, Jairzinho, and myself, who do not live a precarious life. At the same time, today, increasing numbers of the earth's population, people of various skin tones and ethnic extractions, are being reduced to infrahumanity, to what can only ironically be labeled the *democratization of Blackness*, or as Mbembe calls it, the "Becoming Black of the world" (2017, 6).

But in an equally radical vein, Blackness isn't what it used to be. Not all conceptions of Blackness today are synonymous with subjection. The category has a positively charged *alter*, and not just among those people like me who are traditionally referred to as Black who have reworked the signifier. More is at play.

Increasingly, the positively charged alter symbolization of Black-ness operates as a hypercommercialized meta-identity that I term "urban Blackness." As a meta-identity, it need not be explicitly enun-ciated, as in for example a person saying *I am an urban Black*; rather, it solely needs to be performed. In that performance, urban Black-ness grafts itself onto existing ethnoracial identifications and creates an attractive double of these, a double that can only be claimed when a person belonging to the ethnicity being commodified participates in the commercialized meta-identity of urban Blackness. So, you have urban Black Antillean Dutch, urban Black Moroccan Dutch, urban Black native Dutch, and so on. Without the adjective "urban Black," the ethnic noun makes little sense.[2] Below, however, I furnish an explicit illustration of how this works at present. Thus, urban Blackness is the name I give to the increasing consumption and performance of urban popular cultures as styles of being.

With this comes the partial unmooring in the Netherlands of the racial category of urban Blacks, namely the working-class brown-skinned people of sub-Saharan descent living in urban areas of the United States. The musical styles of hip-hop, reggae, salsa, zouk, *kompa*, bachata, *kizomba*, *ritmo combina*, and Afrobeat predomi-nantly produced by African Americans, Afro-Caribbeans, and other similarly racialized groups, including the body politics that goes with them, have become emblematic of coolness in the Netherlands. At its most political, urban Blackness, as it is translated into Dutch settings, is about acknowledging the continuing struggle of the de-scendants of those who survived the Middle Passage and identifying with the subjectivities offered in urban popular culture.

Manu is an example of someone who fully endorses the idea that urban popular culture has to be directed toward bringing into existence a world where the grandchildren of those who were put to work on the plantations would have equal opportunities. He dedicates his art to combatting anti-black racism. So, too, have my childhood friends Sabah and Naima, who connect their fight against Islamophobia to the blight of racial discrimination. They are all part of what Howard Komproe calls his swingbeat society. The people I grew up with, and those I have so far presented in this book, believe like I do in Sam Cooke's anthem affirming that "A Change Is Gonna Come."

Nowadays, however, with the exponential rise of the culture industry, I cannot turn a blind eye to the fact that, increasingly, this utopian dream is being incorporated into the global flows of corporate capitalists, the most powerful agents in our finance-driven world. As a system of global exchange, capitalism has no need for naturalized social identities and their exclusive cultural properties unless they can be made interchangeable. In other words, capitalism needs standardized customers. It is on the basis of this process of homogenization that niches and seemingly heterogeneous identities are marketed. To do so, companies conduct research on specific popular cultures, often employing people traditionally affiliated with those groups, in order to transform styles of being into profitable commodities for corporate interests (Gilroy 2000, 241–78; 2010, 4–54).

This does not imply a vulgar Marxist reading of a transformation of noncommoditized goods and services, based on use value, to their commoditization for exchange value.

Following Jean Baudrillard's (1975, 1981) and Jean-François Lyotard's (1993) critiques, I understand the idea of commodification as an appendix of the nineteenth-century bourgeois fiction of use value. It was this fiction that vulgar Marxist readings erroneously claim that Karl Marx and other nineteenth-century revolutionary thinkers imbibed and projected onto the so-called natives and the wretched in the West, who supposedly lived in a world dominated by use value.[3] The thorough analyses of Baudrillard and Lyotard demonstrate, however, that use value was always the alibi of exchange value. As a myth, use value grounded the capitalist ideology of a hierarchy of needs and humans, whereby those who could afford it seemingly had superior needs. What this mode of distinguishing and totalizing human experience in terms of class obscures is the fact that exchange value has been foundational to every society and social group during the past five hundred years of Western imperialism.

C. L. R. James arrived at similar conclusions. The idea of the primacy of use value was of no value in studying the plantation regimes of the Caribbean—the earliest global expressions of capitalism. Use value, in terms of the plots where Africans and their descendants being reduced to the status of slaves could grow some subsistence crops, came after the fields of sugarcane or the saltpans where they were being worked to death to sweeten or spice the foods of the global privileged had been tended to. James also argued that racialization and gender cannot be fully subsumed by crude economistic understandings of class domination. He did so, however, while remaining within Marxism, yet stretching that critical paradigm to fit the multiplex Caribbean realities that he knew so well.[4] This cardinal difference needs to be registered. So while James implicitly agreed with Lyotard and Baudrillard, who explicitly advocated that many Marxists seemed blind to the fact that oppression and reality were plural affairs that could not be subsumed in any master narrative, he never relinquished his belief that these plural struggles—antiracist, class based, or focusing on gender discrimination—could be pragmatically articulated to further the quest for a decent world order. In the tactic of articulating, one could also refurbish master narratives. James reworked Marxism, demonstrating that the captured and subjugated Africans from whom he and I partially descend were treated as exchangeable objects, thereby revealing that from the inception of capitalism, class was infused with the ideas and practices of "race" and gender.[5]

Therefore, one can credibly argue that, across the spectrum of identity markers, what we are witnessing is an intensification of capitalism's commoditization process known as "sign value." Purchased goods are supposed to define a person primarily or, ideally, in toto. As the feminist philosopher Rosi Braidotti puts it: "This comes down to the imperative: 'I shop, therefore I am'" (2006, 152). The older ideology of exchange value, with use value as its alibi, remains, but nowadays the former becomes the alibi of sign value (Baudrillard 1981; Grace 2000). The discussion in the United States of Euro-American singers such as Elvis Presley and Buddy Holly stealing urban popular culture from African Americans belongs to a way and a moment of thinking about commoditization whereby artistic identities are subordinated to politically recognized ethnoracial identities. The latter are read as more authentic, the rest being stylized as imitative performances (Albrecht 2008).

Growing up in the Netherlands and the Dutch Caribbean, where urban popular culture is an explicitly polyethnic affair and is marketed as such, has led me to have a qualitatively different take on the matter. Urban Blackness is becoming just as *real* as the older ethnoracial identities. What's more, it's my contention that a similar logic is beginning to hold outside of the Dutch world, admittedly the place I know best.

Permit me to explain my point of view by focusing on the global urban pop stars with pinkish skin. Eminem must be able to rap, as Adele must be able to wail soulfully. The fact that they have brown-skinned producers and fans, and explicitly show allegiance to the "authentic" owners of these musical genres, soothes existing nationally induced sensibilities of "race." Hence, they are explicit that their urban style does not cancel out their ethnoracial marking as white. It makes that marking different, as it makes those of their brown-skinned producers different. Eminem and Dr. Dre are classified as white and black rappers.

The focus is increasingly placed on being a rapper. And as rappers or singers, pink-skinned urban artists must vehemently speak out against anti-black racism (Shonekan 2011). Once they comply with these prerequisites, they can win Music of Black Origin (MOBO) awards without being bearers of the right amount of melanin. In fact, they are then even able to lend credibility to up-and-coming brown-skinned artists. To furnish an illustration, the brown-skinned hip-hop icon and producer Dr. Dre endorsed pink-skinned Eminem, who later joined Dr. Dre to endorse the then new kid on the block, 50 Cent. Like the Dr. Dres and Diddys of the pop world, the Eminems and Gwen Stefanis can also become urban Blacks.

Their entrance ticket is the continued consumption and production of urban music and merchandise, the appropriate body politics

as endorsed in video clips, and their acceptance by those historically constituted as blacks who have also bought into this capitalist
logic (i.e., who are in other words also "new and improved" urban
Blacks). In addition, pink-skinned youths who for the most part
consume urban popular culture have to denounce the undeserved
white privileges that come with their inherited ethnoracial identity;
"white" here is understood as a synonym for a version of respectable
middle-class bourgeois culture that looks down on others (Essed
and Trienekens 2008).

Now I am not through sleight of hand implying by way of the
above that "race" is increasingly being subsumed by class in the
United States, the country where most of the Eminems and 50 Cents
of the international scene of urban popular culture hail from. Such
would be folly, given the historical and contemporary record of
that country. The stir caused by, for instance, the case of the pink-
skinned Rachel Doležal, who for many years passed as a leading
black activist, is a telling example. She symbolizes that fact that, as
one scholar aptly put it:

> In the present multiethnic, multiracial [United States] . . . things
> have become ambiguous. The human genome project has dis-
> solved the last stand of scientific belief in racial categories. The
> US Census reminds those filling out forms that the categories
> are based on "self-identification," not biology. Immigration and
> intermarriage are changing the demographics so, for anyone born
> after today, Whites will no longer be the majority. Nonetheless,
> race is not something that will be easily dissolved even if the
> boundaries are starting to blur. The trauma that the United States
> has experienced because of the construction of race is still an
> open wound. Doležal is the ghost that haunts our assumptions
> about race, and tells us we aren't standing on firm ground any-
> more. (Kingstone 2017, 438)

Doležal's defense that she spiritually identified with African
Americans fell on deaf ears. The ground of racial being may be

infirm, but in the United States that has not led to an overall change of heart. This is understandable, given the economic disparities and hatred that African Americans face. Acceptance of the fiction of race will take time and only become a nonissue when concerted material and symbolic efforts are implemented to right the lingering effects of colonial wrongs in that country. In the Netherlands, however, the history of racism is such that urban Blackness, the way I employ the term, becomes thinkable as a meta-identity subtly troubling racial divides. In the country where I live, racist somatic norm images of what an ideal human being should look like did and do play a role (Essed 1991; Essed and Trienekens 2008; Hondius 2009; Jones 2007; Wekker 2016). Yet, in daily life, the American "one-drop rule" and other no less insidious forms of harsh anti-black racism found in the United States were relatively absent in the Netherlands prior to World War II, as there were hardly any brown-skinned people of African descent living there. Class, place of birth, religious affiliation, and political choice mattered most, with anti-black racism operating as a less-acknowledged mechanism. With the mass arrival of brown-skinned men and women from the Netherlands Antilles and Surinam, however, insidious forms of already existing racist attitudes—the implicit institutionalized mechanisms that made many pink-skinned native Dutch consider themselves to be more ideally human than the dark-skinned colonized (never a real point of discussion)—did surface (Jones 2007). Given the contestations of people who look like me and other Dutch against biologically based essentialist notions of difference, the dominant form of distinction explicitly expressed by most pink-skinned native Dutch today is culturalist: "Their culture is incompatible with ours." Once cultural compatibility has been established, negative attitudes based on racist interpretations of somatic differences diminish (the white ideal can be relinquished or put on the back burner). The response of Ans's parents, discussed in chapter 6, is an example of this.[6]

Mention must also be made of the factor of a growing number of pink-skinned Dutch desiring and participating in the cultural style that in my teenage years was fully attributed to hip urban newcomers like myself. Partaking in urban Blackness offers an alternative style of being, as Manu made clear, which unmoors traditional ethnoracial distinctions. It is my contention that in this, the Netherlands reveals a western European trend not sufficiently studied.

Pioneers in the field of studying racism and popular culture in western Europe have long alerted us to the link between urban popular culture—especially music—carrying the signature of positive notions of Blackness, and constructions of new ethnicities and concomitant racial categorizations (Brown 1998; Hall, Galesloot, and Ang 1991; Mercer 1994). From the pioneering work of the Birmingham School of Cultural Studies under the leadership of Stuart Hall, we know that in Great Britain the Black identity marker as a political category and cultural style could encompass the British-born descendants of Afro-Caribbeans, Bangladeshis, Pakistanis, Indians, Africans from both the North and South of that continent, the mixed descendants of enslaved Africans originally brought to Liverpool, and even at times the Irish.[7] Once stretched this far, commoditized through big business, and stripped of the explicitly political connotations that had previously limited the "Black" label to newcomers and those fighting racial injustice, today Blackness as a cultural identity is being stretched even further: for instance, some early studies have revealed that, among their brown-skinned friends, pink-skinned youths in the United Kingdom may sometimes explicitly don the "urban Black" label (Rampton 2018; Hewitt 1986).

Most of the innovative work in this area has been done in the United Kingdom. Similar studies in the Netherlands have not gone far enough in investigating the malleability of Blackness in urban settings. Nor have researchers seriously addressed the ways in which the commoditization of Blackness has rendered less adequate our conceptual and commonsense vocabulary of "race." In the field of sociolinguistics, where urban popular culture is mostly studied, scholars have contented themselves with focusing on how a new lingua franca, *straattaal* (street language), a hybridized Dutch that incorporates and is modified by Sranan Tongo, Arabic, Turkish, and

Papiamento and that is spoken primarily by urban youths with a working-class background, may be involved in transcending ethnic categories (Nortier 2001). I have begun exploring this social development, as I recognize that the relationship between the commoditization of Blackness and consumer capitalism's discovery of urban popular culture has yet to receive sustained attention in the Netherlands. I have done so by following and engaging with young men of various hues in the cities of Helmond, Eindhoven, and Rotterdam who have accepted this new capitalist logic. I am beginning to discern how their acceptance and embrace of urban Blackness implicitly contributes to troubling, taken-for-granted ways of understanding biological and culturally essentialist notions of ethnicity, cultural property, and multicultural living in the Netherlands.

CHAPTER 10

PERFORMANCES OF
URBAN BLACKNESS IN THE
NETHERLANDS

There were moments when Clyde and Jairzinho almost made me forget that to be cool, to perform urban Blackness in a suave and natural way, is not an innate trait. The clothing they and their friends wore, their swag on the dance floor, the way beautiful girls flocked to them, the ease with which they transformed environments into R&B video clips featuring themselves, was amazing. Having visited their homes, and having known them since 2009, I have witnessed how they slowly matured in their performance. They had two left feet when they started practicing hip-hop dances such as the Dougie, and they often went off beat when they sought to write their own rap lyrics. Had I not known better, I would have easily assumed that their current presentation of self had been a longtime component of their identity.

I also knew that their parents had the financial means that allowed the purchase of the clothing and other commodities that came with the urban Black lifestyle. They could afford to purchase the most expensive tickets to see urban superstars like J. Cole or Meek Mill perform, and to take trips to the Costa del Sol in Spain and Montego Bay in Jamaica, all recorded on Instagram. This was not the case with other youngsters whom I encountered.

An example of the latter is Yasin, who as a little boy in the late 1990s used to accompany his older cousins to the youth activities I would organize in Eindhoven. He was a cute but rude six-year-old boy who tried his best to imitate his older cousins. He walked like

them, talked like them, and dreamed like them of being a professional football star and rapper. Yasin and his cousins were fully into
urban popular culture. They wanted to be idols, modern-day demi-
gods like the urban superstars on HBO, MTV, and ESPN. Larger-
than-life figures. In 2009, seeking the means to live like his idols,
Yasin, in late twenties, was convicted for burglary and attempted
manslaughter.

Yasin was not an exception. Many youngsters whose parents
cannot afford their aspiration to perform urban Blackness the
way Clyde and Jairzinho can, do dream of an MTV lifestyle. They
desire cars that are pimped. They long to own *cribs* (houses) that
are way too big to live in, to look as though they were on a Def
Jam–sponsored catwalk twenty-four hours a day. They wanted to
be a *big dog*, a very important person, whose name everyone in the
club recognizes. They literally interpret popular urban Dutch songs
such as "Kluis" (The Safe) and "Ik heb schijt" (I Don't Give a Fuck) to
mean that they must get rich and famous by any means necessary,
as the wider society doesn't care about them. They sell drugs and
other contraband and rob places in order to buy what they need to
perform the most extravagant forms of urban Blackness (the bling
of DJ Khaled and Diddy).

Such experiences lead me to be a bit more cautionary with salutary interpretations of urban popular culture, such as the milder
reading of Ice-T's *Home Invasion* that Howard Komproe proposes.
I know, too, that Appa, who wrote "Ik heb schijt," also has songs that
are more explicitly cries for help by troubled youths in the Netherlands. Think of his hit song "Kijk door mijn Ogen" (Look through
My Eyes), in which he talks about feeling trapped while living in
poverty and having to survive in harsh circumstances.[1]

I can discern Appa's social critique and the way urban popular
culture strengthens conviviality across color lines. Yet I have to also
recognize that the reception of urban popular culture need not be
benign. It can reinforce the "get rich quick or die trying" ethic proposed by the rapper 50 Cent.

I knew from experience that Yasin's older cousins—and Yasin too, I suppose, although I never addressed the matter explicitly with him back then—did believe in and glorify the violence in some of the urban tunes they listened to. Yet, as problematic as the behavior of the Yasins in the Netherlands is, it should not be overblown. Youths who engage in criminal behavior, including Dutch Moroccan youths, are a minority.[2]

The Yasins of the Netherlands do not represent most of the youngsters who are into urban popular culture. The majority of the urban Blacks whom I have encountered do not have parents as wealthy and as influential as those of Clyde and Jairzinho, but they also do not have to hustle and steal to emulate their heroes. One encounters urban Blacks everywhere these days. Many are attending universities and preparing for professional careers.

I came to a full realization of the slow rise of urban Blackness into the Dutch mainstream in my encounter with youngsters in the southern Dutch city of Eindhoven. There, I had the opportunity to ethnographically witness this self-reinvention up close. I saw how Judmar and Koen, a brown-skinned Afro-Antillean and a pink-skinned native, became urban Black. Observing them also helped me recognize how urban Blackness grafts itself onto existing ethnoracial distinctions.

CHAPTER 11

THE TRANSFORMATION OF KOEN AND JUDMAR

Koen used to be the laughingstock of Geldrop, a suburban town adjacent to Eindhoven. He lived in the better part of that town, a place where professionals sought to create a middle-class Valhalla immune from what they considered the uncouth behavior of the offspring of working-class ruffians (many of whom were brown-skinned Dutch). They were seemingly blind to the fact that in their safe enclave, as elsewhere, pestering is unfortunately part of how youths interact with each other. Koen was the boy other teenagers with a surplus of testosterone abused; he was the "not if he was the last man on earth" figure that young teenage girls talk about when fantasizing about sex. He was everybody's football: "Kick him as hard as you can." He used to be a nerd, but not anymore.

Today, Koen is suave, cool, and usually stoned. He sits staring at nowhere, filled with the ecstasy that comes from smoking pot and belonging to the in-crowd. All those days of listening to American hip-hop, trying to be like the ghetto youths while living in middle-class suburbia, were finally paying off.

We are at Judmar's place. A debonair Afro-Antillean Adonis. Judmar recently arrived from Curaçao, where, as a *don dada* (big wheel) with the right family connections and brains, he had owned the world.

For Judmar, the Netherlands was a new world to conquer. So many girls to love, a technical college degree to obtain. Judmar had his work cut out for him, but he was not complaining.

There was only one problem that seemed rather insurmountable for Judmar, which was his lack of proficiency in the Dutch language. He tripped and stumbled all over himself when speaking the tongue. His Dutch had been above average in the predominantly Papiamento-speaking Curaçao. On that island, Dutch was the language of those who do well at school, usually the secure middle class. I had been to Curaçao several times, so I knew that his mastery of Dutch was actually a proverbial case of "in the land of the blind, the one-eyed man is king." Here in the Netherlands, where Dutch is the language of the natives, when he spoke he was deemed just another recently arrived Dutch Antillean who didn't know the difference between the definite articles *de* and *het* or the pronouns *hem* (him) and *haar* (her).

Both lacking what it takes to feel completely comfortable and confident, both attending the same school, both aspiring engineers, Judmar and Koen offered each other a gift that sealed their friendship. Judmar gives Koen's performance of urban Blackness extra credibility, since his skin coincides with older ideas of the ownership of urban music. It matters not that Judmar is middle class and has never set foot in a North American ghetto, where their hip-hop icons emerged from. Koen, for his part, carries the coveted title of native Dutch speaker, and although his *Algemeen Beschaafd Nederlands* (General Civilized Dutch) is of the undervalued, provincial, Brabantic type, he has become Judmar's unofficial Dutch language tutor. What binds Koen and Judmar is the fact that they are both into hip-hop, and with that they seek to perform urban Blackness.

Hip-hop is not enough, Judmar explains to Koen. Even a stiff who lacks the wear and gear can sing along to a popular tune of Drake or J. Cole. To be more authentic, Koen must also learn to show at least a minimum appreciation of reggae, R&B, dancehall, bachata, *kizomba*, and what Judmar terms *kos krioyo* (Antillean salsa). Koen seems to take Judmar's advice to heart as he is also beginning to appreciate these other forms of urban music.

At one of the private fetes for Antillean students, Koen even met Lydia, whom he worships. The fact that he managed to start a relationship with such a beautiful girl as Lydia raises his status. Koen feels like a king, now that Antillean and Surinamese guys shake his hand and are willing to accept him as one of the pack.

He is a *dog* now, a member of the self-proclaimed dog pound of horny multicolored and polyethnic (although mostly darker-skinned) urban youths in Eindhoven, always on the lookout for *chickies* (*dogs* and *chickies* are urban slang in some places in the Netherlands for boys and girls who are into the urban lifestyle; the term *dog* is taken from rap songs, and *chickies* is derived from the English word "chick"). Koen and his friends do their best to conquer as many chickies as possible, as this enhances their prestige. But the chickies are not simply waiting around to be conquered.

They are difficult prey, often in fact preying upon their would-be predators. The chickies have as much bravado as the dogs, proclaiming their sexual and psychological independence just as R&B superstars Beyoncé and Mary J. Blige taught them to do. They, too, fool around. In fact, Koen's dog stature does not make him Lydia's uncontested lover. He knows this, but he has to keep up the appearance that Lydia wants him more than he wants her.

At first, Koen's parents were not too happy with their son's new friends and his newfound dog status. That is, until Judmar made an example of one the Geldrop boys who thought he could still mess with Koen and get away with it. Judmar felt that cuffing Koen's assailant was too much of a respectful gesture; after all, such a clean-cut fellow was no match for him. So instead he slapped him a couple of times. Judmar's opponent bawled like a little child, pleading for mercy, as Judmar grabbed Koen and made him *batié cu skopi* (Papiamento for kick him with your boots).

News of this event spread like wildfire: Koen had become part of a gang of *buitenlanders* (newcomers) who were into heavy crime. To please his parents, Koen invited Judmar over. Being middle class, Judmar knew how to comport himself in such a setting. Judmar explained that since Koen was his friend, he could not stand by idly and watch him be abused. It was his duty to assist. That day, Judmar did everything right. He even offered to do the dishes. "What a dapper and well-mannered young man," Koen's parents must have thought. They told their son that he could take an example from this *Antilliaanse jongen* (Antillean young man), who was living so far away from family and relatives. Judmar could come around at Christmas, Sinterklaas, and other such Dutch holidays. Koen's parents were pleased that their son was never again going to be the *pispaal* (loser) of Geldrop.

The other way around, Koen's gift likewise helped Judmar's confidence to blossom. He was learning two kinds of Dutch: the standard kind, which one needs to succeed in the educational system, and the *straattaal* (street lingo) variant, which is a must for the urban cool. Koen, having lived his whole life in the Netherlands, was proficient in both.

Although Koen wanted to speak only *straattaal* to him, Judmar made sure that Koen remained faithful to his duty as his friend-tutor. In the academic parlance of linguists, one could say that Judmar and Koen were "crossing" (Rampton 2018). They were supposedly using linguistic items and routines that, according to the dominant discourse of ethnolinguistic classifications, they should not use, either because they are not entitled to or because they simply are not supposed to and cannot be imagined to speak anything other than their "own" language variety.

Judmar also made sure to keep Koen on the right path. It was all right to hang out with the dog pound from time to time, but studying hard to get good grades was more important. The same was the case for weed. Judmar was making sure that suburban Koen was not going to become a *koffie shop bewoner* (an addict who spends most of his waking hours in a coffee shop smoking pot).

Respectability—deemed the primary indicator of middle-class status in Europe—is part of the bicultural heritage of Antilleans such as Judmar. Bourgeois culture is not exclusively tied to being European; it is conceived as a transcultural class thing. So, although bourgeois culture was creolized in the Caribbean, it remains distinctly connected with the powerful who today are both brown and pink skinned. Ideally, one has to balance the street bravado of what is called the "reputation culture" (the Afro-Creole complex) with the polite manners of "respectability culture" (the Euro-Creole complex) (Wilson 1969).[1] Judmar reasoned that, in trying to be urban Black, he was learning a new variant of the reputation culture, but he was not giving up completely on respectability.

In Judmar's estimation, it was all right for Eminem to be anti-bourgeois. He was an American. He was rich. Koen, however, had to be antiracist without renouncing his middle-class sensibilities (as this was not considered a white European thing). He had to be both bad and respectable, knowing when to display each.

Becoming versed in *straattaal* was quite a revelation for Judmar. Being born into the identity of an Afro-Antillean and having brown skin like most of the urban artists in the Netherlands was not enough. He had to know when and how to spice up Dutch with primarily Papiamento and Sranan Tongo, some Darija (Moroccan Arabic) and Tamazight (Berber), as well as Turkish, English, and Jamaican patois. If he did not, he was just another Afro-Antillean who could be mistaken for an *antilliaan*, as far as the dogs and the chickies were concerned, instead of an Ántilliaan. The latter were the Afro-Antilleans who combined their ethnicity with urban Blackness the way artists like Kempi and Jayh do. An Afro-Antillean is a nondescript newcomer from the Dutch Antilles who works hard and lives a decent life, but the newcomer must become an Ántilliaan to bask in the good life and attract the most beautiful girls (or boys). The Ántilliaan as urban Black dedicates his hard-earned cash to buying the latest fads, to look as though he jumped off the pages of *Vibe* or *Jet* magazine. He or she will roar as the Dutch comedians of urban popular culture like Komproe make jokes about the stereotypical *antillianen*: the lowlife criminal and ruffian Afro-Antilleans who hate working and prefer collecting unemployment benefits. The *antilliaan*, in short, is a racist characterization of Afro-Antilleans that urban artists have amplified and employ to ridicule. It is a stereotype of a stereotype that is a cash cow. Below, I will present a transcript of a stand-up comedy presentation by Jandino Asporaat that aired on Dutch national TV in 2010. Jandino, whose words I will thereafter analyze, is an Afro-Antillean urban comedian and actor. In his weekly TV program *De Dino Show*, Jandino plays many typecasts that represent a broad range of ethnoracial stereotypes. One of these is Gerrie, a loud and lewd native Dutch woman, whom he depicted during a memorable interview with the North American superstar comedian Kevin Hart.[2] Jandino and Najib Amhali, his Moroccan Dutch counterpart, together broke the Dutch record in 2017 when they organized a comedy show in Feyenoord Rotterdam's football stadium for forty thousand fans. It was the biggest comedy show ever held in the Netherlands and featured cameos by urban artists such as Broederliefde and Sevn Alias, whom I discussed in earlier chapters. Urban popular culture is now mainstream, and artists like Jandino have become household names.

Jandino played with the stereotype of Dutch Antilleans in a comedy sketch in 2010, which is very rich in detail.[3] In the sketch, Jandino is an Afro-Antillean turned hip Ántilliaan whose mother is proud of him. As an Ántilliaan, he has made it. He is part of the fabric of the multiculturalizing Netherlands with transnational links. He informs the audience that his mother telephones friends in the Dutch Antillean islands to tell them about his success, but she also contacts people in places like Morocco and everywhere else. That his mother calls all these other countries indicates that he is a product of the multicultural conviviality that has emerged in Dutch neighborhoods. Like the rapper Sevn Alias, he is the successful Afro-Antillean often viewed as an *antilliaan* who turned Ántilliaan. The crowd hails him and recognizes him as such.

Then Jandino emphatically begins to speak about the *antillianen* who aren't really in his group. Outsiders, however, such as his neighbor, liken him to them. He, too, cannot fully escape the connection. Still, Jandino engages in a subtle play of similarity and difference. The *antillianen* represent the racist stereotype. They are the ones who supposedly just arrived from the Caribbean islands and are committing all kinds of violent crime. Jandino claims that he agrees with Rita Verdonk, at the time a populist Dutch member of Parliament, who had proposed deporting these *antillianen* back to the islands. He admonishes them that they should first integrate into the Netherlands for about four years and then begin their ruckus. That would please the MP.

Jandino them makes a new turn by evoking the mass media's image of social unrest created by non-Western newcomers—and by that he means the stereotyped versions of Surinamese, Moroccan, and Turkish Dutch—who are the counterparts of the *antillianen*. So, here he presents an equation of all these racist stereotypes of brown-skinned Dutch, which then allows him to introduce the *polen*, a racist caricature of the pink-skinned working-class Polish Dutch and other eastern Europeans.

The *polen* are the new menacing "other" that deflect negative attention away from the *antillianen* and other brown-skinned new-comers. The *polen* are aggressive, and everyone is supposedly afraid of them. Except the *antillianen*, of course. They harbor them, and all manner of other stereotyped caricatures of newcomers.

We then arrive at the last twist, as Jandino makes his audience aware that out of the stereotypes used to discriminate against newcomers can emerge cherished and successful identities. The examples he gives are illustrative. Tatjana Šimić, a beloved Croatian Dutch actor and model, is an eastern European "other" like the *polen* who has gone on to achieve national stardom. The same goes for the controversial conservative Somali Dutch MP Ayaan Hirsi Ali. She started as a maligned refugee and, when given a chance, climbed the political ladder, became an international best-selling author, and in 2005 was named by *Time* magazine as of the one hundred most influential people in the world. Though he does not say it, Jandino himself has followed a similar trajectory.

Like Howard Komproe, whom I discussed in chapter 9, Jandino is not one for participating in any politics of fulfillment when it comes to contesting racism in the Netherlands. He wisely avoids explicit conversations about the progressive or conservative po-litical flavors of role models for newcomers. In private interviews, he has made explicit that he will not engage with these matters or with grand-scale social critique. What he does is a politics of transfiguring all categories with the objective of arriving at a future Netherlands where all will be considered valid and validated.

What Jandino does in all of his performances is to collapse the categories of stereotyped and revered newcomer. He does not, however, fully undo the distinctions. The *antillianen* are not the *Ántilliaan*, but they can become it.

I began to appreciate that it was urban popular culture performances like those of Jandino that provided incitement for Judmar to socialize himself to realities in the Netherlands. He had to become cool and successful like Jandino to be seen as an urban Black Ántilliaan. Whenever he was at home, he downloaded video clips of Dutch hip-hop stars such as the Opposites, Ali B, Yes-R, Partysquad, DJ Chuckie, and his favorite band, De Jeugd van Tegenwoordig (the Youth of Today). By watching these clips, he learned how to say *schatje* (sweetie) in a sonorous, bad-boyish way. He learned to play with the language and utter constructions like "Wie denk je wel niet wat je bent?" (Who do you think you be?) instead of the grammatically correct "Wie denk je wel niet dat je bent?" (Who do you think you are?). He even learned how to aggravate his Antillean accent in the urban way, for example, "Je Wwweet het zelfve" (You know it), using an elongated bilabial *w* instead of the Standard Dutch labiodental *w* and adding a final *scha* sound after *zelf*. He also learned facial expressions, dance moves, and how to wear his baseball cap.

To lay claim to the Ántilliaan identity, Judmar had to become Black in the phantasmal, capitalist way of inhabiting that category of identity. The same held for Koen, if he did not want to be seen as just another native Dutch boy who liked urban music. It was possible for both to find role models, as polyethnicity characterizes the Dutch urban popular scene. The superstar dogs and chickies in the Dutch world look much like Judmar and Koen.

However, given the international dimension of this popular culture, in which North American ideas of "race" prevail, Judmar's hue is still implicitly deemed more authentic in the Netherlands.

Capitalism would market his skin tone as a bit more "real," as an index of Black America and "the motherland." Yet without purchasing the appropriate goods, Judmar would just be an *antilliaan*. Attracted by—some would even say heavily hooked on—the commoditized urban ways of being, Judmar and Koen spend many hours singing along and decoding the messages of the clips. Often, these are the misogynist clips that cultural studies experts and civil society groups judge to be totally immoral and dangerous to the civics of gender equality and nonviolence. These are cultural expressions, we are told, that no self-respecting leftist should endorse.

It was on such an occasion, as Koen sat stoned, that "Voor Je Kijken Doorlopen" (Look Straight, Walk On), a video clip of the polyethnic band De Jeugd van Tegenwoordig, was being played on YouTube. It is one of those clips in which the violence and immorality that are part of the urban world are poetically rendered. The clip begins with animated figures named Spuitje, Oliebol, and Flesje (Heroin Needle, Beignet, and Vodka). These vices are supposed to represent the three rappers of the group. While Spuitje, Oliebol, and Flesje are enjoying a pizza, they are disturbed by a pink-skinned junkie who asks them for money to buy food. He speaks with a typical Antillean accent and assures them that he will not use the money to buy drugs. He wants to feel *llekker* (nice). Spuitje, Oliebol, and Flesje react with profanities. After throwing twenty cents at the drug addict, they begin to manhandle him.

Through a perfect camera shot, we, the onlookers, then come to realize that it is two young, pink-skinned Dutch boys, about the age of ten, who are watching this clip. Their tattooed father enters the room with a can of cheap beer, yanks the remote control from their hands, and zaps to another channel. Angrily, one of the boys screams in a stereotypical Surinamese accent: "Vader, wie denk je wel niet wat je bent!" (Father, who do you think you are!). From that moment on, we are shown scenes of the boys stealing, smoking cigarettes, beating up elders, teasing sex workers, and so on. At the end of the clip, a typical, lower-class, overweight, pink-skinned grandma in a jogging suit who also speaks with a Surinamese accent informs us how she let one of the young *buitenlanders* (newcomers) know that they should not mess with her.

Again, we notice that the clip we have been viewing is actually being watched by a television audience consisting of members of the Bond Tegen het Vloeken (Dutch League against the Use of Profanity). When the television presenter asks a representative of this group to react to the clip, we see that he has difficulty finding the appropriate words to describe his disgust. He is rendered speechless, since he has no recourse to the use of profanity, which is an important resource of *straattaal* and the urban lifestyle. It is as though he is speaking a language that is on the brink of extinction or is understood by only certain groups in society. General Civilized Dutch, the privileged speech of the bourgeoisie, is presented as but one of the many types of Dutch spoken in the Netherlands, and it is shown to be a variant of Dutch that is distinctly out of touch with the urban lifestyle.

The latter analysis is mine. Koen compared the character playing the representative of the Bond Tegen het Vloeken to the people who reside in Geldrop, whom he considers to be boring and hypocritical. Judmar simply could not get over the rudeness of the two boys in the clip. He began talking about his mother, who never spared the rod. The other Antillean and Surinamese boys who were in Judmar's apartment also started talking about their mothers and fathers. No way could they imagine being so misbehaved at such a young age (at least, not in front of their parents): "Ta makamba so por" (It is only the children of pink-skinned native Dutch who can do so); "Nan no tin respet" (They do not have any respect for their parents). One of the other Antilleans tapped Koen on the shoulder and asked him: "Hoe komt het jongen; hoe komt het dat jullie zo lau zijn?" (What makes you people so crazy?). One would expect Koen to feel driven into a corner, but this was not the case. He simply stated: "Ik ben een Marokaan, Surinamer, Ántilliaan. Fuck de huidskleur homie ik heb Oranje aan?" (I am a Moroccan, Surinamer, Antillean. Fuck the skin color, my friend. Can't you see I have on orange?). Wearing orange is an allusion to the uniform of the Dutch national football squad, which is symbolic of an encompassing multicultural urban Dutch identity. To this allusion, Judmar replied: "Niks multicultureel, ik ben gewoon hutspot" (Forget that whole multicultural business of separating ethnicities into clear-cut groups. I am just *hutspot*). As a mix of mashed potatoes, carrots, and onions, *hutspot*, considered a typical Dutch dish, is clearly an index of Dutchness here. The two began to laugh, pleased with how they had skillfully quoted hip-hop texts to deconstruct notions of racial difference. The others then joined in. One of them said: "Koen ta konio" (Koen is a real badass).

By appealing to the urban world created by the increasing commoditization of urban popular culture, Koen can always lay claim to the phantasmal Black identity of capitalism. But there is some hard work involved, and from the verbal exchange quoted above, it is clear that Koen may always be put to the test. He must distance himself from White Dutchness while making sure that he is not seen as a wannabe (cf. Hewitt 1986). He has to perform the role of the urban Black native Dutch, like P. Fabergé, one of the pink-skinned rappers of De Jeugd van Tegenwoordig.

An important caveat is that while urban Blackness can unite young men and women of different ethnicities, this should be understood as a potential that may or may not be realized. Urban Black youths may also form groups that have hard boundaries and are less hospitable to those who are seen as ethnoracial outsiders. One group of young men in Rotterdam identifying as Surinamese, for instance, interviewed by anthropologists Leonie Cornips and Vincent de Rooij, were extremely wary of pink-skinned Dutch youths who wanted to be *vernegerd* (Negroized), and they dismissed them as *nepnegers* (fake Negroes). These pink-skinned youths did not understand that they have to perform the urban Black style that coincides with their ethnoracial classification (Cornips and de Rooij 2013).

Now the emergence of this new style of being, this new ethnicity to paraphrase Stuart Hall, raises a set of interesting questions. While I know based on fieldwork that it can bring young men of different ethnicities together, I do not know enough about the gendered constitution of urban Blackness. There is no doubt that in its dominant presentation urban Blackness is heteronormative and masculine. The major figures globally and in the Netherlands—think of Jay-Z and Sevn Alias—perform such bravado. Nonetheless, in the urban world one also encounters Beyoncé and Erykah Badu, and in the Netherlands artists like the rapper Tabitha. What needs to be critically analyzed in detail is the possible transfigurative feminist politics within the heteronormative dominance in urban popular culture, which these female artists are engaged in.

Another crucial matter is the powerful North American presence in urban popular culture. Can the emergence of urban Blackness in the Netherlands fully withstand the weight of older essentialist constructions of "race" and cultural property coming from that part of the globe? US critical race speak is becoming part of the intellectual vocabulary in antiracist circles in the Netherlands. But what about in urban popular culture? It's time to address this issue head on.

CHAPTER 12

WHAT EXACTLY IS THIS THING CALLED RACE TODAY?

Given what I have been arguing throughout this book, it would of course be odd for me to succumb to the fear that urban Blackness is a temporary fad that will eventually be engulfed by the enduring and increasingly overwhelming global presence of older forms of racial essentialisms. That, to be more precise, Afro-Dutch youths will eventually embrace a US-inflected conception of international black nationalism grounded in the myth of a sub-Saharan kinship based on skin, hair, bone, blood, or history. This myth of a unified black identity (in the North American sense of the term) supposedly functions as *the enduring real* of how race is understood by all peoples of sub-Saharan African descent contesting their global subjugation.

I am equally unconvinced by arguments that claim that focusing on the multicultural convivialities one encounters in Dutch neighborhoods, and the recent mainstreaming of urban popular culture, can lead one to be blind to the spectacular rise of virulent forms of indigenous ethnic and racial chauvinisms in Dutch politics (Mepschen 2019; Richard and Duyvendak 2019). The electoral victories of Geert Wilders and Thierry Baudet, populists who flirt with ethnoracial logics, are cases in point. This xenophobic and racist development, which makes newcomers rightfully anxious, can supposedly feed the North Americanization of "race" among Afro-Dutch in the Netherlands.

I appreciate the arguments, but I do not see the Netherlands in those terms. Let me offer some preliminary remarks why not. The rest of this chapter will be a full engagement with these two ways of analyzing Dutch racism.

I see African American racial lore, with its clear-cut division of human beings into black, brown, and white, as part of North American globalization. I take to heart the many excellent anthropological studies that demonstrate that the way these global flows, including the export of African American ideas about "race," are taken up in particular societies is a complicated affair. Some Afro-Dutch seem to wholeheartedly embrace it, while others rework these US ideas about race in ways that would give Afrocentrics a migraine. "How on earth can these black people say that Moroccans are 'black' too!" The fallback position of thinking that the rise of populism in the key of race will set the minds of most Afro-Dutch right, is to platoon formal politics.

Now I am the first to admit that focusing on formal politics as a way of understanding anti-black racism is a useful strategy. Analyzing the state of racism by way of a detailed study of the policies coming out of The Hague, or the ideas of Big Men in Dutch politics spewed in public, provides an important interpretation of the Netherlands. Works that privilege formal politics makes one realize that ethnoracial barbarism is always just around the corner.

We make a cardinal mistake, however, when we present that interpretation as offering the total picture, as a part that explains and stands in for a supposed whole. Formal politics is then presented as that which always matters in the last instance. Popular culture and sociality supposedly follow suit.

One witnesses some hesitation among proponents of this view when faced with the question of economics and its imbrication in popular culture and sociality. There is a recognition that popular culture exclusively framed as a handmaiden of neoliberalism matters; nevertheless, formal politics is still seen as a privileged domain where decisions are made that impact how citizens relate to each other. In addition, some suggest that in these populist times, formal politics enlists popular culture to promote divisions between real people, and newcomers find this kind of response rather unsatisfactory (De Cleen and Carpentier 2010; van Zoonen 2005). This is a case of "what one hand gives, the other takes away." To me, the "politics come first and last" argument is just a transposition of vulgar Marxist analyses of the past (Hall 1992a; Williams 1973). Under all the sophisticated rhetoric of superstructure also having some impact on the base and substructure, economic relations are presented by these types of analyses as the foundation of everything else in a society. C. L. R. James and the cultural studies generation under Stuart Hall, following the pioneering work of Raymond Williams, were right to rail against this simplicity. Vulgar Marxists could not see that "[t]here's always something decentered about the medium of culture, about language, textuality, and signification [as well as, I should add, about musicality and the visual arts], which always escapes and evades the attempt to link it, directly and immediately, with other structures" (Hall 1992a, 284).[1] What comes first and last cannot be decided beforehand, because that complicated complex known as culture—in the sense of the arts, and differing ways of life, created by humans—matters.

Now I have tried to be true to these insights in my own way. As I argued in the introduction and have presented in subsequent chapters, for me, the Netherlands and the wider Dutch world as a signifier stands in for many diverging developments to which are tied particular projects. What I have done is present one of these developments and projects, namely the emerging multicultural convivialities and the ways in which urban popular culture is subtly changing the way "race" is understood. I do not claim to possess a crystal ball to tell the future, its future, or its future impact on other developments or projects, including those taking place in the arena of formal politics.

I would, however, like to present some insights from the social developments and cultural projects I have been charting. It is my contention that despite its manifold contradictions, urban Blackness, that meta-identity that is emerging, is a step away from older conceptions of racial difference. It offers a way of doing antiracism that need not give in to the lure of essentialisms, and it can endure, given the right circumstances; urban Blackness is not a fad.

To me, the distinction between an *enduring real* and a *temporary manifestation* of "race" is but a way of seeing things. I recognize that this way of seeing things has an appeal for scholars and anti-racist activists who are still committed to the idea of there being one overarching truth about how "race" operates in North Atlantic countries. They could counter my perspective by rebutting that, even though I may wish to claim that my being positioned as Black in the Netherlands is different from how I would be positioned if I were living the United States, still, in both these countries and around the world, I will be marked as a Negro (or worse, a nigger). The Afrocentric critical race scholars from the United States who prompted me to write this anthropological study seem to operate under this premise.

Now multiplicity should not be considered the enemy or the opposite of the idea of global historical entanglement. I can agree with scholars who argue that all of us live in the transmodern time born of colonial exploitation and capitalism. I can concede that colonialism had need for the creation and naturalization of "race" and cultural difference, and the same can be said for exclusive notions of ethnonational belonging (Eudell 2016; Gilroy 2000; Mbembe 2017; Quijano 2007; Watson 2001). I can see how the figure of the Negro, the global marker employed for me and all those who look like me, emerged from all this. From the Portuguese voyages to West Africa in the early 1400s followed by Columbus's conquering of the Americas, a global system began to emerge whereby the fates of Africa, the Americas, Europe, and later Asia were intertwined. To justify the ascendancy of the Asian peninsula turned Europe,

"The Christian civilization of the West was mutated into Western civilization at the same time as African cultures were stigmatized as its very polar negation, the absence of civilization, its void." . . . In this context, the pigmentary hereditary variations of peoples from the continent of Africa would be conceptually collapsed into the idea of "Black skin," which "would be confused with the social being of a slave." ... This understanding, one that differed substantially from the self-conceptions of the various societies on the continent of Africa, transformed the "multi-tribal" and "multi-cultural" peoples into a completely new historic entity: the Negro. (Eudell 2016, 48; Eudell is quoting Sylvia Wynter)

It is insights like these that led urban artists like the reggae super-star Peter Tosh to pen the song "African" (1977). There are at least two readings of what Tosh is conveying in this song and in the rest of his oeuvre. In the first reading, he is simply reiterating that for capitalists trading in human flesh, Negro equaled all sub-Saharan Africans. The same was the case for colonial governors enacting "race"-based laws and regulations. Jim Crow and, before that, the French Code Noir enacted in 1658 with its sixteen articles regulating the subordina-tion of enslaved people, and other such slave codes, come to mind (Peabody 2011; Ghachem 1999). Scientific racists added to this by inventing the Negroid race and its original belonging to Africa (part of the geography of management that led to our modern idea of separate continents with their distinct peoples). In most science and philosophy books, one read that the Negro was nothing, had nothing, invented nothing, and thus should be happy that Europeans rescued them from the dark continent. Negro as brown-skinned sub-Saharan is a prime example of a political administrative concept that has wreaked havoc.

To put it bluntly, being marked as Negro became synonymous in many quarters with the status of being the least of all humans. Like all pink-skinned folk, brown-skinned people in a similar social and economic station as the Negro could always say, "We might be down and out, we might be dirt poor, but at least we aren't them!" Even after the legitimacy of the idea of "race" was scientifically demolished in most academic writings, due of course to the Holocaust and the racial logics that fueled the carnage that was World War II, those called "Negro" were still deemed the most underdeveloped humans.[2]

Given this state of affairs, it is understandable that some politi-cally astute persons among those who were deemed Negroes said, "Well, since we are on the receiving end of the idea of 'race', and since we Negroes are from Africa, let us unite around the idea of being Africans in order to contest our subjugation."[3] In the process, they created scientific counternarratives, race-based self-help organiza-tions, and works of culture. The sociological paradigm known as the Black Radical Tradition, which posits that capitalism was from its inception a racial and economic system against Africans, is an example of such a scientific counternarrative (Robinson 1983). The Nation of Islam (NOI) and, before that, the United Negro Improve-ment Organization of Marcus Garvey are examples of self-help race-based institutions. Peter Tosh's "African" is in line with such a tactic in the realm of the arts.

In accepting this reading of Peter Tosh's song, one has to appreci-ate, however, how a second reading more in line with urban popular culture complicates matters. Here, the mystical specificity of Tosh's brand of Rastafari enters. Nowhere in the song does Tosh use the word "Negro." He does not give a wink to Alain Locke and other North American intellectuals who resignified the terms "nigger" and "negroes" into "Negro" with a capital N. Tosh speaks of Africans in rather neutral terms. Neutrality, however, is a first step in his work of reinventing what it means to be an African. There is a subtle meshing of secular history with a spirituality born of the resistance to forced Christian evangelization. That which was resisted was creatively transformed by mixing it with occult motifs identified with Asian and sub-Saharan ways of conceiving living existence. Due to this, being African for Tosh is a secular particularity that summons a mystic universality. One hears this clearest in "Mama Africa," another of his anthems (1983).

Africa is the historical matrix for those whose ancestors were forcefully brought to the New World. For Tosh, Africa is both mother and father. In fact, Africa is a place of bounty, and a place that produces multiplicity. As he sings, there are so many kingdoms and there is so much life. In such a conception, he explicitly rejects the myth of thanking Europe for bringing light to his ancestors and the so-called dark continent. The mystical subtext in all this is the surpassing of the biological idea of a separation of maleness and femaleness into two units. Africa stands for both procreation-enabling genders. We arrive at the preliminary meaning of the Rastafari *I and I*—I am an individual and I am the colonial history I share with others who underwent the experience of transatlantic slavery. But I am more than that at one and the same time, for I am also a particular incarnation of my mother and father, who are both African. Here, one witnesses a denial of a script of coloniality. Conceiving Africa as mother and father is appreciating that, for Rastafari, that signifier also stands for the cradle of humankind. Africa in other words is humanity that fully accepts itself. This Africa, which is diverse in its universality, comes about in relation to the Most High—spirit indivisible from matter. This is the second meaning of the Rastafari *I and I*—Africa as the inspirited Earth communing. It is the work of *Babylon* that seeks to destroy the African matrix, human multiplicity, and concomitantly the spirituality grounding this version of common humanity.

Babylon in Rastafari philosophy stands for both Western powers and those outside of the West who behave in a similar fashion regardless of their skin, hair, or bone. Given that this is the case, and remembering the spiritual universality of Rastafari, we can witness how Tosh had no difficulty articulating the struggle against apartheid in South Africa as well as the subjugation of Palestinians. Oppressive states and their allies are the work of Babylon.

Being African—understood spiritually—in Tosh's conception is not an impediment to solidarity. The Rastafari *I and I* is the universal seed of divinity in each human being that cancels and opens up all historical identity markers to commonality. Therewith, for Peter Tosh, humans' proper name is similar to the name given to Jehovah, namely, I am that I am (we know in incarnate form) (1977).

Tosh's spiritual Rastafari politics, which one also encounters in Bob Marley's oeuvre, Bunny Wailer's ethics, Ziggy Marley's ecumenical livity, and nowadays in the songs of Midnite—at the moment the most popular Conscious Reggae formation—is far removed from racial essentialism. With this particular appreciation of Rastafari, which is part of urban popular culture, one can easily articulate the struggle against global and local forms of anti-black racism to all modes of anti-Blackness. The latter speaks to my structurally informed account of racism. Therein I can accommodate all historically constituted groups from Amazigh to Palestinians, to Native Americans, to Australian Aboriginals, who currently face secondarization based on the idea of their belonging to a separate and lesser race.

Contesting anti-black racism in one's scholarship, politics, and everyday life, taking one's cue from the urban popular culture of Rastafari, is then properly understood as a means to arrive at place in which nonracialism is the rule rather than the exception.

In the Netherlands, I have witnessed many youths draw from Rastafari while they perform urban Blackness. Clyde and Jairzinho did so, as well as Oma Bea's boys and Judmar. This a part of urban popular culture that should not be neglected.

Judmar, for instance, knew all of Bob Marley, Burning Spear, Peter Tosh, and Buju Banton's tunes by heart. He had learned to appreciate Rastafari on Curaçao, where older youngsters taught him that it was about loving Africa, his brown skin, and life in general. Through Judmar, Koen became a fan, and together they attended various reggae concerts in the Netherlands and other parts of Europe.

Clyde and Jairzinho were more into dancehall artists like Konshens and Popcaan. Between tunes glorifying lewdness and the superfly lifestyle, dancehall artists also produce some songs promoting Rastafari ethics. Since summer festivals in the Netherlands feature both dancehall artists and those who perform strictly Conscious Reggae, and since many beautiful girls can be found there, Clyde and Jairzinho did their best not to miss these events. "Rasta Love, je weet toch" (Rasta Love, you know), Clyde once coyly replied when I asked him why he loved attending reggae concerts.

Admittedly there is much contradiction involved. The anticapitalism of Rasta is conveniently neglected for a One Love ideology.

Spending time with these youngsters, however, helped me see how this One Love ideology has tempered the more racially divisive ideas that one encounters in certain forms of US-based hip-hop.

One such race-based ideology is that of the Five Percent Nation, or rather the Nation of Gods and Earths. The Five Percenters as they are popularly called are followers of Clarence X, a former member of the NOI. In founding his own movement, Clarence X maintained the central racial tenet of the ideology of the NOI: all whites are the outcome of a genetic experiment by a black scientist called Yakub in a mythic time (Howard 1998).[4] Today, the status of whites depends on whom one asks. Some Five Percenters maintain the original NOI line that all whites are devils, while others claim that not all exhibit devilish behavior (RZA and Norris 2009, 191).

These contending views are easily explained when one recognizes that, like Rastafari, the Five Percenters are an acephalous movement. Across the board one recognizes that Five Percenters diverge theologically, as well as in terms of practices. To each, his or her own Five Percent ideology is not very far from the mark. There is no church, administration, or canon supervised by high priests that determines when a person may or may not claim to be espousing the correct version of the Five Percenter ideology!

Still, not everything goes, as discernible patterns remain. What remains consistent is the idea that collectively blacks represent divinity. In other words, Five Percenters regard brown-skinned sub-Saharans as the original peoples from whom all other humans descend.

With this comes a series of innovations. The Five Percenters have replaced the Allahu Akbar greeting with "Peace God." According to their ideology, only 5 percent of blacks worldwide have knowledge of their true being, while 85 percent of humankind haven't a clue about their true essence. They are the sheep shepherded by the remaining 10 percent, consisting of blacks, browns, and whites who supposedly know the truth. The numerals and percentages already allude to the fact that for the Five Percenters, Islam is best understood as a Supreme Mathematics on how to live and understand one's life (RZA and Norris 2009, 93). Erykah Badu's popular hit song "On

& On" from the album *Baduizm* (1997) is but one example of how the Five Percenters' message is packaged in urban popular culture. It begins with the idea that the quest to understand oneself brings peace of heart and mind. Knowledge for the Five Percenters is about keenly observing life as it manifests itself—thinking for oneself. It means intensive study, which leads one to recognize, following hints found in science, that blacks are actually the ones referred to in the Bible. They are the ones who made other humans in their image. They are ALLAH, an abbreviation signifying the upright walking creatures who possess Arm Leg Leg Arm Head. In Badu's song, we are reminded that ALLAHs are born under water, meaning in the womb of an Earth: a woman. Earths can either reproduce themselves or create Gods, men. And when one goes back in time to the first Earths and Gods, one arrives in Africa, the land of blacks. The last allusion in Badu's song, namely three dollar and six dimes, which is 360, refers to 360 degrees, a complete circle: the completion of all humans is contained in blacks.

Admittedly, with the exception of Manu and Wendell, the vast majority of the people I spoke to weren't versed in the Supreme Mathematics of the Five Percenters. Some people mentioned an idea of the Five Percenters here and there, but nothing comparable to their more extensive understanding of Rastafari. Most urban Blacks, including Manu and Wendell, love and sing along to the tunes of hip-hop greats such as Erykah Badu, Wu-Tang Clan, Busta Rhymes, Jeru the Damaja, Digable Planets, and Poor Righteous Teachers without fully embracing the Five Percent ideology.

Many seem to merge the teachings of the Five Percenters with the traditional religiosities that they followed. Thus, Mos Def's Sunni Islam informs hip-hop, or the NOI tenets found in the rap records of Public Enemy are placed in the same basket as the Five Percent lyrics of Digable Planets. It is all Islam, Yasin's cousins used to reason. Dutch urban Blacks simply lack sufficient knowledge of the American context to appreciate the difference. Thus, they read for instance Mos Def's Islamic cosmopolitanism as standing in for most of views found in hip-hop with Islamic motifs. Mos Def finds it important in his Islamic message to speak out "against oppression wherever you can. If that's gonna be in Bosnia or Kosovo or Chechnya or places where Muslims are being persecuted; or if it's gonna be in Sierra Leone or Colombia—you know, if people's basic human rights are being abused and violated, then Islam has an interest in speaking out against it, because we're charged to be the leaders of humanity" (Beliefnet n.d.).

The same argument could be made about Christocentric messages in hip-hop. Jairzinho and many of Oma Bea's boys likened Kendrick Lamar, J. Cole, and before them DMX's and Kanye West's appeals to Christianity to the traditional Jesus-centered forms of worship actively practiced by their parents. For them, these rappers, too, became updated messengers of Christian universalism.

I think this confusion and the lack of contextual knowledge among Dutch urban Blacks about racial-religious politics in US-based hip-hop is a good thing. Even at its most open, in the wrong hands, the ideas of black primacy propagated by some of these artists easily slide into black supremacy. The culturally rich panoply of brownish- and pinkish-skinned folk living lives nonreducible to the markers of black and white gets obfuscated by this terminology.

Manu and Wendell told me that the scanty appeal of the Five Percent ideology was not about youngsters simply lacking knowledge. It was also about an implicit understanding that the black nationalist projects of the United States were ill suited to Dutch realities. I had to concede that, even though I knew about the ideology—as I hinted in chapter 6 when I presented an account of "Tarzan" and meeting the parents of my girlfriend at the time—I could not agree wholeheartedly with black privilege. The Five Percent ideology offers an alternative educational system in neighborhoods in the United States where youngsters who look like me feel the neglect of racist state institutions that decimate schools in their vicinity. It gives them pride and a sense of worth and purpose, while amplifying their vocabulary and mathematical skills: the three Rs—reading, writing, and 'rithmetic. In the Netherlands, such state neglect is not the case, and hence the Five Percent ideology has to contend with other ideas that Afro-Dutch are privy to.

This judgment of mine, and that of Manu and Wendell, does not accord with the antiracist politics of many black activist-intellectuals who categorically define themselves as black in the US sense of the term. I am referring to persons such as Quinsy Gario, Kno'Ledge Cesare, Hélène Christelle, and Mitchell Esajas, whom I briefly introduced in chapter 9. As mentioned, these activists engage in a politics of fulfillment, employing a black essentialism that accommodates the funding mechanisms of the Dutch state and NGOs, who prefer clear-cut identities that fit the categories of governance. Since they are beginning to make their mark in Dutch academia, and are moreover my critical interlocutors, I will now address their ideas.

There are manifold political differences among these leading antiracist activists. Let me furnish an illustration. One easily discerns contending lines when zooming in on the struggle against Zwarte Piet, which I discussed in chapter 8. Quinsy Gario campaigns for the full abolishment of the entire festivity, as he deems it part of the Dutch colonial heritage. This has caused him to break ties with Kno'Ledge Cesare, who instead advocates reform of the blackface figure. Once Black Peter is white Peter—once there is no blackface—then Cesare has made it publicly clear that he would also join the celebration. Gario reasons that the removal of blackface is not enough, as it keeps in place the idea of "the white man" as the bringer of gifts. Such is deemed part of the mystification of anti-black racism and an obfuscation of colonial history. This rift, and many more like it, make it hard to present these black activist-intellectuals as a group.

Nevertheless, I see three matters on which they converge. First, they all employ North American critical race speak. Terms such as microaggressions, People of Color, non-Black People of Color, safe spaces, white privilege, institutional racism, race mute institution, trigger warning, and the like have become part of their everyday vocabulary.

The second point of convergence is that they all promote an intersectional agenda, whereby the axes of race, religion, gender, and sexuality are prominent. Especially the latter leads to fierce and welcome criticism of the heteronormativity and misogyny that one encounters among Dutch urban artists. There is no love lost between the artists who employ a politics of transfiguration, especially those who simply promote hedonism, and the black activist-intellectuals doing a race-based politics of fulfillment. The latter claim that these artists are immoral, or are engaging in feel-good politics to make an extra buck; they are accused of being willing slaves to the euro and therefore detrimental to the antiracist and wider intersectional politics of justice. An example of this is the row that ensued in 2016 when a tweet was circulated accusing Sevn Alias of shooting a clip without a single dark-brown model. The tweeter, who goes by the name of emelsculated, expected the rapper to apologize to dark-brown women, but instead Alias lashed back, stating that no dark-skinned girls had applied for the job. He rhetorically asked if he should have waited and paid dark-skinned girls to be in his clip, and sent home the pink-skinned ones who had volunteered and done their best. Alias later removed his tweets but went on to state that he found the whole affair nonsensical:

> I have deleted my comments out of respect for that part of my people who know how to behave. But I continue to stand behind what I said. Don't be a crybaby because the camera is not on you. People work hard to make an awesome video clip, and I find it dis-respectful to white women to say that dark-skinned people have to use more dark-skinned girls in their clips to put them in the spotlight. Again, look at yourself before you blame other people for discriminating against you. The problem begins with you.[5]

Sevn's statement is problematic, advocating a politics that reeks of individual responsibility without addressing structural domination. In addition, it is sexist and shows a lack of understanding of the politics of colorism (see text box 6).

The issue of colorism points to the third convergence, which I have already alluded to, namely that all these figures self-consciously represent themselves as being black and of sub-Saharan African descent. They therewith expect their pinkish-skinned counterparts to categorize themselves as white and allies. Moroccan Dutch and Turkish Dutch who participate in the movements they lead are expected to consider themselves Non-Black People of Color (NBPOC). What this means is that NBPOC who are brown and not black, and allies who are white, should always cede the floor to black activists when it comes to discussions on anti-black racism, and to always be followers or collaborators rather than leaders.

The black activist-intellectuals go on to qualify the identities of being black and African when necessary by foregrounding the place of their own birth or that of their parents. A similar logic then holds. Hélène Christelle, who was born on the African continent, can speak about African matters, and Mitchell Esajas on Afro-Surinamese matters. So only those who hold the specific black identity in question are supposed to lead conversations based upon that identity.

The support of these activist-intellectuals is still rather limited when compared to the ways in which figures like Jandino Asporaat, Howard Komproe, Sevn Alias, or the members of Broederliefde command the attention of millions of Dutch citizens. In addition, given their radical critique, they can't piggyback on the popularity of the latter. One could of course argue that this is understandable given that social movement leaders who directly speak truth to racist power are hardly ever beloved by those benefiting materially and symbolically from being marked as White. What matters is not the size of their following but the way they have astutely positioned themselves as the public intellectual voices of the Afro-Dutch; the popularizers of the academic work of towering Dutch scholars such as Gloria Wekker and Philomena Essed. In that role and given their professional approach and cultural capital, they receive funding and sponsorships from private foundations and municipal governments—part of the explicit adherence in Dutch law to the threefold liberal principles of (1) combating all forms of negative discrimination, (2) promoting participatory citizenship initiatives whereby people take responsibility for their own lives, and (3) realizing not only formal but also substantive equality.

Making use of the possibilities of social media, these black activist-intellectuals are actively busy pushing their cause. In an article published in the renowned Dutch newspaper *NRC Handelsblad*, Quinsy Gario made explicit that circumventing the Dutch media establishment is a deliberate strategy: "We present our criticism of the Netherlands via Twitter and Facebook—far removed from the traditional media. We encounter each other in international gatherings and forums, away from the nauseating reality of discrimination on the basis of 'race,' ethnicity, sex, sexuality, and/or religion. So yes, if you underestimate [our strategy], you will receive a rude awakening."[6]

Interestingly, Gario alerts us to different dimensions of the activist-intellectuals' work in a piece in an established newspaper claiming that he and other black activists are meeting up with kindred souls outside of the Netherlands. Gario's revelation should come as no surprise, given that activism among the descendants of those who were forced into slavery in the Americas has always been international and cutting edge. Why should that of Dutch urban activists be any different? Gario and Esajas, for instance, often attend seminars and conferences in other European countries and the United States, where they give presentations about the workings of racism in the Netherlands.

The Black Archives is a library in Amsterdam run by black activist-intellectuals that emulates the work done by the Schomburg Center in New York.[7] The English name of the institution reveals in some ways its black internationalist orientation. Managed by Mitchell Esajas, the Black Archives organizes lectures and workshops on anti-black racism and documents publications written by and related to brown-skinned sub-Saharans.[8] The library is an apt and timely response to the needs of Afro-Dutch such as Wendell, whom I introduced in chapter 7, who rightfully complained that while coming of age and attending college in the Netherlands, there

---

TEXT BOX 6: ACTIVISTS VERSUS URBAN ARTISTS

Confrontations between these activists and urban artists are recurrent. Frenna, an urban rapper, also faced the brunt of criticism when in a diss track he stated, "Ik ruil een dark skin in voor een Barbie" (I trade in a dark skin for a Barbie). Realizing the way the activists were circulating his words as a form of self-hate, Frenna took to the airwaves to explain. He said: "Met die line bedoel ik meer dat mijn stroom zo hoog is, da tik zo kan switchen. Ik zou nooit een dark skin beledigen. Dat zijn mijn grootste fans. Zonder mijn dark-skinned ladies ben ik echt niemand. Ik zeg eerlijk op het moment van schrijven, dacht ik er niet zo aan. Een Barbie kan van alles zijn. Het heft in mijn ogen niks met huidskleur te maken." (With that line I meant more that my energy is so powerful that I can switch. I would never insult a dark skin. Those are my biggest fans. Without them, I am nothing. Honestly, while writing I did not think deeply. A Barbie can be anything. It has nothing to do with skin color.) Thus, he added a rather halfhearted excuse.

---

was a total absence of literature or intellectual work produced by people who look like us.

The ideas of Gario, Esajas, and Cesare have also been taken up by renowned international media such CNN, the *Washington Post*, and the *Huffington Post*. The intellectual work of these black activists, in other words, feeds into and strengthens a US-inflected metanarrative about who can be considered black. In this metatale, black identity stands solely for persons with what are considered classic sub-Saharan features: dark skin, coiling or curling hair, and an ability to claim genetic ancestry in sub-Saharan Africa. Had one of these black activist-intellectuals written this book, the reader would have been treated to an understanding of the Netherlands that is congruent with what critical race scholars from the United States have come to expect from Dutch works on racism.

Although it radically diverges from my own views on "race," I see no need to immediately dismiss this metanarrative. If, that is, this hailing of people based on how they look and on the supposed genetic flow of their ancestors (an updated version of the meta-physics of blood) is ultimately understood as a political invention. If, that is, these activist-intellectuals recognize that the historical equation of black identity exclusively with brown-skinned people of sub-Saharan descent came about through the work of heretical intellectuals such as W. E. B. Du Bois, Booker T. Washington, Harriet Tubman, Ida B. Wells, Frederick Douglass, Claude McKay, Marlene Nourbese Philip, Mary Seacole, James Baldwin, Amy Jacques Garvey, Aimé Césaire, Claudia Jones, Marcus Garvey, Otto Huiswoud, and Ralph Bunche, to name but a few, who were seeking to unite people trampled by the racial logics operating within capitalism and Western imperialism. If, that is, these black activist-intellectuals understand their work as an attempt to unify the multiplicity of brown-skinned people of sub-Saharan descent, with their forever multiplying experiences and desires, to collectively fight for justice.

Endowed with such an understanding, these leading black activist-intellectuals would have no qualms entertaining the pos-sibility of there being other contending forms of political Blackness. They would not make the mistake that Afro-pessimists and other Afrocentric thinkers do in confusing the work of anti-Blackness's creation of black people for the exclusivity of brown-skinned sub-Saharans owning the black identity marker. They would be able to see that, indeed, "[w]ords do not have a general and fixed meaning, given with language or 'a language.' Instead what they do, evoke, bring about, is always an empirical question. It depends [on, among other things, location, time, context, taste, and purpose to name but a few]" (Mol 2014, 115). My understanding obviously differs from theirs as, for me, the black identity marker does not naturally unify all the people who look like me. There are so many other axes such as differences in wealth and income, education and employment status, citizenship and neighborhood of residence, ethnicity and cultural predilections, and specific moment of enunciation and historical relationship with the Netherlands, which complicate matters. Given this multiplicity, which I do not wish to deny, I choose to rather privilege a structural understanding of Blackness. To repeat, for me,

Blackness is on the one hand a concept I employ to designate those who are being treated as waste regardless of their phenotype or ethnicity. And on the other hand, as urban Blackness, Blackness is an emerging commercial identity signifying style, comfort, and success for those who can afford it. In conversations I have had with Quinsy Gario on this matter, he explicitly agreed that the black identity he and others champion is a historically informed category of subjugation resignified into a political marker. There can be many other versions of political Blackness. They are just doing their part to rid the world of anti-black racism in their own strategically essentialist way, yet they, too, understand that "race" is a social construction.

Gario, however, is one of the few black activist-intellectuals who consistently holds this position. For most, social constructivism does not affect colonial history, which implicitly functions as metaphysics. Their rendition of colonial history, which presents a clear-cut picture of the subjugation of brown-skinned sub-Saharan Africans by pink-skinned Europeans, leads in their estimation to the genesis of a transnational people. Black identity is not an optional identity for an NBPOC or an ally regardless of the lowly station they may occupy. Black identity belongs to sub-Saharan people. It is theirs and theirs alone. Moreover, blacks, too, cannot in their estimation choose not to be black. They simply are black. The basis being this metaphysical understanding of colonial history by which blood, skin, bone, and genetic ancestry slips in through the back door of their social constructivist avowal of race.[9] They sophisticatedly call this essentialist move within their social constructivism, the fact of "frontal reality," which cannot be deconstructed and which they are not willing themselves to question and unmoor. I came to this conclusion in March 2018 after a fierce social media battle that played out on my Facebook wall.[10] I shared a publication of Miriyam Aouragh, a Moroccan Dutch academic who espouses the UK-based understanding of political Blackness that was made famous by the writings of Stuart Hall and Claire Alexander.

Aouragh called the black activist-intellectuals to order for not being radical enough in their intersectional informed politics. She argued that their critique of capitalism was quite limited, and she cautioned them about their black essentialism. She was referring to the idea of making a distinction between NBPOC and black people, and rendering class subsumable to both of these markers. Her intention was to offer friendly critique, as she sided with them in their quest to fully weed out anti-black racism in the Netherlands and the wider world.

The response by the black activist-intellectuals was devastating. Aouragh was attacked to such a degree that, since then, she has not dared to publish or hold public speeches. It was a surreal replay of an experience that Claire Alexander, a leading cultural studies theorist of Asian extraction, related in an article in 2002:

> About eight years ago, while still finishing my PhD on black young men, I was invited to present a paper to the African American studies program seminar at Princeton University. Knowing that my research interests seemed ill-fitting in the American context, and deciding that an upfront defense would be my best shot at forestalling any attack, I prefaced my talk with the explanation that in the British context, "black" included peoples of African and Asian descent. What I had imagined as a minor contextualizing, tactical step actually turned out to be a major diversionary maneuver—after this statement, no one seemed to hear the rest of the paper and the questions returned again and again to this seemingly bizarre British anomaly. (Alexander 2002, 552)[11]

In that piece, Alexander went on to critique US-based academic and popular versions of black essentialism that were slowly beginning to be applied in the United Kingdom. Like with Alexander, although with the debate not being held in a prestigious academic setting, Aouragh's antiracist argument could not be heard. Her intervention was drowned out when she dared to claim blackness as a political identity. She was an NBPOC trying to appropriate blackness. Let me offer a poignant illustration. Hélène Christelle, who is a novelist and stylist of Rwandan background, began by questioning why Aouragh felt that she was entitled to use the work of black thinkers to critique black activist-intellectuals like herself. Aouragh's political Blackness was deemed doubly culpable, appropriating black identity *and* black thought:

> If we, in the here and now, really and honestly pursue being politically black (something of which I am far from convinced), ... honestly and strategically pursue political blackness. Why, then, is systematically only black symbolism used for political blackness? Davis, Lorde, MLK, Mandela, Muhammad Ali, the Black Panthers. Black bodies, black labor. How come the works of honored brown thinkers [here this term refers to Arabic and Amazigh intellectuals from North Africa and the Middle East], like in the article we see mention of Edward Said, the unmentioned Fatema Mernissi, and many others, are rarely used to support arguments that frame political blackness? Why is it mainly black bodies, black lives, black thinkers, and black warriors who have to be stretched to include the whole spectrum of color to the point of tearing? Not the other way around [meaning here brown thinkers]. Who thinks of the intellectual gymnastics done with black people and their lives? Black intellectualism seemingly always has to be applicable for all of us, while we do not demand, expect, or interpret the work of non-black thinkers as such. Being black is the most appropriated and least holy frontal reality.[12]

Christelle went on to critique why Aouragh had such difficulty accepting that black activist-intellectuals did not want their black specificity to be erased by her political blackness. She respected the specificity of activists uniting around the identity of Muslims and feminists, and simply was asking for the same when it comes to black people. Only then could the relationship between brown people like Aouragh and black people like her be seriously addressed. So Auoragh had to relinquish the UK version of political blackness. It was ill fitting, and moreover it shielded activists among the NBPOC such as Aouragh from addressing the anti-black racism in her community.[13]

Once political Blackness disappeared, real work could be done in eradicating anti-black racism and all other intersectional wrongs:

> We are definitely in the Netherlands still discovering how we should relate to one another. This happens within the Afro-Dutch community, but also within the community of color as a whole. I am talking of Islamophobia among non-Muslim black people, anticolonial blackness, anti-black racism among non-black people of color, anti-Rif/Amazigh sentiments, mis-appropriation of Old Egypt and the erasure of black Nubians, anti-Somali sentiments, and misogyny in relation to black women and oriental sexism in relation to colored women [here meaning NBPOC]. We have so much to catch up to [here, the race consciousness of POC and the vocabulary that has developed is judged to be the yardstick].
>
> While we travel together as a Dutch POC community on this journey, being black remains the most appropriated and least holy of all frontal realities. . . . I almost want to say, here you have it. My oh so subjective, oh so negligible blackness. My skin. My blood sweat and tears. My 4c. My sub-Saharan tongue, my hands and feet. Take it, take it all, and put it on. Please tell how it feels and why you so long to have it.[14]

In the first instance, one could say that there is much to commend in Christelle's words. Hers is an intersectional analysis. The activism she stands for is awakening many to the importance of combating anti-black racism in tandem with other related wrongs. Also, the admonition that subjugated groups should engage in self-critique is salutary. However, there are questionable aspects that I cannot fully ignore.

Christelle and other black activist-intellectuals want to address anti-black racism and other intersectional wrongs by remaining firmly attached to the categories of the formal political establishment in the Netherlands and those of US activist-academic circles.

Therein, being labeled black is one of the intersectional identities that a person can be marked with. Once one is accepted by others who are labeled black, then that label becomes their possession: one to be cherished, worked on, and defended in an unjust world. Politics understood as the constitution of a category that supersedes and transforms existing identities is not part of their vista.

A similar critique can be raised with regard to black activist-intellectuals' misunderstanding of the applicability of analytical academic concepts. These are tools that scholars employ to make the messiness of life more amendable to analysis. *Black* and *White* as analytical concepts are not the same as the black and white identity markers of the governing apparatus, communitarian identities, or commerce. The former is ideally used to analyze the workings, contradictions, and hidden causalities of the latter. When Gloria Wekker, the foremost Dutch scholar on anti-black racism, speaks of Whiteness, she is using it as a conceptual tool to analyze the way some pink-skinned native Dutch benefit from a colonial legacy that still has to be fully dismantled (Wekker 2016, 24).

Similarly, urban Blacks and Blackness are analytical categories in my work analysis. I use them to critically interrogate the way intersectionality is erroneously used by activist-intellectuals to promote an exclusivist "race" plus class plus gender plus religion, and so on, understanding of identity whereby they can lay exclusive claim upon blackness.[15] If Blackness is a structural position of domination, then all intersectional identities including US notions of blackness are subsumed by it. In that case, Moroccan Dutch can be black: "[I]t's about racialization and the ascription of blackness—which reminds us, once again, you don't have to be Black to be racialized as Black" (Small 2009, xxvi).

When such is realized, the possibility exists for subjugated people to become politically Black. This is the political Blackness that Stuart Hall and Claire Alexander theorized for the United Kingdom, and what Miriyam Aouragh is promoting in the Dutch case. Blackness on such occasions is reinvented. When that happens, one witnesses

TEXT BOX 7: C. L. R. JAMES 2

The nonracial spirit of C. L. R. James that animates this book, which is substantiated by my research, is that anti-Black racism ends when we all become Black. In other words, when the accursed share is reintegrated into the fold of humanity. It is in fact an old idea, which is beginning to catch on. It is the idea most powerfully articulated during the Haitian revolution. Critical race scholars Paul Khalil Saucier and Tryon P. Woods remind us: "The Black revolutionaries of Saint-Domingue established over two centuries ago that Blackness is freedom's carriage, not racial democracy, justice, or liberty. The Haitian Constitution of 1805 . . . grounds freedom in Blackness proclaiming all Haitian citizens free as Black people, and it explicitly extended this status of Blackness to everyone covered in the Constitution, including a substantial number of mulattos, Germans, and Poles. The Haitian revolutionaries grasped that a political project to make the abject whole must proceed through a radical fidelity to Blackness. . . . [H]uman liberation will always be incomplete, deferred, and anti-Black until and unless it becomes a function of solidarity with Blackness" (2016, 28).

an echo of the anticolonial past—when in Haiti, for instance, Blackness became a category for all those who opposed injustice (Saucier and Woods 2016) (see text box 7).

If one were to attend gatherings of some Black organizations in Britain, one would be surprised to find that they have very few people of African descent. One example is the Southall Black Sisters in London, which involves primarily Bangladeshi and Pakistani women. Other organizations include Blacks, Indians, and other ethnic groups (Small 2009, xxx).

An extra complication arises with the introduction of urban Blackness. The concept signals that the historical connection between the racist workings of colonialism and capitalism are radically being altered. Let me repeat what I argued in chapters 9 and 10.

It was imperative in the heyday of Western imperialism and predatory capitalism, intensifying in the seventeenth century, to systematically promote animosities based on skin and ethnic kin, as these weren't a natural given. The brutal oppression of peoples across the board led to incessant rebellions by many polyethnic bands of subjugated peoples. In addition, to ease consciences and inhibit fellow feeling, the pernicious lie of "race" had to also be sold to the North Atlantic masses who stayed at home. The Negro and Blackness, and Brownness and Whiteness, saw the light of day in this era (Linebaugh and Rediker 2000).

As long as wealthy capitalists benefited materially from ideologies that naturalized peoples' understanding of themselves as belonging to a specific race, they were in accord with North Atlantic state officials. Yet governance was not their leitmotif; rather, making profit was. Rigid naturalization of the idea of race was always a means, and as such was never deemed absolutely necessary. One does well to remember that "[c]apitalism neither loves nor hates social differences. Rather, it exploits them in the short run and erodes them [their cultural specificities] in the long run" (Brown 2005, 106).

Today, the creolized styles of being and the cultural expressions primarily produced by the descendants of those traditionally labeled black have become valuable commodities. The culture industry that markets urban popular culture is a multibillion-dollar enterprise, with larger-than-life figures such as Jay-Z, Dr. Dre, Beyoncé, Rihanna, Oprah Winfrey, and Diddy. Hollywood is coming around as well, with the mega-release and box office success of the epic *Black Panther* movie.

In the Netherlands, far lesser millionaire gods have emerged among the descendants of those who were shipped in chains to the Dutch possessions in the New World. One encounters them especially in the realm of sports. Think of Clarence Seedorf, Nigel de Jong, and Kenley Jansen. Slowly, one is also witnessing a similar development among urban artists like Sevn Alias, Afrojack, and Jandino Asporaat, who live very comfortable lives. In such a world, Blackness will have to be resignified. It cannot be solely the historically inherited category of the dominated. In that resignification, the value of the other intersectional markers will also change. The question of gender, which I signaled in the previous chapter, is caught up in this.

We are at the dawn of a new era with the severing of the agreement between capitalism and governance in the Netherlands and other North Atlantic polities about what "race" should mean in the future. Urban popular culture seems to be going the way of capital whereby blackness as an identity is being transformed into an expensive commodity to be bought and sold. Could the supreme irony be that intersectional black activist-intellectuals in the Netherlands, enamored as they are with the hegemonic ideas coming out of the US activist academy on race and how to combat anti-black racism, may be inadvertently going the way of the populist Dutch politics that they contest?

The time has come to ask a different question than the one I have been trying to answer in this book. Time to politically attend to time.

BY WAY OF CONCLUSION, OR RATHER, ANOTHER QUESTION: WHAT TIME IS IT?

Where worldly and otherworldly beliefs in the possibility of universal justice wither, one still encounters in the hearts of those who strive for a decent world order a devotion to **Time***: that which is always to come, and that which undoes sanctified understandings of what happened and what is happening. For such people, there is a deep recognition that although tomorrow need not be better than today, there is the possibility that it can be. And, given that open-endedness, what they do matters. Since I am such a person, I end this book with an ode to* **You***,* **Time***—that which always offers openings.*

Time, I see that **You** *are beginning to notice her. I can count the wrinkles on her face. One, two, three, four, five . . . Yes, she is getting old, which means I am getting old, too. Your faithful servant, old age, is catching up with us. Let it come, for Sonja is becoming more beautiful and more wise. I, too, am beginning to make sense of why* **You** *brought us together.*

Time, once again **You** *have summoned me to Sonja's abode. Today we are celebrating the rebirth of* **You***. New* **Time***. I am here to honor* **You** *by sharing in Sonja's joy. I am one of the persons she loves without reserve, and she is one of the persons I love unconditionally. After all these years, we are still cool. So cool that I had to be here today.*

Time, **You** *understand that I had to begin this book on the Afro-Dutch experience in the Netherlands by returning to my coming-of-age years in Helmond. In chapters 1 through 3, I present the ways in which Sonja and I and the rest of my polyethnic group of friends,*

Sabah, Naima, Hassan, Wincho, Mercus, Mike, Dragana, Martijn, and Geertje—of Moroccan, Antillean, Moluccan, Surinamese, and native Dutch descent—bridged our differences and bonded for life. Ethnic and religious diversity was the norm in the unruly multicultural working-class neighborhood where most of us resided. We accepted that we had to make it work, and we made it work. Self-interest coincided most of the time with our collective interests. Convivir. Convivencia, Conviviality. I embraced the Netherlands because in my convivial neighborhood I have always felt at home. If culture is a soup that connects and subtly flavors existing and emerging differences, leading to their perpetual transformation in the gumbo of common life, then urban popular culture was what bound Sonja and I and the rest of my friends together. Our culture was a coming together of cultural styles from the United States, Canada, the Antilles, Latin America, England, and a bit of what we found and brought to the Netherlands; a selection of the sounds and styles of cultural life our families sought to enculturate us in. Sonically it was Guy, Jodeci, New Edition, Keith Sweat, Beres Hammond, En Vogue, Bell Biv DeVoe, Johnny Gill, Mary J. Blige, Tony! Toni! Toné!, Karyn White, Janet Jackson, Chaka Demus and Pliers, Bob Marley, Shabba Ranks, Claudius Philips and O.R.E.O., Gibi y su Orquesta, Peter Tosh, Burning Flames, Lauryn Hill, Willy Chirino, Zouk Machine, TLC, Gregory Isaacs, KRS-One, Sanchez, 2Pac, Public Enemy, and more of that good stuff. These musical artists and sports stars like the football players Romário, Regi Blinker, Aron Winter, and Clarence Seedorf were our heroes. The reason I have no problems with the body I do, the body I am, and the body I have is because of urban popular culture.

Time, I am back in Helmond for the day. I don't live here anymore. I took advantage of the opportunities You presented me with. I gained a PhD, traveled the world, found employment at the University of Amsterdam, and today write and teach for a living. Sonja stayed in Helmond and made other choices. She dropped out of school, vacations in Germany and Spain when she can afford to, never reads a book, and today cleans the desks in offices of people who earn a living sitting behind a computer.

Time, *I would later find out by paying meticulous attention to* **You** *that most of the people whose desks Sonja cleans live in other neighborhoods. I now live among them. Most are middle-class native Dutch. Many are trying to come to terms with the changing face of the Netherlands, which multicultural neighborhoods like De Eeuwels represent, with people who mostly look like me and the diversity of the world. I call these people who are trying to come to terms with us, liberals. Some are conscientious and open. Others are self-congratulatory and rather conservative. I was taught by both kinds at the university. They are also the parents of some of the girls I dated. I was welcomed by them, as I was seen as someone who would eventually become like them. Many of them are today my colleagues, friends, and neighbors. I had to write critically but amicably about them in chapters 4 and 5. They still have much to learn about the implicit and explicit negative bias they display toward persons who look like me.*

Time, **You** *taught me to be incredulous about the fact that in North American parlance Sonja is white and I am black. A mode of description that is becoming bon ton in Dutch academia. Sociologists would tell Sonja that she is an inheritor of the wages of whiteness. White privilege. I would be told by historians that I inherited nothing but loss. Black abjection. Yet here we are. Classes apart. It has always been that way. Her family was always hustling, with some trying unsuccessfully to keep a steady job. School meant little to them. My upbringing and family was middle class. Not rich in terms of wealth, but more so in ambition. Education and social uplift was a must in my family. There are many in the Netherlands who resemble Sonja, and many Afro-Dutch whose life can be likened to mine. The big story of racism, with white always on top and black always on the bottom, does not match our reality. Still, it does in statistical terms of course. It's undeniable that pink-skinned native Dutch live more economically comfortable lives than Afro-Dutch. The same can be said for experiences of structural discrimination in, say, the workplace; these are the incontestable facts of Dutch racism. Globally, anti-black racism and anti-Blackness are alive and well. Still, I do not live or view my life, and neither does Sonja hers, in terms of statistics. Statistical time.*

*Abstract time. Academic time. Even, Activist time. All these versions of time are imposters of **You**, **Time**. As an academic I can vouch that Statistical time, Academic time, Activist time, might be useful in pointing to economic and social inequities. My response has been to heed these and yet stay as close as possible to everyday lived realities concerning structural ills. In chapters 6 through 8, I present how I do so by highlighting the lives of Miss Slijngaard, Oma Bea, Wendell, and Sabah. In their capacities as volunteers, social workers, managers of community centers, and policy officers of municipalities, they demonstrate what people who come from these convivial working-class neighborhoods are doing to improve the condition of all Dutch. In their perfect imperfection, these women and men make me hopeful.*

__Time__, did __You__ send her to tempt me? Sonja grabs me by the arm. Time to get up and dance. I act as though I am shy. But I actually want to. I concede. Playing hard to get as always, Sonja smirks. I smile. She knows me well. She knows I love Cache Royale. Sonja can still bust a move. "Dushi what doe je met mij," she crows. She can dance, but singing . . . __Time__, __You__ forgot her in that department. But it doesn't matter. Everyone is singing along.

Everyone. Mike, Hassan, Mercus, Dragana, Martijn, and Naima are here. Wincho is absent. We miss him. Mike imitates Wincho's heavy Curaçaon Dutch accent. Wincho, who had to be taught how to be cool when he migrated to Netherlands to attend college. When he had just arrived in the country, he would wear his pants high up his waist. He was also proud of his tight white jeans. That is, until Mike almost made him cry one day by constantly calling him "papi" and likening him to a Puerto Rican pimp. No mercy. Our dozens. We crack up as Mike pulls up his pants like Wincho, who migrated back to Curaçao. He returned after obtaining his diploma to help develop the place of his birth. Respect.

Sabah isn't here either. She is vacationing in New York. Sabah, a globetrotter with a well-paying job like me. Naima gets up and joins us. Hassan teases her that she is getting fat. Old-age couscous fat. She responds that her man isn't complaining. Later on, she imitates what she considers the rather submissive behavior of Hassan's wife.

Via indirect speech, she jokes that too many men choose brides from Morocco because they can't handle Moroccan Dutch women like her. They choose young girls from Morocco who don't know the ways of the Netherlands, whom they therefore think they can control. But little do they know, Naima jokes on, that their brides are more conniving than them. Hassan's wife doesn't seem to understand. Hassan is silent. Nervous. We laugh. Naima wins. Damn, she is still an ace in playing the dozens. Humor and urban music remain the magic that bridges differences.

Cache Royale is followed up somewhat later by a tune of Frenna and Diquenza, "16 Million." Urban music in the Dutch language. Dutch rap artists topping the charts. Football stars making rap records. Afro-Dutch millionaires. Many more convivial neighborhoods. Things are changing.

Time, *I have become an anthropologist who studies the role of urban popular culture in helping the Netherlands accept* **You:** *its current multicultural condition. Chapters 8 through 10 recount the transformation of the Netherlands through the lens of urban popular culture, which is today one of the dominant styles of being, crosscutting ethnicities and ideas of racial difference. The implicit aesthetic politics of urban artists such as Howard Komproe and Manu van Kersbergen are juxtaposed to how ordinary youngsters today are fully embracing the culture. An example I present in the book is the tale of Judmar, who in many ways resembles Wincho. When I met him, he had just arrived from Curaçao. He lacked the suave and sagacity of youngsters in the Netherlands who were born into the urban. I recounted how together with Koen, a native Dutch who was also a rookie, he was slowly becoming versed in urban popular culture. The difference between my experiences and those of Judmar and Koen is that they have more digital means at their disposal. Via YouTube, the urban radio station FunX, and even more Napster and Spotify, which they receive on their smartphones, they can immerse themselves in the urban 24/7. My generation had to buy records, wait until our artists gave concerts in the Netherlands, or otherwise buy expensive DVDs. Another major difference is that today urban popular culture is becoming part of the*

Dutch mainstream. The Netherlands has a plethora of urban artists, like Ali B and Sevn Alias, who have become household names. Despite anti-black racism and anti-Blackness, we felt centered, like belongers. This generation, even more so.

Time, we all are thankful that Sonja's son, Gerrit, who is almost twenty-seven, is becoming a father. Sonja is of course beside herself. She was worried that his younger sister Milouska would beat him to it. Finally, she is going to be a grandmother. She hopes that Gerrit will be better than his father was. I hope so, too. I also hope better than Milouska's father was. Both were womanizers who did not take care of their children. Sonja did well. She was mother and father with us, her friends chipping in when necessary. And some of us are even becoming family in terms of blood. Well, sort of. Mercus has some relation to Gerrit's girlfriend. Some kind of fourth cousin or something. I smile at the thought of what is being revealed to me. Gerrit is pink-skinned like his mother. Milouska is brown-skinned like her father. Sonja's granddaughter or grandson—she is peeved that Gerrit does not want to tell her the sex of her grandchild—might also show some visible Moluccan signs of her or his mother. The baby will be fully Dutch. Multicultural Dutch like us.

Time, it took me all these years to fully recognize **You. You** are many. **You** are human plurality. **You** are the future always in the present, which ideally can fully demolish our inherited habits of relating to each other in terms racial identities. **You** are **Life** and the radically free possibilities of **Life. You**, **Time**, as **Life** continue to be partially contained by the expulsion of people labeled Black from the realm of human plurality and equality.

Historically, that curse fell on people who look like me. So-called Negroes. Today, it befalls persons of various hues. Through urban popular culture, **You**, **Time**, seem to be summoning us all to redeem that blackened part of the human family; to reincorporate and accept that part of us we expulse and exploit. Only then will we arrive at a place where nonracialism is deemed common sense. Such does not appeal to those urban artists and their fans who are committed to capitalism or those who are more into exclusivist black identity politics.

Both groups seem seduced by idols, in this case Commercial time and
Activist Academic time. For the followers of Mammon, time is money,
and they therefore welcome that today Blackness can be sold as an attractive commodity-identity within urban popular culture. Conversely,
activist-intellectuals are working toward a reformed tribalism: they
seek a racial settlement, with every group respectfully embracing and
recognizing each other's racial belonging. As different as they may
be, both the followers of Mammon and the activist-intellectuals consider the idea of redeeming the blackened part of humanity by way of
everyone incorporating the signifier Black, so that it ceases to be an
accursed share or a thing to be bought and sold, a heretical thought.
Their politics is given sustained attention in chapters 10 and 11.

Different strokes.

In an effort to be true to **You, Time**, as **Life**, by caring for Sonja
and the baby who will soon arrive, I seek to practice nonracialism.
The question any serious scholar working to demolish "race" must ask
themself is, "What am I doing to undo the historical and contemporary effects of anti-black racism and global anti-Blackness in order
for all of us to live in **Time**: for everyone to be given the opportunity
to be a conscientious example of human plurality unfolding outside
of the colonial design of race?"

NOTES

Introduction

1. A similar argument holds for Whiteness of course. As a marker of identity, it is explicitly a product of European imperialism. W. E. B. Du Bois poetically explained the matter in 1920 thus: "The discovery of personal whiteness among the world's peoples is a modern thing,—a nineteenth and twentieth century matter, indeed. The ancient world would have laughed at such a distinction. The Middle Age regarded color with mild curiosity; and even up into the eighteenth century we were hammering our national manikins into one, great Universal Man, with fine frenzy which ignored color and race even more than birth. Today we have changed all that, and the world in a sudden, emotional conversion has discovered that it is white and by that token wonderful! This assumption that of all the hues of God whiteness is obviously inherently better than brownness or tan leads to curious acts; even the sweeter souls of the dominant world as they discourse with me on weather, weal, and woe are continually playing above their words an obligato of tune and tone, saying: 'My poor, un-white thing! Weep not nor rage. I know, too well, that the curse of God lies heavy on you. Why? That is not for me to say, but be brave! Do your work in your lowly sphere, prying the good Lord that into heaven above, where all is love, you may, one day, be born—white!' I do not laugh. I am straight-faced as I ask soberly: 'But what on earth is whiteness that one should desire it?' Then, always, somehow, some way, silently but clearly, I am given to understand that whiteness is the ownership of the earth forever and ever, Amen! . . . Wave on wave, each with increasing virulence, is dashing this new religion of whiteness on the shores of our time" (Du Bois [1920] 2007, 17–18). A whole academic field of study, "Whiteness studies," has emerged since Du Bois's early foray. For examples, see Cian T. McMahon (2015) and Douglas Hartmann, Joseph Gerteis, and Paul R. Croll (2009).

2. Many critical race scholars would find my collapsing of the race versus class distinction an example of racial eliminativist Marxism taken to its logical conclusion. See, for recent examples, Nasar Meer (2018) and Alana Lentin (2016), who argue that the elimination of race obscures its trace. I do not think this is what I am doing. I am taking race seriously while seeking to avoid treating *it* as metaphysics. What I

am making explicit is that any precapitalist conception of inhumanity likened to race that does not involve capitalist-mediated imperialism is one that falls outside of the scope of my reasoning. Moreover, while acknowledging the messiness of histories and of ethnic and cultural identities—and also mindful of antagonisms between the oppressed—I have always regarded the Marxist strategy as working through these particulars to arrive at an open, universal category. The latter is often a particular concept (in this case *Black*) emptied as much as possible of its former significations. As was the case with "all proletariats of the world unite," so, too, Black is a call notwithstanding the manifold different experiences of modern-day capitalist-mediated oppression.

3. I should point out here that the discussion between Afro-pessimists and black optimists (e.g., Frank Wilderson versus Fred Moten), their points of convergence and divergence, is not one I engage with. As a proponent of black optimism, Moten seeks and argues for Blackness as what he terms a paraontological real. He means by that that Blackness cannot be contained by metaphysics or equated to the horror inflicted on black people. There is no direct language to speak of it or for it. We know Blackness by the historical record of humankind trying to deny, tame, and contain it; by its equation with racialized human beings whom dominators deem licensed to exploit and if need be make expendable; and by the way borders are rigidly policed to make sure those who are blackened know their assigned place and stay there. Mysticism (a thinking that does not seek to grasp or tame life, but seeks to flow with it as it sculpts a nonreductive understanding) may be our closest nonviolent path toward acknowledging and coming to terms with Blackness. I have taken Moten and Stefano Harney's musings on Blackness as an invitation to let go of the Christian idea of the complete separation of light (Good) and darkness (Evil). In doing so, I have arrived at a situation in which I can existentially ask in one of my mother tongues, namely Dutch, "Wat als licht niets anders is dan in brand gevlogen duisternis" (What if light is nothing more than darkness that has caught flame?). In other words, what if darkness, likened to the Blackness of a cosmic womb, is not that which also brings about light and life that seeks to deny it (Harney and Moten 2013). Interesting as this appreciation of Blackness is, it is not the focus of this book. I indulge in this interpretation elsewhere (Guadeloupe 2018b). Here, I strictly treat Blackness, or global anti-Blackness, as designating the operation of reifying humans who can then be treated *as if* they were objects. As this has been a planet-wide operation since the capitalist-driven European conquest of the globe, all peoples should recognize Blackness as the accursed share of their ethnic and national identities. Only when we all become Black, in other words fully integrate into our psyches and institutional memory the reality that most have been racially dehumanized in the process of the Western imperial project, will the symbolic power of racism be no more. Then begins in earnest the work of dismantling racist institutional practices

and racial structures whereby we need not refer to each other employing race-based identities. In the meantime, those labeled or implicitly designated Black, for instance blacks and browns, can do the work, as Stuart Hall reminds us to do, by becoming politically Black. What this entails is donning the signifier "Black" as a political identity that is nonracist, in order to combat racism and the economic structures that undergird it. Political Blackness is akin to Marxism's proletariat (see Hall 1991).

4. Black Power–influenced readings of Fanon emphasize the idea of black people suffering from a minority complex. Most are supposedly dissatisfied with their phenotype and dream of escaping their skin by marrying a white person. Implicit therein is that every so-called racial group has its ideal somatic norm image of beauty and propriety. Their first unreflective choice of a partner, and explanation of what is beautiful, is coupled with the norms of their racial group. With New World blacks this is not the case, the argument goes, supposedly because they have a distorted somatic norm image. The work of capitalist-driven European imperialism in shaping all somatic norm images after the invention of race—in other words, having the world population idolize racial images while carnage was the order of the day—is given short shrift in these analyses. So, too, is Fanon's renunciation of these racial imaginaries parading as somatic norm images.

5. It should be noted that Black Brits came into being as an oppositional category pushed by Caribbean, African, Indian, Pakistani, and Bangladeshi newcomers to being excluded from the imaginary of the United Kingdom. As such, from the onset it also included persons of Asian descent.

6. For a succinct summary of this study, registering that most Antilleans in the Netherlands feel at home in the Netherlands, see Jamila Baaziz (2013).

7. The "Windrush generation" is the term used to designate persons from the British Caribbean who arrived in the United Kingdom at the beginning of the post–World War II period. The arrival in England of 450 West Indian passengers aboard the *Empire Windrush* in 1948 has been marked as the symbolic moment of Caribbean migration to the United Kingdom. The privileging of this moment is understandable, as the Caribbean cultural theorist H. Adlai Murdoch reminds us: "[F]igures cited by the British Home Office show that the 15,301 British residents claiming to be born in the Caribbean in 1951 had mushroomed to 171,800 just ten years later and to 304,000 in 1971; by 1981, reflecting a subsequent migration wave made up primarily of children and dependents of previous migrants, 275,000 of Britain's West Indians claimed a birthplace outside the United Kingdom, while 244,000 of them claimed British birth" (2007, 577). For the history and contemporary reality of the Caribbean presence in the United Kingdom, see Murdoch 2007. On the race-based class exploitation that these West Indians and their descendants faced, and never ceased to contest, see Robin Bunce and Paul Field (2011). For a first-person account that also highlights class exploitation through the language of race, see Darcus

Howe (1998). On the Afro-Caribbean presence in the United Kingdom prior to the Windrush generation, see Jeffrey Green (2000).

8. A popular distrust of local politicians is the consistent discourse I have been privy to in the four years I was employed as the president of the University of St. Martin on the island of Sint Maarten from 2014 to 2017. This was a corroboration of my findings conducting fieldwork on the various Dutch Caribbean islands since the year 2000. The same sentiment holds for most Antilleans I have interacted with who reside in the Netherlands. Recent theorizing collected in the edited volume of Linden Lewis (2013) reveals that this is a wider pan-Caribbean sentiment. There is also a general disillusionment with sovereignty among the populations based on their recognition of Western geopolitical dominance and the workings of capitalism.

9. For other examples of works that make explicit the role of race in the modern constitution of the world as divided into cultures and civilizations, see Aníbal Quijano's "Coloniality and Modernity/Rationality" (2007) and Paul Gilroy's *Against Race: Imagining Political Culture beyond the Color Line* (2000).

10. As early as 1938, James reminded Western thinkers of the importance of the Haitian revolution of 1794. He reasoned that only by attending to this revolution could scholars appreciate the historical concretization of the idea of equality and liberty for all. He was going against the dogma of Western liberal thinkers who solely signal the political revolution of 1776 that gave birth to the United States and its follow-up in France in 1791 (James [1938] 1963).

11. Lyrics quoted from Bob Marley's 1976 hit "War" on the album *Rastaman Vibration*. For a sustained meditation on Bob Marley's quest for nonracialism, see Paul Gilroy (2005).

12. James refused to adhere to the theoretical idea of imputing false consciousness to subjugated peoples, or becoming nihilistic about the prospect of a nonracist future in which the unequal workings of capitalism would be acceptable. As one of his premier interpreters, Aldon Lynn Nielsen, put it, James "would reject absolutely the imputation that he was an idealist in the sense of one who believes in a transcendent realm of a priori truth, but he was idealistic in the sense that he was persuaded that mankind would inevitably reach a universal, material ideal of social organization that would eliminate economic exploitation and political oppression" (1997, 124).

13. For a study that reveals James's intellectual and political connection to Lyotard and his foreshadowing of Jacques Derrida's "Spectres of Marx," see *Facing Reality* (James, Lee, and Chaulieu [1958] 1974). James coauthored the book with Cornelius Castoriadis—pseudonym Pierre Chaulieu—and Grace C. Lee. There, one encounters the telling passage, "In the middle of the Twentieth Century a specter is haunting Marxism, keeping it within what is already a graveyard, and when it attempts to come out in the open, ready at the slightest sign of faltering, to show it the way back." For James's forays in forms of theorizing that would later come to be associated

with poststructuralism and postmodernism, see Brett St. Louis (2007), Aldon Lynn Nielsen (1997, 101–23), and Sylvia Wynter (1992).

14. It has become commonplace to transpose Du Bois's concept of double consciousness onto other African diasporic intellectuals, thereby marking their geographic specificity. Examples thereof are Brett St. Louis's *Rethinking Race, Politics, and Poetics: C. L. R. James' Critique of Modernity* (2007) and Nicole King's *C. L. R. James and Creolization: Circles of Influence* (2001). In doing so, the concept of double consciousness is connected to that of creolization and hybridization. Following the radical nonracist spirit of James, who was about fully stamping out racialism, I interpret double consciousness as a circumscription of a creole consciousness within the color lines. Therein I conceptualize creolization as the planetary materialist underpinning of all expressions of a creole consciousness. My appreciation of creolization is indebted to Édouard Glissant (2000), who, starting from the Caribbean, theorizes it as a global condition. We are all creoles because capitalism bolstering Western imperialism, and the resistance to it beginning when Eurocentered colonialism was still the order of the day, have shaped us all.

15. Some examples of academic works that foreground the entangled modern becoming of all peoples are Édouard Glissant's "The Unforeseeable Diversity of the World" (2002); Hilbourne Watson's "Theorizing the Racialization of Global Politics and the Caribbean Experience" (2001); Peter Linebaugh and Marcus Rediker's *The Many-Headed Hydra: Sailors, Slaves, Commoners, and the Hidden History of the Revolutionary Atlantic* (2000); Paul Gilroy's *Against Race: Imagining Political Culture beyond the Color Line* (2000); Aníbal Quijano's "Coloniality of Power, Eurocentrism, and Latin America" (2000); Enrique Dussel's *Philosophy of Liberation* (1985); Aimé Césaire's *Discourse on Colonialism* (1972); C. L. R. James's *Beyond the Boundary* ([1963] 1993); and of course James's seminal work, *The Black Jacobins* ([1938] 1963).

16. For an ethnography that presents multicultural conviviality before the term was coined, see Gerd Baumann (1996).

17. On the life and the impact of Frankie Crocker, see the obituary by the journalist Monte Williams entitled "Frankie Crocker, a Champion of Black-Format Radio, Dies" (2000). Besides urban music, electronic dance music and rock are the major music scenes in the Netherlands. Each produces its own popular culture and new ethnicities, the boundary between urban and EDM being the most porous. In addition, although the degrees vary, these three forms of popular culture are ethnically diverse. Although the *présence Africaine*, to employ Stuart Hall's terminology, is most pronounced in urban music, it is discernible in the other forms as well. Focusing on EDM and rock would produce another understanding of the current dynamics of racism and conviviality in the Netherlands. Alas, I have never done research on these, and as such they will not be discussed in this book.

18. The quotation is taken from KRS-One's hit "Brown Skin Woman" from the *Return of the Boom Bap* album, released by Zomba Records in 1993. See also KRS-One and Marley Marl's *Hip Hop Lives* album (2007), which highlights this form of popular culture as an alternative source of education for downtrodden youths.

19. There is, to my mind, a complementarity between Marxism's call toward a class-based unity of the global subjugated and the idea of political Blackness. What matters, however, is doing the critical work so that the signifier "Black" will not be employed to privilege a specific ethnoracial group, namely brown-skinned people of sub-Saharan descent. The same can be said with respect to the concept of class, which has often been critiqued in critical race theories for implicitly foregrounding the proletariat in the West. Building on C. L. R. James and Oliver Cox, the sociologist Anton Allahar (2015) has sought to do the critical analytical work of recognizing the power of race while foregrounding the multicolored and polyethnic reality of class domination.

20. The questionable notions of heteropatriarchal masculinity displayed in urban popular culture will not receive sustained or systematic attention in this book; foregrounding that important aspect would entail writing a different kind of book. Race as a modality of class as manifested in urban popular culture is my main focus. I recognize that there is a gendered aspect to this. In fact, I have discerned a dominant masculine heteronormativity in urban popular culture. I also, however, cannot get around the fact that some of the leading musical artists such as Beyoncé and Frank Ocean promote a feminist and gay-friendly politics within urban popular culture, which deserves to be analyzed on its own terms. For Beyoncé's views, see Caroline Framke (2016). For scholarly work on arguing for Beyoncé's particular brand of feminist politics, see Nathalie Weidhase's "'Beyoncé Feminism' and the Contestation of the Black Feminist Body" (2015). On the support Frank Ocean received from fellow urban artists who perform heteronormative roles, see James C. McKinley Jr.'s "Hip-Hop World Gives Gay Singer Support" (2012). For a more in-depth analysis, see Frederik Dhaenens and Sander De Ridder's "Resistant Masculinities in Alternative R&B? Understanding Frank Ocean and The Weeknd's Representations of Gender" (2015). I plan to do research on this matter in the follow-up to this project.

Chapter 1

1. This text, which was published in 2013 (Guadeloupe 2013b), was read out at the funeral of a dear friend. The original letter was written in English, which signals that urban popular culture in the Netherlands is a multilingual affair. Many of the song texts mix various languages, even though Dutch predominates. Urban popular culture's multilingual style implicitly signals a move away from the grounding of ethnic absolutism in linguistic exclusivity. Portions of the subsequent sections also appeared in the 2013 article.

Chapter 2

1. For an early academic study of this phenomenon, highlighting the role of Afro-Surinamese youngsters, see Livio Sansone (1992).

Chapter 3

1. The clip can be found on YouTube at https://www.youtube.com/watch?v =j8dUUvzV3DU.

2. The original quotation in Dutch reads: "Ik ben van West gekomen, daar waren alleen maar mocro's om me heen. Toen kwam ik in Almere terecht en daar waren weer alleen maar Marrokkanen. Zo was het gewoon . . . Je moet het zo zien—elke dag ben ik met Marokkanen. Elke jaar gaan zij naar huis en komen ze terug en vertellen ze mij hoe mooi het daar is. Dan word ik parra. Ik ben nog niet eens in Suriname geweest, terwijl ik half Surinaams ben. Maar die verhalen die ik hoor over Marokko, de foto's en filmpjes die ik zie . . . Ik kan mezelf daarin meer vinden."

Chapter 4

1. Frantz Fanon's *Black Skin, White Masks* (1967), first published in 1952, has to my mind been wrongly taken to demonstrate that most Afro-Caribbeans suffer from an inferiority complex. Fanon is actually diagnosing a pathology suffered by middle-class brown-skinned men in Paris. I read *Black Skin, White Masks* as a contribution that presents the reader with "perfectly" functioning brown-skinned neurotics in a racialist and racist world. Fanon, however, demonstrates that the perfection of Afro-Caribbean neurotics is actually an imperfection, an alienation that they share with their pink-skinned counterparts. Both, and the rest of us, will have to undo ourselves of inherited identities marked by race. See, in that light, Judith Butler's "Violence, Non-Violence: Sartre on Fanon" (2006). Butler connects Fanon's radical invocation of a nonracial world to his anticapitalist humanism in his other seminal text, *The Wretched of the Earth* (2004; first published in 1961).

2. For a discussion on the impact of these older forms of African American music in Europe, see Paul Gilroy's *The Black Atlantic: Modernity and Double Consciousness* (1993, 72–110).

3. On my sojourn to Sint Maarten, see my "Exploring the Non-Ordinary Dimensions of Decoloniality" (Guadeloupe 2018a).

4. I have to also mention Karin Willemse and Francien van Driel, who form a trio with Tine Davids in their academic focus. For a taste of their mode of doing feminist anthropology, see Davids's "Trying to Be a Vulnerable Observer: Matters of Agency, Solidarity and Hospitality in Feminist Ethnography" (2014); Willemse's "'Everything I Told You Was True': The Biographic Narrative as a Method of Critical

Feminist Knowledge Production" (2014); and Davids and van Driel's "The Unhappy Marriage between Gender and Globalisation" (2009).

5. See my coauthored articles "Yu di Kòrsou, a Matter of Negotiation: An Anthropological Exploration of the Identity Work of Afro-Curaçaons" (Allen and Guadeloupe 2016); and "Conclusion: Post-Script on Sex, Race and Culture" (Geschiere and Guadeloupe 2016), both in Jan Willem Duyvendak, Peter Geschiere, and Evelien Tonkens's edited volume *The Culturalization of Citizenship*.

Chapter 5

1. I take from Aníbal Quijano that, in order for one not to fall into the trap of thinking of the global elite as pink skinned, one needs to distinguish Eurocentered colonialism from Western imperialism. Quijano explains: "A relation of direct, political, social and cultural domination was established by the Europeans over the conquered of all continents. This domination is known as a specific Eurocentered colonialism. In its political, above all the formal and explicit aspect, this colonial domination has been defeated in the large majority of the cases. America was the first stage of that defeat, and afterwards, since the Second World War, Asia and Africa. Thus the Eurocentered colonialism, in the sense of a formal system of political domination by Western European societies over others seems a question of the past. Its successor, Western imperialism, is an association of social interests between the dominant groups ('social classes' and/or 'ethnies') of countries with unequally articulated power, rather than an imposition from the outside" (Quijano 2007, 168).

2. Thus I am not advocating a full-scale rejection of the insights of the Frankfurt school, but a way of having them complemented by the more hopeful analysis of James and his heirs such as Stuart Hall. See also Brian W. Alleyne (1999), who also argues that Marxism is best served by critically combining the insights of James and Adorno.

3. Urban popular culture contains spiritualist strands that often go unnoticed. For examples of scholars who offer a sustained analysis of this phenomenon, specifically hip-hop's infusion of Islamic motifs, see Khatija Bibi Khan (2012) and Hisham Aidi (2004). For Rastafari, see Joseph Thompson (2012) and Timothy Rommen (2006). A classic in this field remains Michael Eric Dyson's *Reflecting Black: African-American Cultural Criticism* (1993).

4. The original text in Dutch reads: "De meeste burgers hebben kennelijk geen oog voor de vreemde discrepantie tussen hun eigen gewone, veilige leven en de gruwelijke jungle die volgens de media om de hoek van hun gezellige straat begint." Van Rossem, an essayist and political commentator, places the mediation of mass media front and center in the growing fear of newcomers and the symbolization of the multiculturalizing Dutch world as a jungle. Mention must also be made that the jungle metaphor has a wider purchase outside of the Netherlands. One

encounters various online articles that present asylum seekers and other refugees from the former colonized world as dangerous beings from the jungle. See, for instance, E. J. Bron (2019). Deep ruminations on the historical and transnational linkages that have led the jungle metaphor to appear throughout Europe and the wider North Atlantic exceeds the scope of this book. Still, what is of interest is that in the Dutch urban scene the negative racist connotations of the jungle metaphor are being co-opted and resignified. It is about the full acceptance of the jungle, a stand-in for the multicultural "now." See the popular tune "Jungle" on the album *Hard Work Pays Off 2* by the award-winning Dutch rap formation Broederliefde (2016), which I discuss below in this chapter (videoclip at https://www.youtube.com/watch?v=Lqzl7XMgKMc).

5. For a historical analysis on how the Dutch political establishment and the general populace is recognizing the wrong that was transatlantic slavery, see Gert Oostindie (2010). For an article highlighting the role of the Afro-Surinamese grassroots activists, see Markus Balkenhol (2011). For a critical reflection that highlights the few historical voices in the Netherlands of the 1700s who were crying in the wind, see Alex van Stipriaan (2014).

6. The Rotterdam-based rap group Broederliefde is truly a phenomenon. No other Dutch group or artist has held the number 1 spot in the Dutch charts as long as they have. Their Dutch-language CD *Hard Work Pays Off 2* (2016) spent fourteen consecutive weeks at the number 1 spot.

Chapter 6

1. The phenomenon of social relatedness evoking biologically based kinship terms is a recurring anthropological theme. For a study on this matter in urban settings, see Gerd Baumann (1995).

Chapter 7

1. Academic treatises on the racial underpinnings of Black Peter do not address the festivity on Aruba, Bonaire, and Curaçao. Kees Broere (2017) describes the manner in which everyone has to paint themselves white or black during the festivity on these islands.

2. Belafonte, an artistic intellectual extraordinaire, was the first to produce an album—*Calypso*—that sold one million copies worldwide.

3. Due to the fact that, in 2018, fascist groups openly sought to violently attack the peaceful protests against Black Peter, prominent government officials and captains of industry have come out with statements that the tradition will have to change to reflect the current diversity of the Netherlands. They advocate slow change, however.

This is still unacceptable to Kno'Ledge Cesare and other antiracist activists. Thus one can expect the annual protest to continue.

4. In 2013, I explained the predicament of the two camps not understanding each other's discourse in one of the last radio interviews I did before my four-year hiatus to Sint Maarten, with friend and colleague Alex van Stipriaan (https://www .funx.nl/news/funx/19611-het-einde-van-zwarte-piet).

Chapter 8

1. As I write, there is work being done to address the question of diversity and representation of the multiculturalizing reality of the Netherlands in Dutch institutions of higher learning. At the University of Amsterdam, none other than Gloria Wekker chaired a diversity report that argued that more had to be done on that terrain. Quoting from the report: "In 2015/2016, 14% of all students registered at the University of Amsterdam had a non-Western background, understood in the sense that at least one of their parents was born in a 'non-Western' country.... When we exclude international students, this share is 13%. Although this roughly equals the national average (12% of university students in the Netherlands have a non-Western background), this 13% is relatively low when compared with the Vrije Universiteit Amsterdam (21%) and Erasmus University Rotterdam (22%), which find themselves in cities with comparably high shares of youth of non-Western descent. Of the employees who filled in the survey, 11% have a non-Western background, which drops to a mere 4% when we exclude the international professionals. For a university that presents itself as firmly rooted in the city of Amsterdam—which has recently become a majority-minority city—this is unsatisfactory" (Wekker et al. 2016, 5). See also Wekker's *White Innocence: Paradoxes of Colonialism and Race* (2016, 72–76).

2. The ideas in this chapter are based on a 2014 article I coauthored with Vincent de Rooij entitled "The Promise of a Utopian Home, or Capitalism's Commoditization of Blackness."

3. The track is on Amier Papier's compilation album *Hard Voor Weinig*, vol. 1 (2010).

Chapter 9

1. A vital point of contention that surely deserves correction is Mbembe's omission of serious consideration of the foundational role of Portugal and Spain in the promulgation of anti-blackness. As a correction, see, among others, Demetrius L. Eudell's "From Mode of Production to Mode of Auto-Institution: Sylvia Wynter's Black Metamorphosis of the Labor Question" (2016); Hilbourne Watson's "Theorizing the Racialization of Global Politics and the Caribbean Experience" (2001); and Aníbal Quijano's "Coloniality of Power, Eurocentrism, and Latin America" (2000).

2. How the articulation of urban Blackness to new digital technologies will affect the workings of our colonially inherited ideas of race is an important and fascinating matter that unfortunately will not be addressed in this book. The reader should, however, take into consideration that many urban popular culture artists and fans, going way back to George Clinton and P-Funk, promote sci-fi futurist thought to demolish anti-black racism. On this matter, see Alexander Weheliye's "'Feenin': Posthuman Voices in Contemporary Black Popular Music" (2002).

3. The prevalence of this type of vulgar Marxist reading, whereby Marxism was presented as an exclusively European paradigm, prompted critical race scholars such as Cedric Robinson (1983) and Anthony Bogues (1997) to promote and advocate for a Black Radical Tradition: an anticapitalist organic scholarship produced by the descendants of the captured Africans who survived the New World plantations, salt mines, and other ruthless regimes of forced labor. Other prominent thinkers such as Aimé Césaire (1972) made similar critiques while remaining Marxists.

4. For a thorough argumentation of this point, see Sylvia Wynter (1992) and Anthony Bogues (1997). Both authors argue that James's Caribbeanness led him to reject orthodox Marxism to attend to race and gender. For a counterargument that James could find all the resources to articulate racism and gender within Marxist theory, see Anton Allahar (2015).

5. Hence, when an Afro-pessimist scholar such as Frank Wilderson argues in his 2003 article "Gramsci's Black Marx" that "[c]apital was kick-started by the rape of the African continent" and that "[t]his phenomenon is central to neither Gramsci nor Marx," he and other Afro-pessimists omit that it was for the Marxism of C. L. R. James. Wilderson should know this, given that one of his inspirations is Orlando Patterson's conceptualization of slavery as social death (natal alienation whereby the exploited African and her descendants are rendered kinless, stateless, and property to be exploited). Influenced by James, Patterson theorized this conception of slavery within the Marxist paradigm. What I am correcting, a matter that cannot be taken up at length here, is that, similar to the manner in which James could incorporate postmodern concerns within his brand of Marxism, he could do the same with regard to an Afro-pessimist's rightful interventions against vulgar Marxist analyses.

6. The Netherlands is a schoolbook example of this wider western European mode of accommodating postcolonial difference. The historian Guno Jones (2007), who has published on this matter, argues that the explicit, biologically based racism of the late 1940s, which became prevalent with the arrival of Indo-Europeans and Indonesians, gradually gave way in the 1950s to assimilationist strategies. There was thus a gradual shift from the notion of biological incompatibility between white Dutch men and women and brown-skinned Dutch men and women of Indonesian extraction to a situation in which the latter could be assimilated and diluted into pinkish Dutchness through intermarriage. However, the newcomers from the Moluccas

who also arrived in the 1950s, but who were colonial soldiers and thus seen as threat, were segregated and discriminated against. Together with the Surinamese and other politically astute old- and newcomers who contested Dutch racism, they rebelled. This is an important part of the expression of the 1950s to 1970s global civil rights moment in the Netherlands. In conjunction with the culmination in the 1970s of the full dismantling of the Dutch pillar system—whereby society was subdivided into religious and ideological units—a new version of the Netherlands emerged. The Netherlands was transformed from a deeply religious and politically conservative country into Europe's beacon of tolerance and progressiveness, and a defender of secularism in the public domain. This has led to the current hegemonic Dutch ideal whereby race should not matter at all—even though it does—once cultural compatibility has been established. For studies discussing the emergence of the post–World War II hegemonic Dutch norm, characterized by fervent anticlericalism and the defense of social democracy, consult Oskar Verkaaik's *Ritueel burgerschap: Een essay over nationalisme en secularisme in Nederland* (2009). See also Peter Geschiere's *The Perils of Belonging: Autochthony, Citizenship, and Exclusion in Africa and Europe* (2009) for a comparative perspective.

7. Rod Earle and Coretta Phillips write: "Distinguished by not being White and English, those with origins in Britain's former colonial territories across the globe—from Antigua and Barbados in the West Indies, Pakistan, India, and Sri Lanka in … Asia, Cyprus in the Mediterranean to Nigeria and Uganda in Africa—asserted a positive and collective solidarity. … [T]he concept of political Blackness was forged as a form of cultural and political resistance against the hegemony of whiteness and its associated racism. … It was reference to a struggle that even, somewhat tentatively, included some White groups, such as the Irish, owing to their particularly close and troubled relationship with British imperialism. … After all, the signs in shop windows advertising rooms to rent in the 1950s and 1960s were as likely to say 'No Irish' as they were to say 'No Niggers.' … Thus, for a time, and in its time, political Blackness was not so much a signifier of skin color but a potent symbol of a binary and oppositional political identity that operated across diverse ethnicities, cultures, histories, and traditions" (Earle and Phillips 2013, 115). Earle and Phillips cite Bill Rolston and W. W. Daniel in the above passage. For an informative discussion on the internal and external dynamics that led to the weakening of political Blackness, see Claire Alexander (2018).

Chapter 10

1. The song can be found on Appa's album *Straatfilosoof* (2007a) and is also available on YouTube at https://www.youtube.com/watch?v=U-oPj2Yg1dw.

2. For the most recent statistics that show a sharp decrease in crime among all youths in the Netherlands, see Centraal Bureau voor de Statistiek (2017).

Chapter 11

1. On the lack of gender sensitivity in Peter Wilson's theory, see Jean Besson (2002). On recognizing how respectability and reputation continuously reconstitute and reinforce each other, see Shalini Puri (2003).

2. A clip of Jandino engaging Kevin Hart is available at https://www.youtube .com/watch?v=EWqJbwLEByo.

3. For the sketch, see https://www.youtube.com/watch?v=HV2oIYALSFw.

Chapter 12

1. Raymond Williams was on to the same thing when he deconstructed the base-superstructure divide in the 1970s thus: "[I]f we come to say that society is composed of a large number of social practices which form a concrete social whole, and if we give each practice a certain specific recognition, adding only that they interact, relate and combine in very complicated ways, we are at one level much more obviously talking about reality, but we are at another level withdrawing from the claim that there is any process of determination" (1973, 7).

2. The antiracist narrative that emerged after the Holocaust did not sufficiently address anti-black racism. For a theoretical exposition of this point, see Barnor Hesse (2004).

3. For clear statements on how this idea has been a recurring one, see Abiola Francis Irele (2005).

4. In addition to the myth of Yakub, one encounters other founding tales on the origin of pink-skinned people. To offer an illustration, here is how the genesis is described by public historian Rudolf R. Windsor: "Major mutations or changes took place among the descendants of Japheth. This is obvious because of their white skin. In other words, they were black at one time but their skin changed to white. This phenomenon can be understood in view of the total world population. Over two-thirds of the population of the world consists of colored people. That is a ratio of 2–1. Two out of Noah's three sons remained black. We know this to be true because many of the people throughout Africa, Asia, Latin America, and the islands in the Pacific Ocean are yellow, brown or, black" (1969, 22).

5. The original text in Dutch reads: "Ik heb m'n bericht maar verwijderd uit respect voor het deel van m'n volk dat zich wel weet te gedragen, maar ik sta nog steeds achter wat ik heb gezegd. Niet huilen als het licht niet op jou schijnt. Mensen werken hard om een toffe clip in elkaar te zetten [sic] en ik vind het disrespect naar blanke vrouwen toe om te zeggen dat donkere mensen, donkere meisjes in clips moeten gebruiken om donkere mensen meer in het licht te zetten. Nogmaals, kijk naar jezelf voordat je anderen de schuld geeft van discriminatie. Het probleem begint bij jezelf."

6. The original text in Dutch reads: "Wij delen onze kritiek op Nederland via Twitter en Facebook—ver weg van de traditionele opiniepagina's. Wij vinden elkaar op internationale verzamelplaatsen, buiten de verstikkende dagelijkse realiteit van uitsluiting op basis van ons ras, etniciteit, sekse, seksualiteit en/of geloof. Dus ja, bagatelliseer je dat, dan krijg je de wind van voren" (Gario 2016). See also an article recognizing the power of black twitter among antiracist activists in the country (Bahara 2015).

7. For an introduction to the remarkable life of the Afro–Puerto Rican intellectual Arturo Alfonso Schomburg, see Jesse Hoffnung-Garskof (2001).

8. See Mitchell Esajas's self-penned article "Nederland is niet Onschuldig" (2017). See also the explicit interview with his partner, Jessy Abreu, on the objectives of the Black Archives (Blokker and Chorus 2016).

9. In many ways this is but a Dutch example of ethnoracial entrepreneurship: ideologues who translate the grievances of subjugated peoples into ethnic absolutist terms. See Anton Allahar (2004), who discusses the matter as it relates to Trinidad and Tobago.

10. For the discussion, see https://www.facebook.com/francio.guadeloupe/posts/1830754740330254.

11. Alexander, being of East Indian descent, could not claim black identity in the US academic setting. Given her experiences, she is critical of the wholesale acceptance of US-derived "critical race theories speak" in European intellectual settings. There are, however, many ways to skin this cat. In "Koning Schaak: Mannen Prijzen als Stijloefening" (2006), Annemarie Mol also implicitly notes the difference between the American and European contexts when she relates how her Pakistani immigrant taxi driver did not consider himself black. This was something she took for granted, habituated as she was to political Blackness. For the taxi driver, however, blacks—African Americans—were poor, dangerous people whom he as a stranger in America was weary of. Mol could then settle for describing him as an Asian immigrant. That narrative shifted quickly as the taxi driver made *her* the precarious stranger (immigrant). He then took on the role of the settled American seeking to guide the immigrant. The persons Mol was staying with included African Americans who were comfortably middle class. Mol registers the abjectness attributed to African Americans—as an ideology that does not correspond to reality—but goes on to make another point. She avers that we recognize that the everyday messiness of life makes the analytics of academia porous. As such, the task of anthropologists may be to minutely follow what is happening and what happened—and therewith offer radical redescriptions that challenge academic orthodoxies. It is a daunting challenge. This book is an attempt to do so.

12. The original text in Dutch reads: "Als we in het hier en nu, inderdaad een oprecht politiek zwart-zijn nastreven (hetgeen ik nog verre van overtuigd van ben),

maar stel, dat we een oprecht en strategisch politiek zwart-zijn zouden nastreven. Waarom wordt dan voor dat politiek-zwart zijn, systematisch zwarte symboliek ingezet? Davis, Lorde, MLK, Mandela, Muhammad Ali, the Black Panthers. Zwarte lichamen, zwarte arbeid. Hoe komt het dat de werken van gehonoreerde bruine denkers als de in dit artikel genoemde Edward Said, de onvermelde Fatema Mernissi, en velen anderen zelden aangehaald worden om argumenten te staven die het politiek zwart-zijn kaderen? Waarom zijn het hoofdzakelijk zwarte lichamen, zwarte levens, zwarte denkers en zwarte strijden die moeten worden gerekt en strakgetrokken om het gehele spectrum van kleur te omvatten tot scheurens-toe. En niet andersom. Wie staat er stil bij wat die intellectuele gymnastiek zwarte mensen en levens kost? Zwart intellectualisme lijkt ten alle tijden toepasbaar te moeten zijn op ons allen, terwijl we datzelfde niet eisen of verwachten of interpreteren van en uit het werk van niet-zwarte denkers. Zwart-zijn is de meest geapprorieerde en minst heilige frontale realiteit van alle heilige huisjes." Taken from a discussion on my Facebook wall, at https://www.facebook.com/francio.guadeloupe/posts/1830754740330254.

13. Triggered by the Facebook debate, Mitchell Esajas went on to write an extensive piece on the Black Archives blog (2018) criticizing the idea of political Blackness. He also took Auoragh to task for not respecting the differences between the Black Radical Tradition and Marxism.

14. The original text in Dutch reads: "We zijn, zeker in Nederland, nog steeds aan het ontdekken hoe we ons tot elkaar moeten verhouden. Dat gebeurt binnen de Afro-Nederlandse gemeenschap, maar ook binnen de gemeenschap van kleur in haar geheel. Ik heb het dan over islamofobie onder niet-moslim zwarte mensen, anti-continentaal-zwartzijn, anti-zwart racisme onder niet-zwarte mensen van kleur, anti-rif sentimenten, misappropriatie van oud-Egypte en het uitwissen van zwarte nubians, anti-Somali sentimenten, mysoginoir tov zwarte vrouwen en oriëntalistische seksisme tov bruine vrouwen. We hebben nog zo zo veel in te halen. Terwijl we die reis samen als NL poc gemeenschap afleggen, blijft zwart-zijn naar mijn constatering tot dusver dus de meest geapproprieerde en minst heilige van alle frontale realiteiten. . . . Ik wil bijna zeggen, hier heb je het. Mijn oh zo subjectieve, oh zo verwaarloosbare zwart-zijn. Mijn huid. Mijn bloed zweet en tranen. Mijn 4c. Mijn sub-Saharaanse tong, mijn handen en voeten. Neem het, neem het allemaal en trek het aan. Vertel me vooral nadat je erin gekropen bent, waarom je er zo naar hunkerde." Excerpt from my Facebook wall, at https://www.facebook.com/francio.guadeloupe/posts/1830754740330254.

15. For a clear statement by the scholar who coined the term, arguing that intersectionality should not be mistaken for black feminist particularity, see Kimberlé Crenshaw (2010).

BIBLIOGRAPHY

Adorno, Theodor W., and Max Horkheimer. 1997. *Dialectic of Enlightenment*. Translated by John Cumming. London: Verso.

Aidi, Hisham. 2004. "'Verily, There Is Only One Hip-Hop Umma': Islam, Cultural Protest and Urban Marginality." *Socialism and Democracy* 18, no. 2: 107–26.

Alba, Richard, and Jan Willem Duyvendak. 2019. "What About the Mainstream: Assimilation in Super-Diverse Times." *Ethnic and Racial Studies* 42, no. 1: 105–24.

Albrecht, Michael Mario. 2008. "Acting Naturally Unnaturally: The Performative Nature of Authenticity in Contemporary Popular Music." *Text and Performance Quarterly* 28, no. 4: 379–95.

Alexander, Claire. 2002. "Beyond Black: Re-Thinking the Colour/Culture Divide." *Ethnic and Racial Studies* 25, no. 4 (July): 552–71.

Alexander, Claire. 2018. "Breaking Black: The Death of Ethnic and Racial Studies in Britain." *Ethnic and Racial Studies* 41, no. 6 (May): 1034–54.

Allahar, Anton. 2004. "Ethnic Entrepreneurship and Nationalism in Trinidad: Afrocentrism and *Hindutva*." *Social and Economic Studies* 53, no. 2 (June): 117–54.

Allahar, Anton. 2015. "Marxist or Not? Oliver Cromwell Cox on Capitalism and Class Versus 'Race'." *Canadian Journal of Latin American and Caribbean Studies* 39, no. 3: 1–25.

Allen, Rose Mary, and Francio Guadeloupe. 2016. "Yu di Kòrsou, a Matter of Negotiation: An Anthropological Exploration of the Identity Work of Afro-Curaçaons." In *The Culturalization of Citizenship: Belonging and Polarization in a Globalizing World*, edited by Jan Willem Duyvendak, Peter Geschiere, and Evelien Tonkens, 137–60. London: Palgrave Macmillan.

Alleyne, Brian W. 1999. "Cultural Politics and Globalized Infomedia: C. L. R. James, Theodor Adorno and Mass Culture Criticism." *Interventions* 1, no. 3: 361–72.

Amier Papier, comp. 2010. *Hard Voor Weinig* (album). Vol. 1. Amsterdam: Hard Voor Weinig Records.

Amier Papier, Brakko, and Manu. 2010. "Wat Ik Zie" (remix). YouTube, October 12. Available at https://www.youtube.com/watch?v=ottY-hJSaFo.

Appa. 2007a. *Straatfilosoof* (album). Amsterdam: TopNotch Records.

Appa. 2007b. *Ter Beschikking van de Straat* (album). Amsterdam: not on label.

Appiah, Kwame Anthony. 2005. *The Ethics of Identity*. Princeton, NJ: Princeton University Press.

Arrindell, Rhoda. 2014. *Language, Culture, and Identity in St. Martin*. Philipsburg, Sint Maarten: House of Nehesi.

Asante, Molefi K. 2006. "A Discourse on Black Studies: Liberating the Study of African People in the Western Academy." *Journal of Black Studies* 36, no. 5 (May): 646–62.

Baaziz, Jamila. 2013. "Antillianen Voelen Zich Thuis in Nederland." Caribisch Netwerk, January 14. Available at https://caribischnetwerk.ntr.nl/2013/01/14/antillianen-voelen-zich-thuis-in-nederland/#:~:text=Bijna%20driekwart%20(72%20procent)%20van,of%20soms%20last%20van%20heimwee.

Badu, Erykah. 1997. *Baduizm* (album). London: Universal Records.

Bahara, Hassan. 2015. "De Power van Black Twitter." *De Groene Amsterdammer*, June 24. Available at https://www.groene.nl/artikel/de-power-van-black-twitter.

Baldwin, James. 1998. *Baldwin: Collected Essays*. New York: Library of America.

Balkenhol, Markus. 2011. "Emplacing Slavery: Roots, Monuments and Politics of Belonging in the Netherlands." *African Diaspora* 4, no. 2: 135–62.

Baudrillard, Jean. 1975. *The Mirror of Production*. Translated by Mark Poster. St. Louis: Telos Press.

Baudrillard, Jean. 1981. *For a Critique of the Political Economy of the Sign*. Translated by Charles Levin. St. Louis: Telos Press.

Baumann, Gerd. 1995. "Managing a Polyethnic Milieu: Kinship and Interaction in a London Suburb." *Journal of the Royal Anthropological Institute* 1, no. 4 (December): 725–41.

Baumann, Gerd. 1996. *Contesting Culture: Discourses of Identity in Multi-Ethnic London*. Cambridge: Cambridge University Press.

Belafonte, Harry. 2009. "Man Piaba." YouTube, June 24. Available at https://www.youtube.com/watch?v=LvN6-RK66Bo.

Belafonte, Harry, and Michael Shnayerson. 2012. *My Song: A Memoir of Art, Race and Defiance*. New York: Vintage.

Beliefnet. n.d. "You're Gonna Serve Somebody." Available at https://www.beliefnet.com/entertainment/music/2001/04/youre-gonna-serve-somebody.aspx.

Benítez-Rojo, Antonio. 1992. *The Repeating Island: The Caribbean and the Postmodern Perspective*. Translated by James E. Maraniss. Durham, NC: Duke University Press.

Berrios-Miranda, Marisol. 2004. "Salsa Music as Expressive Liberation." *Centro Journal* 16, no. 2 (Fall): 159–73.

Besson, Jean. 2002. *Martha Brae's Two Histories: European Expansion and Caribbean Culture-Building in Jamaica*. Chapel Hill: University of North Carolina Press.

Blakely, Allison. 1993. *Blacks in the Dutch World: The Evolution of Racial Imagery in a Modern Society*. Bloomington: Indiana University Press.

Blokker, Bas, and Jutta Chorus. 2016. "Hoe Dekoloniseer je de bibliotheek?" *NRC Handelsblad*, September 30. Available at https://www.nrc.nl/nieuws/2016/09/30/hoe-dekoloniseer-je-de-bibliotheek-4541967-a1524367.

Bogues, Anthony. 1997. *Caliban's Freedom: The Early Political Thought of C. L. R. James*. London: Pluto Press.

Bogues, Anthony. 2003. *Black Heretics, Black Prophets: Radical Political Intellectuals*. New York: Routledge.

Botman, Maayke, Nancy Jouwe, and Gloria Wekker, eds. 2001. *Caleidoscopische Visies: De Zwarte, Migranten- en Vluchtelingen-Vrouwenbeweging in Nederland*. Amsterdam: Koninklijk Instituut voor de Tropen.

Braidotti, Rosi. 2006. *Transpositions: On Nomadic Ethics*. Cambridge: Polity Press.

Broederliefde. 2016. *Hard Work Pays Off 2* (album). Amsterdam: TopNotch Records.

Broek, Aart G. 2017. "Zijn Knecht Staat te Lachen." Neerlandistiek: Online Tijdschrift voor Taal en Letterkundig Onderzoek, October 22. Available at https://www.neerlandistiek.nl/2017/10/zijn-knecht-staat-te-lachen/.

Broere, Kees. 2017. "In Willemstad is Piet vooral Donkerzwart en Sint Wit Geschminkt." *Volkskrant*, November 18. Available at https://www.volkskrant.nl/nieuws-achtergrond/in-willemstad-is-piet-vooral-donkerzwart-en-sint-wit-geschminkt~b444c3d2/.

Bron, E. J. 2019. "De Jungle van Calais is symbool voor de EU-politiek." Verzamelde Vertalingen van E. J. Bron, August 30. Available at https://ejbron.wordpress.com/2016/08/30/de-jungle-van-calais-is-symbool-voor-de-eu-politiek-update/.

Brown, DeNeen L. 2018. "How Aretha Franklin's 'Respect' Became an Anthem for Civil Rights and Feminism." *Washington Post*, August 16. Available at https://www.washingtonpost.com/news/retropolis/wp/2018/08/14/how-aretha-franklins-respect-became-an-anthem-for-civil-rights-and-feminism.

Brown, Jacqueline Nassy. 1998. "Black Liverpool, Black America, and the Gendering of Diasporic Space." *Cultural Anthropology* 13, no. 3 (August): 291–325.

Brown, Wendy. 2005. *Edgework: Critical Essays on Knowledge and Politics*. Princeton, NJ: Princeton University Press.

Bunce, Robin, and Paul Field. 2011. "Obi B. Egbuna, C. L. R. James and the Birth of Black Power in Britain: Black Radicalism in Britain 1967–1972." *Twentieth Century British History* 22, no. 3 (September): 391–414.

Butler, Judith. 2006. "Violence, Non-Violence: Sartre on Fanon." *Graduate Faculty Philosophy Journal* 27, no. 1: 3–24.

Carpentier, Alejo. 1995. "On the Marvelous Real in America." In *Magical Realism: Theory, History, Community*, edited by Lois P. Zamora and Wendy B. Faris, 75–88. Durham, NC: Duke University Press.

Centraal Bureau voor de Statistiek. 2017. "Criminaliteit tussen 2012 en 2016 gedaald." March 1. Available at https://www.cbs.nl/nl-nl/nieuws/2017/09/criminaliteit-tussen-2012-en-2016-gedaald.

Césaire, Aimé. 1972. *Discourse on Colonialism*. Translated by Joan Pinkham. New York: Monthly Review Press.

Chamoiseau, Patrick. 2018. *Migrant Brothers: A Poet's Declaration of Human Dignity*. Durham, NC: Duke University Press.

Condé, Maryse. 2004. *Tales from the Heart: True Stories from My Childhood*. New York: Soho Press.

Cone, James H. 1997. *God of the Oppressed*. New York: Orbis Books

Cornips, Leonie, and Vincent de Rooij. 2013. "Selfing and Othering through Categories of Race, Place, and Language among Minority Youths in Rotterdam, the Netherlands." In *Multilingualism and Language Diversity in Urban Areas: Acquisition, Identities, Space, Education*, edited by Peter Siemund, Ingrid Gogolin, Monika Edith Schulz, and Julia Davydova, 129–64. Amsterdam: John Benjamins.

Crenshaw, Kimberlé W. 2010. "Close Encounters of Three Kinds: On Teaching Dominance Feminism and Intersectionality." *Tulsa Law Review* 46, no. 1 (Fall): 151–89.

Danticat, Edwidge. 2011. *Create Dangerously: The Immigrant Artist at Work*. New York: Vintage.

Davids, Tine. 2014. "Trying to Be a Vulnerable Observer: Matters of Agency, Solidarity and Hospitality in Feminist Ethnography." *Women's Studies International Forum* 43 (March–April): 50–58.

Davids, Tine, and Francien van Driel. 2009. "The Unhappy Marriage between Gender and Globalisation." *Third World Quarterly* 30, no. 5: 905–20.

De Cleen, Benjamin, and Nico Carpentier. 2010. "Contesting the Populist Claim on 'the People' through Popular Culture: The 0110 Concerts versus the Vlaams Belang." *Social Semiotics* 20, no. 2: 175–96.

DeCosmo, Jan. 1995. "To Set the Captives Free . . . Religion and Revolution in Bob Marley's Music." *International Journal of Comparative Race and Ethnic Studies* 2, no. 2: 63–79.

De Jong, Lammert. 2009. "Implosie van de Nederlandse Antillen." *Justitiële Verkenningen* 35, no. 5: 11–32.

De Jong, Lammert. 2010. *Being Dutch, More or Less: In a Comparative Perspective of USA and Caribbean Practices*. Amsterdam: Rozenberg.

De Keijzer, Yannick. 2015. "Dit is het Eerlijkste Interview met Sevn Alias Ooit." *Ballinnn'*, October 7. Available at http://ballinnn.com/dit-is-het-eerlijkste -interview-met-sevn-alias-ooit/.

Dhaenens, Frederik, and Sander De Ridder. 2015. "Resistant Masculinities in Alternative R&B? Understanding Frank Ocean and The Weeknd's Representations of Gender." *European Journal of Cultural Studies* 18, no. 3 (June): 283–99.

Du Bois, W. E. B. (1903) 2007. *The Souls of Black Folk*. New York: Cosimo.

Du Bois, W. E. B. (1920) 2007. *Darkwater: Voices from within the Veil*. New York: Cosimo.

Dussel, Enrique. 1985. *Philosophy of Liberation*. Translated by Aquilina Martinez and Christine Morkovsky. New York: Orbis Books.

Duyvendak, Jan Willem, Peter Geschiere, and Evelien Tonkens, eds. 2016. *The Culturalization of Citizenship: Belonging and Polarization in a Globalizing World*. London: Palgrave Macmillan.

Dyson, Michael Eric. 1993. *Reflecting Black: African-American Cultural Criticism*. Minneapolis: University of Minnesota Press.

Earle, Rod, and Coretta Phillips. 2013. "'Muslim Is the New Black': New Ethnicities and New Essentialisms in the Prison." *Race and Justice* 3, no. 2 (April): 114–29.

Eaton, Sherry C., Jonathan N. Livingston, and Harriette Pipes McAdoo. 2010. "Cultivating Consciousness among Black Women: Black Nationalism and Self-Esteem Revisited." *Journal of Black Studies* 40, no. 5 (May): 812–22.

Esajas, Mitchell. 2017. "Nederland is Niet Onschuldig" *Joop*, July 20. Available at https://joop.bnnvara.nl/opinies/nederland-niet-onschuldig.

Esajas, Mitchell. 2018. "Lessen uit een verborgen geschiedenis van de Zwarte Radicale Traditie." Black Archives, March 28. Available at http://www.theblackarchives.nl/blog/lessen-uit-een-verloren-geschiedenis-van-de-zwarte-radicale-traditie.html.

Essed, Philomena. 1991. *Understanding Everyday Racism: An Interdisciplinary Theory*. London: SAGE.

Essed, Philomena, and Isabel Hoving, eds. 2014. *Dutch Racism*. New York: Rodopi.

Essed, Philomena, and Kwame Nimako. 2006. "Designs and (Co)Incidents: Cultures of Scholarship and Public Policy on Immigrants/Minorities in the Netherlands." *International Journal of Comparative Sociology* 47, nos. 3–4 (August): 281–312.

Essed, Philomena, and Sandra Trienekens. 2008. "Who Wants to Feel White? Race, Dutch Culture and Contested Identities." *Ethnic and Racial Studies* 31, no. 1: 52–72.

Eudell, Demetrius L. 2016. "From Mode of Production to Mode of Auto-Institution: Sylvia Wynter's Black Metamorphosis of the Labor Question." *Small Axe* 20, no. 1 (March): 47–61.

Fanon, Frantz. 1967. *Black Skin, White Masks*. Translated by Charles Lam Markmann. New York: Grove Press.

Fanon, Frantz. 2004. *The Wretched of the Earth*. Translated by Richard Philcox. New York: Grove Press.

Fields, Karen E., and Barbara J. Fields. 2012. *Racecraft: The Soul of Inequality in American Life*. London: Verso.

Framke, Caroline. 2016. "A Rare Beyoncé Interview Reveals Her Thoughts on Feminism, 'Formation,' and Police Brutality." *Vox*, April 6. Available at https://www.vox.com/2016/4/6/11373442/beyonce-elle-interview-feminism-police.

Gario, Quinsy. 2016. "Witte Man Moet Mij Niet de Les Lezen" *NRC Handelsblad*, June 18. Available at https://www.nrc.nl/nieuws/2016/06/18/witte-man-moet-mij-niet-de-les-lezen-2797153-a1506703.

Gario, Quinsy. 2017. "De Gettoïsering van het Gedachtegoed van Martin Luther King Jr." *One World*, April 11. Available at https://www.oneworld.nl/achtergrond/de-gettoisering-van-het-gedachtegoed-van-martin-luther-king-jr/.

Geschiere, Peter. 2009. *The Perils of Belonging: Autochthony, Citizenship, and Exclusion in Africa and Europe*. Chicago: University of Chicago Press.

Geschiere, Peter, and Francio Guadeloupe. 2016. "Conclusion: Post-Script on Sex, Race and Culture." In *The Culturalization of Citizenship: Belonging and Polarization in a Globalizing World*, edited by Jan Willem Duyvendak, Peter Geschiere, and Evelien Tonkens, 203–18. London: Palgrave Macmillan.

Ghachem, Malick W. 1999. "Montesquieu in the Caribbean: The Colonial Enlightenment between *Code Noir* and *Code Civil.*" *Historical Reflections / Réflexions Historiques* 25, no. 2 (Summer): 183–210.

Gilroy, Paul. 1993. *The Black Atlantic: Modernity and Double Consciousness*. Cambridge, MA: Harvard University Press.

Gilroy, Paul. 2000. *Against Race: Imagining Political Culture beyond the Color Line*. Cambridge, MA: Harvard University Press.

Gilroy, Paul. 2004. *Postcolonial Melancholia*. New York: Columbia University Press.

Gilroy, Paul. 2005. "Could You Be Loved? Bob Marley, Anti-Politics and Universal Sufferation." *Critical Quarterly* 47, nos. 1–2 (July): 226–45.

Gilroy, Paul. 2006. "Multiculture in Times of War." *Critical Quarterly* 48, no. 4 (Winter): 27–45.

Gilroy, Paul. 2010. *Darker Than Blue: On the Moral Economies of Black Atlantic Culture*. Cambridge, MA: Harvard University Press.

Glissant, Édouard. 1989. *Caribbean Discourse: Selected Essays*. Charlottesville: University Press of Virginia.

Glissant, Édouard. 2000. *Poetics of Relation*. Translated by Betsy Wing. Ann Arbor: University of Michigan Press.

Glissant, Édouard. 2002. "The Unforeseeable Diversity of the World." Translated by Haun Saussy. In *Beyond Dichotomies: Histories, Identities, Cultures, and the Challenge of Globalization*, edited by Elisabeth Mudimbe-Boyi, 287–96. Albany: State University of New York Press.

Gosa, Travis L. 2011. "Counterknowledge, Racial Paranoia, and the Cultic Milieu: Decoding Hip Hop Conspiracy Theory." *Poetics* 39, no. 3 (June): 187–204.

Grace, Victoria. 2000. *Baudrillard's Challenge: A Feminist Reading*. London: Routledge.

Green, Jeffrey. 2000. "Before the Windrush." *History Today* 50, no. 10 (October): 29–35.

Guadeloupe, Francio. 2006. "Love When Love Could Not Be: An Example of Romantic Love from the Caribbean." *Etnofoor* 19, no. 1: 63–70.

Guadeloupe, Francio. 2009. "Their Modernity Matters Too: The Invisible Links between Black Atlantic Identity Formations in the Caribbean and Consumer Capitalism." *Latin American and Caribbean Ethnic Studies* 4, no. 3: 271–92.

Guadeloupe, Francio. 2013a. "Curaçaons on the Question of Home: The Lure of Autochthony and Its Alternatives." In *Caribbean Sovereignty, Development and Democracy in an Age of Globalization*, edited by Linden Lewis, 189–207. New York: Routledge.

Guadeloupe, Francio. 2013b. "The Netherlands, a Caribbean Island: An Auto-ethnographic Account." *Agathos* 4, no. 2: 83–93.

Guadeloupe, Francio. 2018a. "Exploring the Non-Ordinary Dimensions of Decoloniality." In *Smash the Pillars: Decoloniality and the Imaginary of Color in the Dutch Kingdom*, edited by Melissa Weiner and Antonio Carmona Baez, 125–36. Lanham, MD: Lexington Books.

Guadeloupe, Francio. 2018b. "Paying Attention to 'Spanish Radio Stations' in the Netherlands: An Essay on the Potential of Urban Popular Culture as Anti-Racism." *Etnofoor* 30, no. 2: 83–94.

Guadeloupe, Francio, and Vincent de Rooij, eds. 2007. *Zo Zijn Onze Manieren . . . Visies op Multiculturaliteit in Nederland*. Amsterdam: Rozenberg.

Guadeloupe, Francio, and Vincent de Rooij. 2014. "The Promise of a Utopian Home, or Capitalism's Commoditization of Blackness." *Social Analysis* 58, no. 2 (June): 60–77.

Haley, Alex. (1965) 2010. *The Autobiography of Malcolm X, as Told to Alex Haley*. London: Penguin Books.

Haley, Alex, and David Stevens. 1993. *Queen: The Story of an American Family*. New York: Avon Books.

Hall, Stuart. 1991. "Old and New Identities, Old and New Ethnicities." In *Culture, Globalization and the World-System: Contemporary Conditions for the Representation of Identity*, edited by Anthony D. King, 42–68. London: Macmillan.

Hall, Stuart. 1992a. "Cultural Studies and Its Theoretical Legacies." In *Cultural Studies*, edited by Lawrence Grossberg, Cary Nelson, and Paula A. Treichler, 277–94. New York: Routledge.

Hall, Stuart. 1992b. "What Is This 'Black' in Black Popular Culture?" In *Black Popular Culture*, edited by Michele Wallace and Gina Dent, 21–33. Seattle: Bay Press.

Hall, Stuart. 1994. "Cultural Identity and Diaspora." In *Colonial Discourse and Post-Colonial Theory: A Reader*, edited by Patrick Williams and Laura Crisman, 392–403. London: Harvester Wheatsheaf.

Hall, Stuart. 1996. "Minimal Selves." In *Black British Cultural Studies: A Reader*, edited by Houston A. Baker Jr., Manthia Diawara, and Ruth H. Lindeborg, 114–19. Chicago: University of Chicago Press.

Hall, Stuart. 1999. "Whose Heritage? Un-Settling 'The Heritage,' Re-Imagining the Post-Nation." *Third Text* 13, no. 49 (Winter): 3–13.

Hall, Stuart. 2001. "Negotiating Caribbean Identities." In *New Caribbean Thought: A Reader*, edited by Brian Meeks and Folke Lindahl, 24–39. Mona, Jamaica: University of the West Indies Press.

Hall, Stuart, and Les Back. 2009. "At Home and Not at Home: Stuart Hall in Conversation with Les Back." *Cultural Studies* 23, no. 4 (July): 658–87.

Hall, Stuart, Hansje Galesloot, and Ien Ang. 1991. *Het Minimale Zelf en Andere Opstellen*. Amsterdam: Socialistische Uitgeverij Amsterdam.

Harney, Stefano. 1996. *Nationalism and Identity: Culture and the Imagination in a Caribbean Diaspora*. London: Zed Books.

Harney, Stefano, and Fred Moten. 2013. *The Undercommons: Fugitive Planning and Black Study*. New York: Minor Compositions.

Harris, Wilson. 1970. *History, Fable and Myth in the Caribbean and Guianas*. Tacarigua, Trinidad and Tobago: Calaloux Publications.

Hartmann, Douglas, Joseph Gerteis, and Paul R. Croll. 2009. "An Empirical Assessment of Whiteness Theory: Hidden from How Many." *Social Problems* 56, no. 3 (August): 403–24.

Helsloot, John. 2012. "*Zwarte Piet* and Cultural Aphasia in the Netherlands." *Quotidian* 3: 1–20.

Hesse, Barnor. 1997. "It's Your World: Discrepent M/Multiculturalisms." *Social Identities* 3, no. 3: 375–94.

Hesse, Barnor. 2004. "Im/plausible Deniability: Racism's Conceptual Double Bind." *Social Identities* 10, no. 1: 9–29.

Hewitt, Roger. 1986. *White Talk Black Talk: Inter-Racial Friendship and Communication amongst Adolescents*. Cambridge: Cambridge University Press.

Hira, Sandew. 2009. *Decolonizing the Mind: Een Fundamentele Kritiek op het Wetenschappelijk Kolonialisme*. The Hague: Amrit Consultancy.

Hoffnung-Garskof, Jesse. 2001. "The Migrations of Arturo Schomburg: On Being *Antillano*, Negro, and Puerto Rican in New York, 1891–1938." *Journal of America Ethnic History* 21, no. 1 (Fall): 3–49.

Hondius, Dienke. 2009. "Blacks in Early Modern Europe: New Research from the Netherlands." In *Black Europe and the African Diaspora*, edited by Darlene Clark Hine, Trica Danielle Keaton, and Stephen Small, 29–47. Urbana: University of Illinois Press.

Howard, John R. 1998. "The Making of a Black Muslim." *Society* 35, no. 2 (January): 32–38.

Howe, Darcus. 1998. "Fifty Years after SS *Windrush* Docked, We Should Remember That We Came, Not Simply as Black Immigrants, but as Members of the Working Class." *New Statesman*, June 12, 30.

Huijnk, Willem, and Iris Andriessen, eds. 2016. *Integratie in Zicht? De Integratie van Migranten in Nederland op Acht Terreinen Nader Bekeken*. The Hague: Sociaal Cultureel Plan Bureau.

Hunter, Marcus A., and Zandria F. Robinson. 2016. "The Sociology of Urban Black America." *Annual Review of Sociology* 42 (July): 385–405.

Ice-T. 1993. *Home Invasion* (album). Los Angeles: Priority Records.

Irele, Abiola Francis. 2005. "What Is Africa to Me? Africa in the Black Diaspora Imagination." *Souls* 7, nos. 3–4: 26–46.

Jackson, Michael. 2013. *Lifeworlds: Essays in Existential Anthropology.* Chicago: University of Chicago Press.

James, C. L. R. (1938) 1963. *The Black Jacobins: Toussaint L'Ouverture and the San Domingo Revolution.* New York: Vintage.

James, C. L. R. 1980a. "Black Power." In *Spheres of Existence: Selected Writings,* 221–36. London: Allison and Busby.

James, C. L. R. 1980b. "Dialectical Materialism and the Fate of Humanity." In *Spheres of Existence: Selected Writings,* 70–105. London: Allison and Busby.

James, C. L. R. 1980c. *Notes on Dialectics: Hegel, Marx, Lenin.* London: Allison and Busby.

James, C. L. R. 1986. "Cricket and Race." In *Cricket,* 278–79. Edited by Anna Grimshaw. London: Allison and Busby.

James, C. L. R. 1992a. *American Civilization.* Edited by Anna Grimshaw and Keith Hart. Oxford: Blackwell.

James, C. L. R. 1992b. "Black Studies and the Contemporary Student." In *The C. L. R. James Reader,* 396–97. Edited by Anna Grimshaw. Oxford: Blackwell.

James, C. L. R. 1992c. *Every Cook Can Govern: A Study of Democracy in Ancient Greece and Its Meaning for Today.* Detroit: Bewick Editions.

James, C. L. R. 1992d. "Letters to Constance Webb." In *The C. L. R. James Reader,* 127–52. Edited by Anna Grimshaw. Oxford: Blackwell.

James, C. L. R. (1963) 1993. *Beyond the Boundary.* Durham, NC: Duke University Press.

James, C. L. R. 1996. *On the "Negro Question."* Edited by Scott McLemee. Jackson: University Press of Mississippi.

James, C. L. R., Grace C. Lee, and Pierre Chaulieu. (1958) 1974. *Facing Reality.* Detroit: Bewick Editions.

Jones, Guno. 2007. *Tussen Onderdanen, Rijksgenoten en Nederlanders: Nederlandse Politici over Burgers uit Oost en West en Nederland, 1945–2005.* Amsterdam: Rozenberg.

Kelley, Robin D. G. 2002. *Freedom Dreams: The Black Radical Imagination.* Boston: Beacon Press.

Khan, Khatija Bibi. 2012. "Erykah Badu and the Teachings of the Nation of Gods and Earths." *Muziki* 9, no. 2: 80–89.

King, Nicole. 2001. *C. L. R. James and Creolization: Circles of Influence.* Jackson: University Press of Mississippi.

Kingstone, Lisa. 2017. "Blackface, Passing or Coming Home." *Patterns of Prejudice* 51, no. 5: 432–38.

KRS-One. 1993. *Return of the Boom Bap* (album). New York: Zomba Records.

KRS-One. 2017. *The World Is Mind* (album). New York: R.A.M.P. Entertainment.

KRS-One and Marley Marl. 2007. *Hip Hop Lives* (album). New York: Koch Records.

Lentin, Alana. 2016. "Eliminating Race Obscures Its Trace: Theories of Race and Ethnicity Symposium." *Ethnic and Racial Studies* 39, no. 3 (February): 383–91.

Lewis, Linden, ed. 2013. *Caribbean Sovereignty, Development and Democracy in an Age of Globalization*. New York: Routledge.

Linebaugh, Peter, and Marcus Rediker. 2000. *The Many-Headed Hydra: Sailors, Slaves, Commoners, and the Hidden History of the Revolutionary Atlantic*. Boston: Beacon Press.

Lyotard, Jean-François. 1984. *The Postmodern Condition: A Report on Knowledge*. Minneapolis: University of Minnesota Press.

Lyotard, Jean-François. 1993. *Libidinal Economy*. Translated by Iain Hamilton Grant. Bloomington: Indiana University Press.

Maharaj, Gitanjali. 1997. "Talking Trash: Late Capitalism, Black (Re)Productivity, and Professional Basketball." *Social Text* 21, no. 50 (Spring): 97–110.

Maldonado-Torres, Nelson. 2008. *Against War: Views from the Underside of Modernity*. Durham, NC: Duke University Press.

Marcuse, Herbert. 1964. *One-Dimensional Man: Studies in the Ideology of Advanced Industrial Society*. Boston: Beacon Press.

Marley, Bob. 1976. *Rastaman Vibration* (album). London: Island Records.

Mbembe, Achille. 2017. *Critique of Black Reason*. Durham, NC: Duke University Press.

McGrane, Sally. 2013. "The Netherlands Confronts Black Pete." *New Yorker*, November 4. Available at https://www.newyorker.com/culture/culture-desk/the-netherlands-confronts-black-pete?fbclid=IwAR22-SgpNfSklQW4bS-rv6KL5SPQgn4aUNvj-ZAKOMiBwEW8XEcXaPf5mpI.

McKinley, James C., Jr. 2012. "Hip-Hop World Gives Gay Singer Support." *New York Times*, July 6. Available at https://www.nytimes.com/2012/07/07/arts/music/frank-ocean-draws-praise-for-declaring-his-homosexuality.html.

McMahon, Cian T. 2015. "The Pages of Whiteness: Theory, Evidence, and the American Immigration Debate." *Race and Class* 56, no. 4 (April–June): 40–55.

Meer, Nasar. 2018. "'Race' and 'Post-Colonialism': Should One Come before the Other?" *Ethnic and Racial Studies* 41, no. 6 (May): 1163–81.

Mehta, Brinda J. 2010. "Indianités francophones: Kala Pani Narratives." *L'Esprit Créateur* 50, no. 2 (Summer): 1–11.

Mepschen, Paul. 2019. "A Discourse of Displacement: Super-Diversity, Urban Citizenship, and the Politics of Autochthony in Amsterdam." *Ethnic and Racial Studies* 42, no. 1: 71–88.

Mercer, Kobena. 1994. *Welcome to the Jungle: New Positions in Black Cultural Studies*. London: Routledge.

Michaels, Walter B. 2006. *The Trouble with Diversity: How We Learned to Love Identity and Ignore Inequality*. New York: Metropolitan Books.

Michielsen, Dido. 2019. *Lichter dan Ik*. Amsterdam: Overamstel Uitgevers.

Mills, Charles, W. 2006. *The Racial Contract*. Ithaca, NY: Cornell University Press.

Mintz, Sidney W. 1996. "Enduring Substances, Trying Theories: The Caribbean Region as *Oikoumenê*." *Journal of the Royal Anthropological Institute* 2, no. 2 (June): 289–311.

Mol, Annemarie. 2006. "Koning Schaak: Mannen Prijzen als Stijloefening." *Tijdschrift voor Genderstudies* 9, no. 3: 63–78.

Mol, Annemarie. 2014. "Language Trails: 'Lekker' and Its Pleasures." *Theory, Culture and Society* 31, nos. 2–3: 93–119.

Morant, Kesha M. 2011. "Language in Action: Funk Music as the Critical Voice of a Post-Civil Rights Movement Counterculture." *Journal of Black Studies* 42, no. 1 (January): 71–82.

Moten, Fred. 2008. "Black Op." *PMLA* 123, no. 5 (October): 1743–45.

Moten, Fred. 2013. "Blackness and Nothingness (Mysticism in the Flesh)." *South Atlantic Quarterly* 112, no. 4 (Fall): 737–80.

Murdoch, H. Adlai. 2007. "'All Skin Teeth Is Not Grin': Performing Caribbean Diasporic Identity in a Postcolonial Metropolitan Frame." *Callaloo* 30, no. 2 (Spring): 575–93.

Nielsen, Aldon Lynn. 1997. *C. L. R. James: A Critical Introduction*. Jackson: University Press of Mississippi.

Nortier, Jacomine. 2001. *Murks en Straattaal: Vriendschap en Taalgebruik Onder Jongeren*. Amsterdam: Prometheus.

Nzume, Anousha. 2017. *Hallo Witte Mensen*. Amsterdam: Amsterdam University Press.

Oomen, Mar. 2019. *Missievaders: Een Familie Geschiedenis van Katholieke Wereld-verbeteraars*. Amsterdam: Uitgeverij Atlas Contact.

Oostindie, Gert. 2008. "History Brought Home: Postcolonial Migrations and the Dutch Rediscovery of Slavery." Paper presented at the Postcolonial Migrants and Identity Politics workshop, Internationaal Instituut voor Sociale Geschiedenis/ Koninklijk Instituut voor Taal-, Land- en Volkenkunde, Amsterdam.

Oostindie, Gert. 2010. *Postcolonial Netherlands: Sixty-Five Years of Forgetting, Commemorating, Silencing*. Amsterdam: Amsterdam University Press.

Oostindie, Gert, and Peter Verton. 1998. *Ki sorto di Reino? / What Kind of Kingdom? Visies en verwachtingen van Antillianen en Arubanen omtrent het Koninkrijk*. The Hague: Sdu.

Patterson, Orlando. 1972. "Toward a Future That Has No Past: Reflections on the Fate of Blacks in the Americas." *Public Interest* 27 (Spring): 25–62.

Patterson, Orlando. 1977. *Ethnic Chauvinism: The Reactionary Impulse*. New York: Stein and Day.

Patterson, Orlando. 1980. "Language, Ethnicity, and Change." *Journal of Basic Writing* 3, no. 1 (Fall–Winter): 62–73.

Patterson, Orlando. 2000. "Race Over." *New Republic*, January 10. Available at https://www.unz.com/print/NewRepublic-2000jan10-00006/.

Patterson, Orlando. 2005. "Four Modes of Ethno-Somatic Stratification: The Experience of Blacks in Europe and the Americas." In *Ethnicity, Social Mobility, and Public Policy: Comparing the US and UK*, edited by Glenn C. Loury, Tariq Modood, and Steven M. Teles, 67–121. Cambridge: Cambridge University Press.

Patterson, Orlando. 2006. "The Last Race Problem." *New York Times*, December 30. Available at https://www.nytimes.com/2006/12/30/opinion/30patterson.html?fbclid=IwAR2F0E78rdHOYzn9-KUR0PcpalYBwyfQxbUSeZLrJ5ou SOHGJjhAdku6kyk.

Peabody, Sue. 2011. "Slavery, Freedom, and the Law in the Atlantic World, 1420–1807." In *The Cambridge World History of Slavery*, vol. 3, *AD 1420–AD 1804*, edited by David Eltis and Stanley L. Engerman, 594–630. Cambridge: Cambridge University Press.

Pennycook, Alastair. 2007. "Language, Localization, and the Real: Hip-Hop and the Global Spread of Authenticity." *Journal of Language, Identity and Education* 6, no. 2 (June): 101–15.

Perry, Marc D. 2008. "Global Black Self-Fashioning: Hip Hop as Diasporic Space." *Identities: Global Studies in Culture and Power* 15, no. 6: 635–64.

Phillips, Caryl. 2013. *Color Me English: Migration and Belonging before and after 9/11*. New York: New Press.

Poor Righteous Teachers. 1996. *New World Order* (album). New York: Profile Records.

Price, Richard. 2017. "Créolisation, Creolization, and Créolité." *Small Axe* 21, no. 1 (52): 211–19.

Public Enemy. 1990. *Fear of a Black Planet* (album). New York: Def Jam Records.

Puri, Shalini. 2003. "Beyond Resistance: Notes toward a New Caribbean Cultural Studies." *Small Axe* 7, no. 2 (September): 23–38.

Quijano, Aníbal. 2000. "Coloniality of Power, Eurocentrism, and Latin America." *International Sociology* 15, no. 2: 215–32.

Quijano, Aníbal. 2007. "Coloniality and Modernity/Rationality." *Cultural Studies* 21, nos. 2–3 (March–May): 168–78.

Rampton, Ben. 2018. *Crossing: Language and Ethnicity among Adolescents*. 3rd ed. London: Routledge.

Rapport, Nigel. 2008. "Gratuitousness: Notes towards an Anthropology of Interiority." *Australian Journal of Anthropology* 19, no. 3 (December): 331–49.

Reed, Adolph L., Jr. 1999. *Stirrings in the Jug: Black Politics in the Post-Segregation Era*. Minneapolis: University of Minnesota Press.

Rivera-Rideau, Petra R. 2013. "'Cocolos Modernos': Salsa, Reggaetón, and Puerto Rico's Cultural Politics of Blackness." *Latin American and Caribbean Ethnic Studies* 8, no. 1: 1–19.

Robinson, Cedric J. 1983. *Black Marxism: The Making of the Black Radical Tradition*. London: Zed Press.

Rommen, Timothy. 2006. "Protestant Vibrations? Reggae, Rastafari, and Conscious Evangelicals." *Popular Music* 25, no. 2 (May): 235–63.

Rorty, Richard. 2006. *Take Care of Freedom and Truth Will Take Care of Itself: Interviews with Richard Rorty*. Edited by Eduardo Mendieta. Stanford, CA: Stanford University Press.

Rosengarten, Frank. 2008. *Urbane Revolutionary: C. L. R. James and the Struggle for a New Society*. Jackson: University Press of Mississippi.

RZA and Chris Norris. 2009. *The Tao of Wu*. New York: Riverhead Books.

Sansone, Livio. 1992. *Schitteren in de Schaduw: Overlevingsstrategieën, Subcultuur en Etniciteit van Creoolse Jongeren uit de Lagere Klassen in Amsterdam 1981–1990*. Amsterdam: Het Spinhuis.

Saucier, Paul Khalil, and Tryon P. Woods, eds. 2016. *Conceptual Aphasia in Black: Displacing Racial Formation*. Lanham, MD: Lexington Books.

Sexton, Jared. 2008. *Amalgamation Schemes: Antiblackness and the Critique of Multiracialism*. Minneapolis: University of Minnesota Press.

Shonekan, Stephanie. 2011. "Sharing Hip-Hop Cultures: The Case of Nigerians and African Americans." *American Behavioral Scientist* 55, no. 1 (January): 9–23.

Small, Stephen. 2009. "Introduction: The Empire Strikes Back." In *Black Europe and the African Diaspora*, edited by Darlene Clark Hine, Trica Danielle Keaton, and Stephen Small, xxiii–xxxviii. Urbana: University of Illinois Press.

St. Louis, Brett. 2007. *Rethinking Race, Politics, and Poetics: C. L. R. James' Critique of Modernity*. New York: Routledge.

Standley, Fred L., and Louis H. Pratt, eds. 1989. *Conversations with James Baldwin*. Jackson: University Press of Mississippi.

The-Dream. 2014. *Black* (EP). Los Angeles: Capitol Records.

Thomas, Greg. 2018. "Afro-Blue Notes: The Death of Afro-Pessimism (2.0)?" *Theory and Event* 21, no. 1 (January): 282–317.

Thompson, Joseph. 2012. "From Judah to Jamaica: The Psalms in Rastafari Reggae." *Religion and the Arts* 16, no. 4: 328–56.

Tosh, Peter. 1977. *Equal Rights* (album). New York: Columbia Records.

Tosh, Peter. 1983. *Mama Africa* (album). London: EMI Records.

Trouillot, Michel-Rolph. 2003. *Global Transformations: Anthropology in the Modern World*. New York: Palgrave Macmillan.

Van Rossem, Maarten. 2009. "Populisme de Ziekte van de Democratie." Maarten! Available at https://www.maartenonline.nl/nl/content/110945/populisme-de -ziekte-van- de-democratie.html.

Van Stipriaan, Alex. 2014. "De Achterkant van Vrijheid, Gelijkheid, Broederschap: Nederland en Zijn Slavernijverleden." *Tijdschrift over Cultuur & Criminaliteit* 4, no. 3: 68–80.

Van Zoonen, Liesbet. 2005. *Entertaining the Citizen: When Politics and Popular Culture Converge.* Lanham, MD: Rowman and Littlefield.

Verkaaik, Oskar. 2009. *Ritueel burgerschap: Een essay over nationalisme en secularisme in Nederland.* Amsterdam: Aksant.

Vété-Congolo, Hanétha. 2014. "Créolisation, Créolité, Martinique, and the Dangerous Intellectual Deception of 'Tous Créoles!'" *Journal of Black Studies* 45, no. 8 (November): 769–91.

Walcott, Derek. 1998. *What the Twilight Says: Essays.* New York: Farrar, Straus and Giroux.

Wald, Elijah. 2012. *The Dozens: A History of Rap's Mama.* New York: Oxford University Press.

Walker, Alice. 1983. *In Search of Our Mothers' Gardens: Womanist Prose.* Orlando: Harcourt.

Warren, Calvin L. 2017. "Black Mysticism: Fred Moten's Phenomenology of (Black) Spirit." *Zeitschrift für Anglistik und Amerikanistik* 65, no. 2 (June): 219–29.

Watson, Hilbourne. 2001. "Theorizing the Racialization of Global Politics and the Caribbean Experience." *Alternatives: Global, Local, Political* 26, no. 4 (October): 449–83.

Weheliye, Alexander G. 2002. "'Feenin': Posthuman Voices in Contemporary Black Popular Music." *Social Text* 20, no. 2 (Summer): 21–47.

Weidhase, Nathalie. 2015. "'Beyoncé Feminism' and the Contestation of the Black Feminist Body." *Celebrity Studies* 6, no. 1: 128–31.

Weiner, Melissa F. 2014. "E(RACING SLAVERY): Racial Neoliberalism, Social Forgetting, and Scientific Colonialism in Dutch Primary School History Textbooks." *Du Bois Review* 11, no. 2 (Fall): 329–51.

Wekker, Gloria. 2016. *White Innocence: Paradoxes of Colonialism and Race.* Durham, NC: Duke University Press.

Wekker, Gloria, Marieke Slootman, Rosalba Icaza, Hans Jansen, and Rolando Vázquez. 2016. *Let's Do Diversity: Report of the University of Amsterdam Diversity Commission.* Amsterdam: University of Amsterdam.

Werbner, Pnina, and Mattia Fumanti. 2012. "The Aesthetics of Diaspora: Ownership and Appropriation." *Ethnos* 78, no. 2: 149–74.

West, Cornel. 1993. *Race Matters.* Boston: Beacon Press.

Wilderson, Frank B., III. 2003. "Gramsci's Black Marx: Whither the Slave in Civil Society?" *Social Identities* 9, no. 2: 225–40.

Willemse, Karin. 2014. "'Everything I Told You Was True': The Biographic Narrative as a Method of Critical Feminist Knowledge Production." *Women's Studies International Forum* 43 (March–April): 38–49.

Williams, Monte. 2000. "Frankie Crocker, a Champion of Black-Format Radio, Dies." *New York Times*, October 24. Available at https://www.nytimes.com/2000/10/24/ nyregion/frankie-crocker-a-champion-of-black-format-radio-dies.html.

Williams, Raymond. 1973. "Base and Superstructure in Marxist Cultural Theory." *New Left Review* 82 (November–December): 3–16.

Williams, Richard. 1995. "Orlando Patterson Interview." *Sociological Forum* 10, no. 4 (December): 653–71.

Wilson, Peter J. 1969. "Reputation and Respectability: A Suggestion for Caribbean Ethnology." *Man*, n.s., 4, no. 1 (March): 70–84.

Windsor, Rudolf R. 1969. *From Babylon to Timbuktu: A History of the Ancient Black Races Including the Black Hebrews.* Chicago: Lushena Books.

Wynter, Sylvia. 1992. "Beyond the Categories of the Master Conception: The Counterdoctrine of the Jamesian Poiesis." In *C. L. R. James's Caribbean*, edited by Paget Henry and Paul Buhle, 63–91. Durham, NC: Duke University Press.

Wynter, Sylvia. 2003. "Unsettling the Coloniality of Being/Power/Truth/Freedom: Towards the Human, After Man, Its Overrepresentation; An Argument." *CR: The New Centennial Review* 3, no. 3: 257–337.

INDEX

ABOUT THE AUTHOR

A social and cultural anthropologist by training, Francio Guadeloupe has worked at major universities in the Netherlands. In addition, he served for four years as the president of the University of
St. Martin on the binational island of Saint Martin and Sint Maarten
in the Caribbean. He is currently employed at the University of
Amsterdam in the Netherlands. His publications include *Chanting
Down the New Jerusalem: Calypso, Christianity, and Capitalism in
the Caribbean* (2009).